This is a book that can change your life. If men will read this great work, it will change their hearts and their marriages. This is no quick-fix, instant-solution approach to our problems as men. In fact, to become the new man that Steve describes requires much pain. But Steve helps us see the hope for change and bluntly challenges every man to not stay the same.

He speaks from his own experiences while quoting those who have been in the valley and made it to the top of the mountain. He also speaks from experience on the value of us men connecting with other men, holding each other accountable and encouraging each other to do the right thing.

Old Man New Man is an encouragement to stay the course, to persevere through difficulty and wait for God to reveal His purpose in the midst of pain. The new man that Steve describes is the man I want to be. It is a man of character who knows what he believes and who believes in the reality of a God who has called us to a higher purpose.

If you have been struggling with anything from a longing for a father who was never there to masturbation or financial freedom, Steve provides a way of escape as he addresses so many tough issues for us men. I have looked at certain issues with new insight because of Steve's keen sense of reality and his deep wisdom.

It is my prayer that every man would read *Old Man New Man*, because it is never too early or too late to grow into the man God has called us to be. Thank you, Steve, for a book that has given me new wisdom and solid directions on how I can become a new man every day for the rest of my life.

—STEPHEN ARTERBURN
CEO, NEW LIFE CLINICS AND WOMEN OF FAITH

Old Man New Man is a great practical treatment of the REAL male issues facing men today. Steve writes this book compassionately and positively so men can reach their personal destiny in Christ.

—DOUGLAS WEISS, PH.D.
AUTHOR, *THE FINAL FREEDOM*

The prophet Job said, "Just as my mouth tastes good food, so my mind tastes truth when I hear it." This is a book that has the taste of truth that is so good. It is not what men are born with, but what men are reborn with that gives them the character and quality of real manhood. This is not a book for a man content to be a male, or the one who aspires only to being a man, but this book is for the man who desires to be the covenant man God created him to be.

The truest Christian is always the finest gentleman. Reading this book won't make you a "gentleman," but putting it into practice will make you a "Christian gentleman."

Stephen Strang writes as precisely and decisively as he does everything else in life. His walk with God through life has given him an understanding of what it is to be Christlike, and he presents it in a humble, mature manner that allows a man to learn principles and gain wisdom in a most unique way.

There is a maxim that says: "Good salesmen never sell a product; they only help people meet their needs." Another is: "You can get anything you want in life by helping others meet their needs." A good product sells only because of its service to meet needs. Meeting needs is the easiest way to get wealth. Stephen's book can be a way to get wealth, and wealth can get riches, but the main thing this book does is help meet the needs of a man. This book is a product of life—of Stephen's life. It took a lifetime of living and learning to make this book what it is. I commend Stephen for writing it, and I recommend that you read it—not skim it—read it! After you have read it, go back and take the key points that apply to you, put them into practice, and you will be on your way to having a life that is rich in truth and wealthy in character. Thank you, Stephen, for this book.

–Dr. Edwin Louis Cole
President and Founder, Christian Men's Network

Stephen Strang goes "where no man has gone before" by addressing issues that are important to men that no one seems to want to talk about. He tackles these issues head-on, without mincing words and with a sound scriptural foundation. By drawing on many personal experiences as well as those of the many men he has met all over the world, this book will minister to and encourage any man who reads it. I have seen firsthand the unfolding of the vision Steve has had to help men reach their fullest potential in Christ, and this book is a key part of that vision. The passion God has given him for this calling will be obvious to anyone who picks up this book.

–D. Scott Plakon
President, Nationwide Publishing Company, Inc.

OLD MAN NEW MAN

I f you are like most men, you feel the constant pressure of temptation. You want to live right . . . but more often than you care to admit, you fail. But there is a way to escape—a way to break free of the struggles of your past and into a Christian life that "works," a life pleasing to God.

Old Man New Man is a refreshing look at the issues men have faced throughout history—issues you face today: anger, rage, denial, fear, guilt and shame—and their deadly effect. This book can help you:

- Get a vision for your life
- Change the way you think
- Attain sexual purity
- Deal with fatherlessness issues
- Improve your marriage
- Care for your "temple"
- Develop lasting male relationships
- Find mentors to help you

Old Man New Man is a classic example of a "how-to" book, providing you with study questions at the end of each chapter and more resources on a special website. It is an excellent resource for:

- Personal study
- Men's groups
- Pastors' sermons
- Cell group discussions
- Retreats
- Devotions with sons
- Mentoring

STEPHEN STRANG, one of the world's leading Christian communicators, is president and founder of Strang Communications Company. He is an executive coach, men's group facilitator and publisher of *New Man* magazine, founded in 1994 to *"renew men in purpose and passion in Christ."* The readership of *New Man* magazine exceeded 500,000 in 1997—making it one of the world's most-read Christian men's magazines.

The magazine features articles on marriage, career, finances, faith in action, spiritual instructions, health, male sexuality (from a Christian perspective) and fathering.

New Man magazine is part of a stable of award-winning magazines published by Strang Communications Company, including *Charisma, Ministries Today, SpiritLed Woman, Vida Cristiana* (in Spanish) and two trade journals, as well as books, church curriculum and Internet.

Stephen Strang has arranged for the author's share of the proceeds to be given for men's ministry. See details at www.oldmannewman.com.

OLD MAN
NEW MAN

STEPHEN STRANG

OLD MAN NEW MAN by Stephen Strang
Published by Creation House
A part of Strang Communications Company
600 Rinehart Road
Lake Mary, Florida 32746
www.creationhouse.com

Unless otherwise noted, all Scripture quotations are from the Holy Bible, New Living Translation, copyright © 1996. Used by permission of Tyndale House Publishers, Inc., Wheaton, IL 60189. All rights reserved.

Scripture quotations marked KJV are from the King James Version of the Bible.

Scripture quotations marked THE MESSAGE are from The Message, copyright © 1993, 1994, 1995. Used by permission of the NavPress Publishing Group.

Scripture quotations marked NAS are from the New American Standard Bible. Copyright © 1960, 1962, 1963, 1968, 1971, 1972, 1973, 1975, 1977 by the Lockman Foundation. Used by permission. (www.Lockman.org)

Scripture quotations marked NIV are from the Holy Bible, New International Version. Copyright © 1973, 1978, 1984, International Bible Society. Used by permission.

Scripture quotations marked NKJV are from the New King James Version of the Bible. Copyright © 1979, 1980, 1982 by Thomas Nelson, Inc., publishers. Used by permission.

Scripture quotations marked TLB are from The Living Bible. Copyright © 1971. Used by permission of Tyndale House Publishers, Inc., Wheaton, IL 60189. All rights reserved.

Interior design by Pat Theriault

AUTHOR'S NOTE: The stories in this book come from my personal experience with people over time in the various places where I have lived and worked. Names, places and identifying details have been changed and altered to protect the privacy and anonymity of the individuals to whom they refer. Some persons referenced are actually composites of a number of people who share similar issues and are equally protected with names and information changes to protect privacy. Those whose first and last names are given are real individuals. With the exception of those persons, any similarity between names and stories of individuals described in this book and individuals known to readers is coincidental and not intended.

Library of Congress Catalog Card Number: 00-107274
International Standard Book Number: 0-88419-741-7
0 1 2 3 4 5 6 7 VERSA 8 7 6 5 4 3 2 1
Printed in the United States of America

To my sons, Cameron and Chandler.
My prayer is that you both will be new men in Christ,
following the example you see in your dad.

Contents

Internet Resources . . . .*xiii*

Foreword by Jack Hayford . . . .*xv*

A Note to Any Women Readers . . . .*xix*

Introduction by Stephen Strang . . . .*xxi*

Section I
The Problem With the Old Man

1   Men: Must We Struggle to Serve Christ? 1

2   Fatherlessness: The Root of the Problem 15

3   Sexual Problems: Are They Always an Issue? 31

4   Three Steps Forward: Two Steps Back 55

Section II
The Solution Is Becoming a New Man in Christ

5   Salvation: Brings New Life 65

6   Deliverance: Breaks Sin's Hold 83

7   Receiving the Holy Spirit: Empowers Your Life 105

8   Accountability: Keeps You in Touch 121

Section III
Getting Your Act Together

9   Getting a Life Vision: Finding Your Purpose 149

10   Renewing Your Mind:
        Changing the Way You Think 165

11   Ordering Your Finances:
        Gaining Freedom to Soar 181

12   Working on Your Marriage:
        Making It Great 203

13   Impacting Your Children:
        Speaking the Father's Blessing .225

14   Caring for Your Body: Getting Into Shape 243

15   Developing Male Relationships .259

16   Becoming a Man of God 281

        Appendix: Important Reading for New Men 301

        Notes 307

Acknowledgments

My wonderful wife, Joy, to whom I owe a great debt of gratitude, has stood with me through thick and thin and has seen God's purposes in my life, even when my faith was weak. She is my best friend and partner in every sense of the word. She is also the most godly woman I know (other than my mom!). In spite of my imperfections, she has always respected my position as head of our home, and she has continually told me that I am a man of God with a destiny and purpose. As I write this, she has loved me and believed in me for twenty-eight fantastic years. Joy, I know I have told you this many times, but I love you more than you will ever know.

My sons, Cameron and Chandler, are the two most important "men" in my life. As I write this, Cameron is a mature man of twenty-four, and Chandler is a maturing thirteen-year-old. God has His hand on each of them, and I am so thankful for them both. Guys, I love you very much.

I also thank the men in my "GOLF Group" (which stands for "Group of Loyal Friends") who have walked the Christian walk with me for nearly eight years. Christianity is not something we practice alone—we do it in community. And these men form part of my community of believers. They have prayed with me about this book and kept me accountable to meet my deadlines. Over the years they have made my life much richer because I have known them: Scott Plakon, Scott Nelson, Bob Minotti, Gene Koziara and Brian Walsh. Scott Plakon in particular made it his responsibility to keep me accountable to write when I preferred to procrastinate.

New Man magazine managing editor Robert Andrescik has been a blessing. This book is an outgrowth of the ministry and vision of *New Man*. He labored over the manuscript and gave me great ideas and tips. He also helped us create the extensive website that accompanies this book.

Joel Kilpatrick's help as a researcher and writer was invaluable. The process caused me to learn to deeply respect Joel's keen mind, spiritual insights and rock-solid integrity.

The team at Strang Communications has been great to work with: Dave Welday has worked me with for more than nineteen years and prodded me patiently to finish this book; Rick Nash is largely responsible for the shape and format the book has taken; Barbara Dycus helped fill in the holes and turn the manuscript into a finished book while meeting an almost impossible deadline; Mike Janiczek, Jay Griffin and Carol Wilde believed in the book and pre-sold thousands of copies. Thanks also to Dottie McBroom, Bob Cruz, Carol Duffie and the rest of the team.

And last but not least, I thank my Lord and Savior Jesus Christ, who saved me at five years of age and who did not give up on me when I was a rebellious teenager bent on sowing a few wild oats. Thankfully I came back to Him just days before turning twenty years old, and I have served Him faithfully ever since. He is the One who took my "old man" nature and made me a "new man in Christ." Thankfully, He did not give up on me when the change was not instantaneous. If I have learned anything on my Christian walk, I thank Jesus for helping me share it with you in this book.

Internet Resources

Old *Man New Man* is more than just a book. When you purchased a hardcover copy, you received a one-year subscription to *New Man* magazine. Many things in the book, including the writing style and layout, mimic the style of the magazine. Now, the book becomes interactive through the Internet.

If you log on to www.oldmannewman.com, you will be able to access much more information than we were able to cram in to the 337 pages of this book. If we quote from an article in *New Man,* you can go to the website and read the entire article.

We list all the book references in the book appendix. You can find where to buy a copy (if the book is still in print), and where appropriate you can link to a website or get more material than what we reference.

In the text there are icons that list the web address and some area being dealt with such as "Find Help For Sexual Addictions." It is an indication there is something on the website about what is being discussed in the chapter. Think of it as a print version of a hyperlink.

The website also contains many articles on related topics that we have published in *New Man* or that we got permission to put on the site. And as time passes, the site will develop and grow.

On the site you can give you comments about the book and you can tell us what you like and don't like. In some cases we will put on information on one chapter, and if we get a good response, we will come back later and do it for the other chapters. In that way, the website will continue to evolve and improve.

Notice the material on chapter 2 on "Fatherlessness: The Root of the Problem." We included a way to study this each day. If you like it, let us know so we can do more of this. You can find more questions on the website.

Sound interesting? I hope so. That website is for you and it's password protected. Web surfers can't access it. Only readers of this book. You can only find the user ID and the password here:

User ID: oldman
Password: newman

Use it. Learn. Be challenged. And enjoy it.

Foreword
by Jack Hayford

Let me say it first: *Sir, this is as practical a book on manhood that you will find anywhere!* I do not expect to be challenged on that. Forgive me for being so direct, and let me assure you—I do not "owe" this commendation to anyone (even though the author is a good friend). But . . .

Having spoken to stadiums full of men (and heard some of the nation's best speakers do the same), and . . .

Having watched thousands of men in my own congregation move into sensible, godly manhood (for over twenty-five years, "building men" was at the highest priority in my leadership strategy as pastor of The Church On The Way in Los Angeles), and . . .

Having written nationally published books for men and reading, as well, many of the finest by internationally recognized "voices to men," I still say it—right here, right now . . .

This is the most thoroughgoing book on "moving forward in manhood" you will find anywhere! So, I have said it—"as practical as any," "most thoroughgoing of all." Why so positive?

First, because Stephen Strang has touched all the bases.

If I published a "curriculum" for building a godly, fulfilled, sensible, solid man (and I have), there is nothing I would include that this book does not have already. Steve has done a phenomenal job doing two things: 1) He has synthesized the writings of many of today's insightful authors and distilled their wisdom into practical pointers you and I can put to work; and 2) he has complemented this with helpful guidelines born of his own rich experience, all expressed with forthright candor and personal self-disclosure.

Second, because Steve has a passion to help men like us.

That he is the publisher of the most widely distributed men's magazine in the world dedicated to building godly men was not merely a *business* decision. Steve was answering the call of the Holy Spirit upon his own heart; he was saying yes to God and yes to you and me as brothers in Christ. That second yes means, "I want to do everything I can to help you and me to be the maximum men God wants us to become through the power of the Holy Spirit."

Third, Steve has not been hesitant to keep our feet to the fire on the toughest issue all of us men deal with: sexual purity.

I doubt there is one guy in a thousand who has not wrestled with keeping a pure mind or with steeling himself against the temptation to indulge in porn, masturbation or other unworthy self-indulgences or with refusing to yield turf to the whispering demons always at hand to suggest some flirtatious activity. His sensitive, sensible and scriptural way of dealing with this constant bugaboo challenging the most godly of committed guys is realistic—and genuinely helpful.

Finally, Steve is unafraid to remind us that, at the bottom line, we need more than the resolve of a good disciple of Jesus. We also need the power that comes only when you and I come to the feet of Jesus—to receive the fullness of the Holy Spirit on New Testament terms.

So, there is practical and powerful truth here. And, I am done with my foreword . . . except to say one more thing.

I want to add that there is one more reason this book is so

filled with worth, hope and promise. The reason? The man who wrote it is as real as his writing is pointed and practical. Stephen Strang is a humble, teachable brother in Christ, who is also a creative, successful, visionary leader. To meet him is *not* to be impressed with fancy footwork or humanistic dynamism. Instead, it is to simply be reminded that *faithfulness* pays, hard work is still in vogue and *good guys* still win. Especially when they commit to learn a lifelong walk with our Lord Jesus Christ.

This book will help you do more of that.

—Dr. Jack W. Hayford
Founding Pastor, The Church On The Way
Chancellor, The King's College and Seminary
Van Nuys, California

A Note to Any Women Readers

This is a book for men. It is NOT a book for women.

That is not to say some women will not read the book anyway. You may be one of them. Maybe you are reading it to better understand the man you love. But be forewarned; *men look at things differently than women do.* They process things differently. They even struggle with different issues in life and in their walk with God.

A secular author wrote a best-selling book titled *Men Are From Mars, Women Are From Venus.* That humorous phrase exemplifies the differences between the two sexes.

I have written this book because I saw a need. Almost without exception, men who read it seem to feel, "Finally, someone understands how I feel; someone is showing me the way. Maybe there *is* hope for me."

One friend who saw an advance copy of the book sent me an e-mail to encourage me. "This book will change lives," he wrote. "It will encourage men to get together to open up, discuss and overcome issues that have plagued many for decades."

That is the response I am hoping for.

On the other hand, some of the women who read advance copies have had a different reaction. One called some of the stories in the book "yucky." Another "stopped reading due to getting quite upset."

The problem is that many men struggle with some very serious issues. They have no one to talk to or to show the way. They struggle in silence until one day they snap and do something really weird like abusing the ones they love or even abandoning the family altogether.

Would it not be good if we could help those men before it is too late?

Life is a series of decisions. I try to make this point in the book again and again. Each of us must make a decision to follow Jesus. Then we must make a decision to put off the old man and to say no when temptation comes our way.

No book has all the answers. But I hope my book will give men a few answers to point them to Jesus. I have tried to make clear that there is a life in God where there is victory over what the Bible calls the "old man." Men can soar like an eagle to new heights spiritually. But first they need to get a basic understanding of who they are in Christ and get help—sometimes even deliverance—from the strongholds Satan may have put in their lives.

This book is written to men from a male perspective to offer hope to men who may feel as the apostle Paul felt when he said, "Why do I do the things I don't want to do?" Paul found his hope in a Christ who could transform him into a new man in Christ. I want the men who read this book to find that hope also.

This book is written from that perspective. So, woman reader, please remember this: If this book helps the men in your life, then ultimately it will also be of great help to you in your relationships with those men.

Introduction

I was trained to be a newspaper reporter and learned to write in the short, clipped style that newspapers use. For the past twenty-five years, I have been a magazine editor and publisher, so I have learned to write for the "skip and jump" reader, including the ones who begin at the inside back page and read the magazine backwards, stopping to read whatever catches their eye.

In my first book (authored alone), I use some of these techniques to help you through *Old Man New Man*. We have tried to make it easy to read, from the short sentences and paragraphs of newspaper style, to the type font we chose, to the way we laid out each chapter. Across from each chapter opening is "A clip from *New Man*" on the chapter topic, meant not only to be an "art element," but also to draw you into the chapter itself.

Throughout the book we pulled interesting quotes to grab you as you thumb through the pages. We laid it out in three easy-to-follow sections that outline the problem, present the solution and then tell you how to get your act together.

Then, to make the book interactive, we have an extensive Notes section with complete source information for everything I cite—and for the testimonies I quote. We have created a website where you can read an entire article from *New Man* from which we may have quoted. An attractive icon on a page calls your attention to where you can get more information online. Or you can look in the book appendix to find out how to get a book from which we may have quoted.

We want feedback from you. Go online to write me a "letter to the author" telling what you thought about the book—especially if your life was impacted. You may also post your thoughts for all to see who visit the website at www.oldmannewman.com. Use the user id **oldman** and the password **newman**. It is **case sensitive** so type all lowercase leaving no spaces.

A lot of hard work and prayer has gone into this book. I consider this to be an outgrowth of my ministry to men in each issue of *New Man* magazine. In fact, if you purchased a hardcover copy of the book, you will receive a one-year subscription to *New Man*—if you send us your name and address on the bind-in card provided.

I have tried to open my heart and life in a way that may help you on your odyssey toward becoming a new man in Christ. God has a wonderful destiny for you. You do not need to stay mired down in your past. You were meant to soar and to grow in faith as you develop a greater hunger for God. It is a journey I am taking with you.

—STEPHEN STRANG
LAKE MARY, FLORIDA
AUGUST 8, 2000

Section I

The Problem With the Old Man

Small Beginnings

As Christians we are always planning ways to get free from sin. We certainly aren't dreaming up ways to cover sin and get away with it. But we go around with our heads down, feeling condemned because we aren't perfect yet. The fact that we are susceptible to condemnation reveals our deep caring and longing to please God. Those desires are a manifestation of the ever-increasing glory of God in our lives.

The rubble of the past is being cleared away. Slowly but surely, a foundation in God is being laid. Some day a beautiful temple will rise from the ruins. Begin shouting "Grace! Grace!" right now. Have confidence that "He who began a good work in you will perfect it" (PHIL. 1:6, NAS).

Don't underestimate the grace of God. Don't despise the day of small beginnings. Don't say, "I'll never be any different. I'm always going to be in bondage to lust, anger and covetousness. I'll never be free." The glory of God is already at work in your life. Thank Him for the sincere desire you have to break free from sinful habits and walk in the Spirit. Those small beginnings are firm steps in the direction of full maturity.[1]

—Mike Bickle

Chapter 1

Men: Must We Struggle to Serve Christ?

OLD MAN — Struggles with fleshly temptations and problems.

NEW MAN — Lives in God's power above the problems.

Are there things in your life with which you are not satisfied? Do you sometimes feel alone—as if you have nowhere to turn? Are you trying to live for God, but continue to battle the same lusts and sins that have dogged you for years?

Maybe you are disappointed with your career, your marriage or your health. Maybe your walk with God is not all you dreamed it would be. Maybe deep down inside you wish you had close friends with whom you could be open or an older, more experienced mentor to guide you through choppy seas.

If these struggles sound familiar, you are not alone. I have met literally hundreds of Christian men in the course of leading the company I founded nineteen years ago. Through conferences, my work with *New Man* magazine and in other venues, I have seen how most Christian men sincerely want to live overcoming lives—but they feel alone.

- Far too many do not have a real mentor.

- Far too many feel disconnected from a life-enhancing, life-changing community of believers.

■ Far too many have never really been strengthened and established in the Christian faith. So they toss to and fro, as the Bible puts it, never really becoming whom they can become in Christ.

■ Far too many men are floundering on the treacherous shoals of that thing called *midlife*. Sometimes it is so bad it becomes a crisis. Other times it is just a *malaise*—to use the word Jimmy Carter made famous.

■ And even though there may be times when we overcome spiritually or have great emotional highs at a conference or at church, it seems the same problems and temptations continue to nip at our heels—or even overwhelm us.

While struggles exist, there is a realm in the Spirit where we can live above the problems. There is a place in God where we put off the "old man" and become the "new man" that Christ has purposed for us to become. That is what this book is about. It is to help you move from where you are to where you can be in Christ. Of course, we never really "arrive" spiritually. But as we grow spiritually, we can begin to soar like an eagle—not stay around the barnyard with all the turkeys, or worse yet, wallow in the mire like a bunch of pigs.

The Christian life is not something you live alone, as we all know. It is meant to be lived in real relationship with others. The key word for many men is *real*—not churchy, religious or insincere. The Bible talks about working through our salvation with fear and trembling (Phil. 2:12, KJV). Yet too many men walk alone: alone with the fear, alone with the hurts, alone with the temptations, alone with their doubts, alone with their loneliness. They confide a limited amount in Christian "friends," but the struggles run much deeper. No one shows them how to turn the corner from what the Bible calls "the old man" to becoming a "new man" in Christ.

Like so many children reared in pastors' homes, I trusted Jesus Christ as my Savior early—age five to be exact. I was a good kid, made good grades and followed the rules. My father ministered in the Assemblies of God, and as I was growing up I heard him talk about a deeper experience with the Holy Spirit available to Christians, which was called the *baptism of the Holy Spirit.*

I wanted all that God had to offer, and at the age of twelve I received the baptism of the Holy Spirit that my father taught about. It was genuine, life-changing, unforgettable—and is the motivation for much of what I do today. The experience let me know a bit of the power of God. I knew God was real, but in all honesty, even as a "preacher's kid" I received little or no training in how to live the Christian life.

> ## I lived for Christ some of the time and for Satan some of the time— the same pattern I see lived out all too often in the lives of many Christian men I know.

My hormones changed at age thirteen, and at the exact moment when this good and eager-to-please child began to be tempted by sin, my dad went off to graduate school in another state. It all made complete sense—on paper. My parents had a strong marriage, and they hated the idea of being apart. But they also had a mortgage, my mom had a good job and my dad was going to come back to his existing job after getting his doctorate. They decided it was better if Dad went off to graduate school while the rest of us stayed behind.

My dad could not have left at a worse time.

The results were devastating. At a time when I needed a strong male influence, I lived in what was essentially a single-parent home. During those two pivotal years I became more and more rebellious, testing the waters of sin and living a double life of which my parents were completely unaware. I was definitely hanging around the wrong crowd, even though I never completely lost touch with my Christian friends.

The result, as you can imagine, was one mixed-up, unhappy teenager. I knew God was real, but the sinful nature—the "old man"—was strong and tenacious. I simply did not know how to live a victorious life. I lived for Christ some of the time and for Satan some of the time—the same pattern I see lived out all too often in the lives of many Christian men I know. I would repent at the altar at a revival service and backslide within a month or two. I finally got fed up with the hypocrisy of my life. I decided that if I could not be a good *Christian*, then I would be a good *sinner*. Being honest with myself was more attractive than being a hypocrite.

Was that right or logical? No. But that was how my life went for several years. I joined a fraternity and sowed the wild oats I was not allowed to sow at home. For a while, the "hell raising" was fun, like enjoying some forbidden fruit. But it was not satisfying. I knew I was doing wrong. I had learned enough scriptural concepts that I knew I would spend eternity in hell if I did not get right with God. Increasingly I was disillusioned by the wickedness I saw all around me—and within me. I felt alone, almost afraid.

As I look back, I see that I finally came to the end of my self in the middle of my university career—as a sophomore at the University of Florida. I decided to turn my life over to Christ without reservation. Now I understand that the Holy Spirit had been hounding me the entire time. I made a decision to follow Christ. I did not answer an altar call; instead, I spent several evenings walking alone around the campus, crisscrossing the campus green where I could pour out my heart to God. After so many years of up-and-down Christianity, I remember telling God, "This time it has got to work!"

I do not say that *I got saved*. I had a salvation experience when I was five. Yet I was in a backslidden stage. I needed to come back to God. And when I did, the Holy Spirit began to teach me how to be the "good" Christian I longed to be. This event in January 1971 was a *life-changing experience*. With God's help, I have lived for Him since then.

It has not always been smooth. I have had my ups and downs. I know what it is to feel that pull of sin and to have to consciously renew my mind when it seems that every fiber of my being wants to give in. Much of this book deals with renewing the mind. Over the years I have learned what it is to become a "new man" in Christ. As the Bible says, "Old things are passed away; behold, all things are become new" (2 Cor. 5:17, KJV).

I am no expert. God knows I have not arrived. I am the first to say I am a "sinner saved by grace." In fact, one of the struggles I have had to deal with as I have worked on this book for the past year is the conflict between giving advice on how to live for God and knowing well the weaknesses in my own life.

One night not long before this manuscript was ready for the printer, I sat and talked to my wife about our own problems of communication. Actually, she did most of the talking.

I had been under some sort of cloud, my time priorities were all messed up and I had not been focusing on the marriage at all. "What kind of advice," Joy wanted to know, "are you going to give other men on how to have a good marriage?"

Ouch.

However, as I have written I have found that the days I feel most inadequate are the days the words flow the most freely. Writing this book has been an exclamation point to the words of the apostle Paul, who declared, "When I am weak, then I *am* strong" (2 Cor. 12:10, emphasis added). Maybe that is because God uses the weak things to confound the wise.

I have had to overcome many things in my own life. Apart from the grace of God, I can be small-minded, able to find the cloud in every silver lining and unable to do anything more than just "get by" financially. But as I have come under God's mighty hand, He has given me a measure of success. I have had the privilege of traveling the world—hopefully with something to share with other men.

I began this book because mentoring men and showing them the way has become a passion of mine—and because it seemed that, for all the men's books out there, precious few were addressing the issues that men came to me about. I was tired of not having answers for them, and that in turn prompted me to write this book.

But the writing experience has made me drill deep into my own heart and life, not just to find stories and examples to use to help you, but to discover those areas that God is still working on in *me*. It is not how successful you are, if your name is on a company (as mine is), if you have met famous people or whatever else we might consider worthy of admiration or imitation.

In fact, as the book has progressed I have come to realize that in some ways I am dealing with what has come to be called *men's ministry*. And maybe here is where I begin to feel inadequate. If I compare myself to other men whose names are associated with men's ministry, I am not a rousing coach like Bill McCartney; I am not the father everyone wishes they had like Edwin Louis Cole; I have not been a successful real estate mogul like Patrick Morley. And while I am thankful for where God has brought me, at midlife I know I am not where I need to be or where God will take me in the future. In many ways, I am still becoming the "new man in Christ" that I write about in this book.

Many men lack meaningful friendships and desire real intimacy with other men.

But I know from personal experience that God is real. He *did* change me—and He *is changing* me "from glory to glory" as the Scriptures say (2 Cor. 3:18, KJV). I know that even though Satan comes to "steal and kill and destroy," Jesus has come "to give life in all its fullness" (John 10:10). That is not just a recitation to me. It is an actual fact that I have seen played out in my own life. He really has given me life in all its fullness, and I am thankful for that. So like a man in the desert who has only one cup of water, I offer that to you if you are thirsty for a drink.

The good news of the gospel is that God, through His mercy, makes us new men in Christ. That is the thrust of this book. When temptation comes—and we both know it seems to be ever present—there is a way of escape. It is possible to overcome whatever is in our past—hurt, sins, guilt, wrong choices, damaged relationships—to become new men in Christ. I want to show you how.

In this book, through the stories of men who have been through any number of situations and through the advice of some of the people I respect most in their fields, you will see that God longs to lead us out of sinful and controlling life patterns. You will see how you can change and be renewed.

The Real Issues

I spent a lot of time talking with friends and colleagues during the writing of this book. Throughout the book, you will meet some of these men; in most cases their names will have been changed. (And, where indicated, I have sometimes included a longer version of their testimonies on our website.) Collectively, my interviews gave me a glimpse into what specific areas men feel they need help with.

Lusts, temptations, masturbation and pornography

Many men still struggle with the ghosts of their past. Some have been sexually abused as children or young men. Or, their struggles with lust or pornography—and often masturbation—continue to haunt them, making them feel there will never be victory. Single men face their own issues with lust and frustrated sexual desire.

Marriage issues

Sexual issues creep into the marriage bedroom as well. Many men feel trapped in less than perfect marriages—often due to their own inability to provide Christian leadership in the home or because no one ever showed them a model of being a Christian husband. Men with sexual addictions often lose interest in their wives, leaving them sexually frustrated and compounding the problems of the marriage.[2]

Fathering issues

Many men did not have a good relationship with their fathers, and they lack the knowledge about how to father the next generation. Or they make the same mistakes in fathering with their own children that their fathers made with them. Some have never had a positive male role model in their lives, and they find it hard to interact with their children in healthy, positive ways. There is an innate something in men that causes us to reach out for the fathers we never had, or who were emotionally unavailable, or even to feel a need to be *re*-parented.

Aging issues

Middle-aged men often face their own mortality for the first time when their parents die—just as they notice their own libido is dropping. They begin to recognize that peers and friends the same age as they are have begun to deal with declining issues. They find they cannot do everything that they used to be able to do. Often these concerns dominate their thoughts and make them irritable and hard to be around. They feel as if no one understands them, and they feel that they cannot open up because they have no one to trust with their innermost thoughts.

Underlying loneliness

Many men said they lack meaningful friendships and desire real intimacy with other men. Few had a good relationship with their dad or siblings. Most wanted close friends, but felt they must keep on a mask or others will not like them. They know they need male companionship and accountability. They long for a confidant or a mentor to help them, but they do not know where to turn. And even if those friends were there, they do not have friendship skills to help them be a friend or mentor to others.

Loneliness is a major factor in sexual addictions. How many men surf the porno sites with their wives watching? Very few, if any. Loneliness breeds problems if we let it do so.

One man I interviewed mentioned the importance of accountability—the kind spoken of in Galatians 6:1–2, which says, "Dear brothers and sisters, if another Christian is overcome by some sin, you who are godly should gently and humbly help that person back onto the right path. And be careful not to fall into the same temptation yourself. Share each other's troubles and problems, and in this way obey the law of Christ."

> ## Too many of us feel trapped in a life that is nothing like the life we imagined, one that is going way too fast.

Accountability is vitally important to each one of us. But it needs to be the kind spoken of in these verses. Most men do not share what is really going on. Sometimes an accountability group can be just someplace to "hang out with the guys." Real accountability does more than sharpen us, give us new ideas and give us courage to stand—real accountability helps us become more like Christ and helps us to break the hold of things that hinder us from that. One man put it to me as learning "how to be themselves in God."

Lack of life vision

Many men I talked to seemed to have lost their purpose or become cynical. They doubted that God could use them to accomplish something lasting and meaningful in this life. Maybe you have seen the television commercial where children talk about what they want to be when they grow up, solemnly offering answers such as "a brown-nose" or "have a dead-end job." The pathos in this commercial is so thick you could cut it with a knife. The point is, too many of us feel trapped in a life that is nothing like the life we imagined, one that is going way too fast.

Lack of spiritual power

Our lament is the same as the lament of the prophet Habakkuk: "I have heard all about you, LORD, and I am filled with awe by the amazing things you have done. In this time of our deep need, begin again to help us, as you did in years gone by. Show us your power to save us. And in your anger, remember your mercy" (Hab. 3:2).

We hear stories all around us of the power of God to break addictions, deliver from sin and make lives work—but it always seems to happen to someone else. We feel empty, inept, powerless to live the lives we know God wants us to live. Alone, discouraged and weak, we fake it and hope no one notices.

Men want to know the will of God. They want to know the purpose they have, but often they are clueless. Where to turn? Who to help? How to change? We feel as the disciples must have felt as they gathered in the upper room after the death of Jesus. They had no idea of the power they were about to receive—they only knew they had none at that moment.

Financial and career goals

Having success—or not having it—can both bring problems. Often when men succeed, the benefits of their success seem to pull them in the direction of the cares of this world. But the opposite is also true; when there are not enough finances to pay the bills, or men's careers are not going forward the way they should, those men feel defeated and depressed.

Health issues

At every juncture of life, health issues concern men. Young men may become obsessed with meeting the world's standards for the "cool, attractive, with-it" appearance. Or they may become so focused on reaching their own career goals that they neglect taking care of themselves properly and suffer from stress or the effects of "workaholism." Men in their middle years must face emerging health issues that never affected them before—as well as the recognition that they are no longer the fine specimens of youth that they used to be. Older men face health issues almost daily, and they struggle to feel good about being in the declining years of their health—and lives.

Finding Answers

As the founder and publisher of *New Man*, I believe God has given me a vision for ministering to men in a new way. This book is an outgrowth of that vision. In fact, if you purchased the hardbound version of this book, you received a free one-year subscription to *New Man*. This way our journey through the struggles and joys of manhood can continue through the pages of the magazine.

In *New Man* magazine and in this book, I will tell the stories of men just like you who struggle. I will also share the testimonies of men who have turned the corner on their struggles and experienced victory—and who begin to soar in spiritual things, hungry for more of God and a life of holiness and fulfillment.

Writing this book (my first to author alone) is part of my vision to minister more directly and personally to men such as you and to help show you the way.

It bears repeating: I do not have all the answers. But in my odyssey, God has helped me overcome many struggles and to have great faith for helping other men. I know God can change you. It is more than a legalistic approach to try harder and commit to self and others not to sin. It is developing a passion for Jesus and knowing Him intimately.

Someone has said that living the Christian life is not *difficult*, it is *impossible*—that is, *without the power of the Holy Spirit.*

Though I do not have all the answers, I can tell you what has worked for me and what is working for others. I can offer hope. I can give you what God has given me. And I can trust the Holy Spirit to speak to you in the pages of this book and to put within your heart a deep, deep hunger for more of Him.

The Bible says that hope is what faith is made of (Heb. 11:1). I used to struggle with "faith confessions" in which I prayed for things that did not exist and I knew logically might never exist. It did not seem honest to say something existed that I knew did not exist.

But then I learned that hope is the first step toward faith, and hope does not say something is when it is not; hope merely says, "It is possible."

I direct my hope toward God because He can do all things. I personally have that hope in Him. I can say honestly that anything "is possible"—even for you.

That is because right now somewhere in the world an impossibly broken marriage is being repaired; someone given up to die of cancer is being healed; someone struggling with seemingly hopeless sexual addictions is finally being set free. Jesus is at work right now making things right in thousands, even millions of lives around the globe. I want to be one of them. I want you to be one of them, too.

This book will tell stories of men who have struggled and won over the lusts, temptations and problems that seem common to all men. I believe it will provide hope that there is a better way, that it is possible to become a new man in Christ and to develop the passion for God that is the goal of the Christian life.

I deal with practical issues in the last section of the book to help you see measurable improvement in the key areas of our lives as men—particularly in your own life. It is my way of mentoring you to move to the next level.

With God's help, you do have the power to change. No matter where you are in your Christian walk—whether a new believer or someone who has followed Jesus for a long time—there *is* hope that you can attain your full destiny in Christ.

There is a place of maturity that awaits you and a destiny that beckons you. This book will help you along the way.

A book is by its very nature a humble offering, yet I know there are stories and testimonies of victory in the following chapters that will convey the difference that the power of God can make in your life. My prayer is that God will reach through these paragraphs and grab hold of your heart in a way that shakes you loose of some sin or gets you back into right relationships with other people. I am eager to hear from you as we journey together toward the "new man" in God that He has destined us to be.

Let us begin the journey by discussing what I believe is at the root of the problem—fatherlessness.

Talk about it   Think about it

Men: Must We Struggle to Serve Christ?

Author's note: I want this book to be useful, so at the end of each chapter I have prepared some questions. Why? Because it is useful to reflect on what you have read if you are to learn from it. Plus, I believe many men's groups will want to use this book for small group discussion. I have tried to give something for the individual reader as well as for groups.

For more information on this topic (which we will add to as time passes) check out our www.oldmannewman.com website. Use the user id: **oldman** and the password **newman**. These are **case sensitive,** so use all lowercase letters and leave no spaces.

1. In a group setting: What do you hope to get out of this study? As an individual: What motivated you to buy this book? What do you want to happen in your life as a result of reading this book?

2. Discuss this statement on page 6, "But I know from experience that God is real. He *did* change me—and He *is changing* me 'from glory to glory' as the Scriptures say" (2 Cor. 3:18, KJV). When did God become more than a word for you?

There are nine crucial areas in the lives of men. They are:

- Lust issues
- Marriage issues
- Fathering issues
- Aging issues
- Loneliness
- Lack of life vision
- Lack of spiritual power
- Financial and career goals
- Health issues

If you could experience breakthrough in just one of these areas, which would it be, and why?

A clip from

New Man July/August 1994

What Will Your Kids Engrave on Your Tombstone?

Many men suffer at the hands of a man who is a father in the biological sense only. As part of one research project, thousands of men were asked what kind of epitaph they would give their fathers. The results reflected a variety of relationship types quoted in *New Man* magazine.

"Here lies my dad. Always gone; still is."

"Here lies my dad. He did not demonstrate love to his sons."

"Here lies my dad, a hard-working man full of pride who died lonely."

"Here lies my dad. If your actions matched your talk, you would be awesome."

Others were happier:

"Here lies my dad. One of my best friends and a real neat guy."

"Here lies my dad, a man who encouraged his children to reach for their dreams."

"Here lies my dad, a man to model my own life by and try to equal."

"Here lies my dad, one of the men I most admire."[1]

Chapter 2

Fatherlessness:
The Root of the Problem

OLD MAN — Suffers with the limiting destructive effects of a father-wound.

NEW MAN — Walks in a new destiny from his perfect heavenly Father.

A major source of hurt for men is their sense of fatherlessness. Recently I interviewed a fifty-two-year-old friend of mine whose father had been dead for ten years. I was impressed by this man's sincerity and love for the Lord.

But my friend had lived a messy life. By his own admission, he had also become a sex addict like his dad before him. Before God got hold of him, he had two failed marriages, lost a successful business that had earned him nearly $200,000 a year and had a cocaine habit. Hitting bottom made him call out to God.

As he told me his testimony that day, the only time he choked up was when he talked about his dad. His dad was a hard-drinking, hard-working womanizer who was never close to any of his children and never told them he loved them. He fought continuously with his wife, which made her lean on the oldest son for emotional support. It was something the boy was not equipped to handle.

The result was a boy with low self-esteem who did not know how to connect emotionally with anyone—least of all a woman.

Years later my friend finally heard his dad say he loved him. It happened when he was thirty years old and was in the hospital for some minor surgery. His dad visited him, and as he left the hospital room, my friend called out to him, "Dad, I love you," to which his father replied, "I love you, too." My friend broke down in tears. "Dad, do you realize that is the first time I have ever heard you say 'I love you'?" he said. To which his dad replied, "I thought you knew."

The Father-Wound

Boys don't automatically know their fathers love them. When there is silence instead of supportiveness, ambivalence instead of affirmation, doubt instead of confidence, it leaves a huge hole that various authors have dubbed the "father-wound." My friend's example is a classic case. When it comes to a father's love, silence is crippling, not golden.

"I am still waiting for my father to talk to me about sex and success, money and marriage, religion and raising kids," a *Men's Health* magazine editor confessed after his father died. "The shame of it is, I don't know a man my age who does not feel as if he is navigating his life without a map."

> Inflicting father-wounds on your children is not inevitable, nor do you have **to carry the pain of your father-wound for the rest of your life.**

Gordon Dalbey, author of several pioneering books in this field, wrote this: "This epidemic 'father-wound' has been the finest revelation from the secular men's movement of God's momentous work among men today. Tragically, the growing mainstream Christian men's movement has largely ignored it—even though God has displayed its truth clearly in Scripture."[2]

I cannot agree more. As I explain later in this chapter, I have my own father-wound, and I have never known a man who did not have one. But inflicting father-wounds on your children is not inevitable, nor do you have to carry the pain of your father-wound for the rest of your life.

I am painfully aware of this issue, and I am determined by the power of God not to pass it along to my two sons, although I have come to realize I have already repeated with my sons some of the mistakes my dad made with me. "No pain seems to strike more deeply in the heart of a man than to be abandoned by his dad–either physically or emotionally. And it makes it difficult for many men to relate then to our Father God, who is the only one who can heal this wound," as Dalbey writes. Yet Dalbey's the expert here, not me, so I'll share some of the points he makes:

- Jesus came to reconcile humanity to the Father (John 14:8–13). Nowhere in this world is the impetus for that reconciliation more keenly felt than in relationship with our earthly fathers.

- That's why the enemy of God is hell-bent to make us deny not only the father-wound itself, but the Fatherhood of God. He promises to cover this deep shame in men today by urging us into a variety of compulsive/addictive behaviors, from drugs and pornography to workaholism and religious legalism.

- The father-wound is a wound of absence. Therefore, it is harder to recognize than other wounds—and ultimately, more destructive.[3]

If a man who is suffering from a father-wound will honestly acknowledge the wound, he can begin to grieve the pain and then move away from it. But there is no human power that can heal the wound and allow you to move into your destiny in God. Only Jesus can heal it. Only Jesus can overcome the sin nature and restore us to a right relationship with God—the Father of us all. Dalbey writes: "Only the dignity of sonship can overcome the shame of abandonment."[4]

Christians have a task—neither to worship manhood nor to curse it, but to redeem it, as Dalbey puts it so well. Only when we face our shame and hand it to Jesus can we heal from it. Jesus takes our wretched, sinful "old man" and, through His miraculous work of redemption, hands the "new man" back to us—fully redeemed and set free from the bondages of the old man.

Dalbey also makes this point: Men who have not allowed Jesus to do His redemptive work in their lives cannot know the resurrection power Christ can give. Instead they try to hide their wounds, often living a Christian life that nothing is more than a façade—a whited sepulcher—together and attractive on the outside, but filled with the stench of sin within.

Most men today long to feel secure in their manhood. But they are locked in, paralyzed by sin, overwhelmed by the emptiness of having been abandoned by their fathers.

But when a man—any man, every man—cries out to Jesus with his pain, that pain can be put to death, Dalbey writes. Jesus will fill that man with the love of his heavenly Father who enables men to see their fathers as God sees them—lonely, abandoned by their own fathers and incapable of modeling manhood. Jesus will teach us to see our fathers as we see ourselves—hopeless and destitute without our Father God.

Healing fatherlessness
oldmannewman.com

Dalbey believes that "a boy cries from his father's wounds; Dad hurts you, and you cry. A man cries for his father's wounds, as an intercessor. This leads him into compassion for Dad, and by grace, forgiveness—and at last, freedom from the generational cycle of destruction—to walk in his own true destiny."[5]

Edwin Louis Cole, writing in *New Man*, says this:

> **Fatherlessness is far more than just the absence of the father. Fatherlessness is the absence of concern for the family. But the core problem of fatherlessness is actually childishness—immature males in men's bodies . . . Maturity does not come with age, but with the acceptance of responsibility.**[6]

"Immature males in men's bodies" are men suffering the gripping pain of an open father-wound. The acceptance of responsibility for their display of fatherlessness is only possible when they have acknowledged their wound, handed it to Jesus and allowed Him to complete His redemptive work in their lives. The "old man" is the immature male in a man's body. The "new man" is fully mature in Christ—a destiny available to all men regardless of their age.

> # The core problem of fatherlessness is immature males in men's bodies.
> ## Maturity does not come with age, but with the acceptance of responsibility.

One survey by the National Center for Fathering showed that only a third of men considered their father their male role model. (Nearly 20 percent said they had no male role model.)[7] To see what the lack of a good father can do to a life, read the monthly newsletter from Exodus International, a Christian ministry that helps homosexuals overcome that lifestyle through the redeeming power of Christ. It is remarkable how many men mention their fathers in the first few paragraphs of their testimonies.

One recovering homosexual wrote: "Dad was always working to support our family of five children. Unfortunately, his constant worries about money left him short-tempered and critical. He had little time to spend with us, and as I grew older, I began to resent him."[8]

Another stated: "The inner pain started early in my life. At the age of five, I promised my mother that I would care for her, in light of the abuse we all suffered from my father . . . But I craved attention from [other boys] to replace what was missing from my father."[9]

Another said that his father's absence caused a deep loneliness in his life. "It was a hurt that was temporarily forgotten as I plunged into gay relationships," he wrote.[10]

Finally, one man put in words what has probably been the response of many men to the sense of fatherlessness they felt:

> **When I was a child, I didn't know that my father loved me . . . Though he did not mean to hurt me, I felt rejected and began to shut him out emotionally.**[11]

Of course, many other factors caused these men to veer into homosexuality, but what if the strong presence of a father had been there? Surely, many of them would have been spared their own bad choices had they received proper direction at critical times.

Then there are those like Avery Johnson, point guard for the San Antonio Spurs. Johnson had a healthy, even enviable relationship with his father. Avery came from a big family. His father was the rock of the family. Although his father died a few years ago, Avery found it easy to honor him, because he was always there for him. He believes that is one reason he is headed in the right direction—becoming the type of father, husband and man he believes God wants him to be. "I have no regrets now that Dad is gone," he says. "We lived life to the fullest together. Not only did we talk about basketball and family, we could talk about the Lord anywhere, anytime."

Avery remembers the day he gave his life to Christ. "I walked up to my dad with this look on my face. He said, 'You don't even have to say it. When are you getting baptized?' I said, 'Seven, tonight.' He said, 'I'll be there.' When a father and son are close, there's something almost supernatural that happens between them."[12]

Being a father is very important. Fathering my two sons, Cameron and Chandler, is very high on my list of priorities—

He was always there
▶ oldmannewman.com

over career, over spending time with my men's group, over everything except my relationships with my God and my wife. I do not want to make any mistakes in my relationship with them that could create a father-wound in their lives. Yet as high a priority as I place on it, my older son, Cameron, remembers me as being distant and away from home a lot on business trips when he was young. There was time we spent together when he was tiny, which I called *together time.* But Cameron remembers that my body was there, but my mind was far away. Thankfully, Cameron has found it in his heart to forgive my shortcomings as a father and is off to a great start in his career as a young visionary who wants to reach his generation for Christ.

Eleven years after Cameron was born, his brother, Chandler, came along. I am much closer to Chandler at an early age than I was with Cameron at the same age. I hope Chandler will not feel the same sort of regret when he grows up that Cameron tells me he used to feel.

Why do I share this? It is not because I like admitting it even to myself or to my wife, let alone to the tens of thousands of people who will read this. And everything in me wants to point out that if graded on the curve as a dad, I think I would still get a good grade. I share it to let you know that even when we think we are doing a good job of parenting, we often fall short. We are not necessarily being the dad our children need.

But there is hope. Perpetuating your father's mistakes perpetuates your pain into the next generation. But you do not have to make the same mistakes. The power of God can heal you. Keep reading to see how God has done this in the lives of many men—and how He can do this in your life.

I believe the Spirit of God can "re-parent" you and give you the power to parent your children. And the Word of God can show you how to be a perfect father—exactly the father God created you to be with your own children. You can break the generational curse of the father-wound—and I will show you how.

Needed—Fathers Who Father

There is no getting around it—God created fathers to be with their children. Children thrive under a father's loving care, just as we thrive as God's children under His loving care. In an article he wrote for *New Man,* Mike Yorkey, a writer from San Diego, states: "When it comes to raising kids, most fathers understand they get what they put into it. Usually within ten to twenty years they see the fruit of their labor."[13] We can see these fruits of a father's labor in many of the famous sons and daughters who are receiving media attention—such as golf great Tiger Woods, rising tennis stars Serena and Venus Williams and, a great Christian example of fatherhood, Franklin Graham, son of Billy Graham.

But most of us have to deal with at least some of our father's shortcomings.

Preston Gillham talks about recovering your father's fumble, using a football term to illustrate what we can do when our fathers fail. He says that men all over the world wrestle with questions related to masculine doubt and male insecurity. He makes an important point:

> When fathers fail
> oldmannewman.com

> But regardless of whether your dad fumbled the ball or handed it off to you definitively, the point remains: Your heavenly Father has placed His capable and determined hands on the ball, and while handing it off to you, He has blessed you as a man. He is proud to call you His friend and His son.[14]

Honor Your Father

Ken Canfield, writing for *New Man* magazine, gave these tips for honoring your father. Whenever you do this, it becomes "father's day" in a sense.

Affirm him

If you want to honor your father but don't know where to

begin, one suggestion from Dennis Rainey's book *The Tribute* is to make a list of memories related to your father. (If that relationship involves a lot of pain or abuse, you would be wise to go through this process with help from a competent counselor. You may have some healing to do before honoring your father is possible.) These positive memories should provide plenty of ammunition to barrage your dad with expressions of honor and blessing.

Forgive him

Forgiveness faces the facts, with all the pain, and then consciously decides not to hold those actions against a person. In forgiving, you remove the tie between past actions and present relationship. And your father's actions will no longer determine your emotions, thoughts and behavior. Through forgiveness, you gain freedom and power—important assets to your own success as a dad.

Engage him

As two adults, your relationship can be more of a friendship than it is ever been. Make an effort to stay in touch, and go out of your way to include him in family activities. Affirm and esteem him, and look for common interests you can develop and share together.

Involve him

As a granddad your father probably has a childlike wonder when it comes to his grandkids, and he is honored when you encourage him to be involved in their lives. You can also honor him by telling your children about him—about what life was like for him as a child, about what he has accomplished in his life, about his qualities as a father. (This one works even if your father has passed away.)

It is your father's deep desire to pass on something positive—skills, values and traditions—to the coming generation. In a culture where he may feel "in the way" or "out of touch," you can honor him by affirming the vital contribution he can make to your life and the lives of your children.[15]

A father's blessing
oldmannewman.com

I encourage you not to let "old man" thinking continue to hinder your relationship with your father. As you become a new man, all you have to lose is the pain of the past, and you stand to gain a great friend. Do it for him; do it for you.

Gary Smalley gives an excellent real-life example of this. Smalley's father treated him well as a young boy, but when he became a teenager, his father became angry, demanding, aloof and controlling. "To be honest, I probably dishonored my father as much as anything," Smalley wrote. "He died when I was in high school, and I cannot recall that I had ever treated him as a valuable person."

When Smalley became a Christian, he was convicted by the verse, "'Honor your father and mother.' This is the first of the Ten Commandments that ends with a promise. And this is the promise: If you honor your father and mother, 'you will live a long life, full of blessing'" (Eph. 6:2–3). He decided to list all the good traits his father had. This exercise gave him a sense of appreciation and honor for his dad that he had never felt before. Then he listed all the negative things he felt he could not honor in his father's example, but instead of dwelling on them, he decided to do the opposite of each one in his own life.

For example, when he detected himself becoming distant from his own children, he spotted it as a negative trait and reminded himself to connect with them instead. "Yes, [my father] ruined relationships with his disease of selfishness, but I got vaccinated in the process!" he wrote.[16]

Author Patrick Means, in his excellent book titled *Men's Secret Wars*, says that the father-wound cripples a son with the message that he doesn't measure up as a man. He writes, "For this reason, most men experience the wound left by their father as a deeper and more painful wound than the wound left by their mother. This point was graphically illustrated in a true story told by Richard Rohr.

"A friend of his, a nun, was working in a men's prison. One spring an inmate asked the nun to buy him a Mother's Day card to send home. She agreed. But word traveled fast in the prison; soon hundreds of inmates were asking for cards. So the nun contracted a greeting card manufacturer, who happily sent crates of Mother's Day cards to the prison. All the cards were passed out.

"Soon afterward the nun realized that Father's Day was approaching and, thinking ahead, once again called the card manufacturer, who responded quickly with crates of Father's Day cards. Years later, the nun told Rohr, she still had every one of them. Not one prisoner requested a card for his father."[17]

My Own Example

My dad was, by nearly every measure, a good father. He was a Christian man who never smoked or drank. I never heard him swear the entire time I was growing up. When he died a few years ago, he had been married to my mother for nearly forty-eight years.

Yet to me he was always distant. I remember as a child thinking he was always away, either visiting parishioners when he pastored, working long hours to put himself through graduate school or spending even longer hours preparing for classes or counseling students when he taught in a Bible college.

When he did "play catch" with me or go to a school function, I had the distinct feeling he would rather have been doing something else. Now that I reflect on it, maybe this is the same thing Cameron felt from me a generation later. I never felt approved by my dad. Maybe I developed a tendency to overachieve to try to prove something to him.

My dad would tease us in belittling ways. For example, he had nicknames for my brother and sister and I that were the wrong gender—Guinevere for me, Gertrude for my brother and Walter for my sister—as if we were each born the wrong sex. And as we would travel and see a tumbled-down old house that was overgrown with weeds, he would point out that was our dream home. His oddball humor probably made no lasting marks on us (other than the fact I remember it so clearly so many years later), but I took it to mean that somehow there was something wrong with us.

Later in life, as I achieved some success, my dad always said he was proud of me. But at a time when I was striving to think big and to achieve some goals, I felt he had settled into a pattern of small goals. He was perfectly content to work for a small salary, live in small houses and drive an inexpensive car. But he didn't have to settle for this—he was an intelligent, talented and gifted man who just was not looking for more in life.

I am merely telling you how I felt. I am not trying to say that my dad was a failure—he was not. In fact, he was the first in our extended family to earn a doctorate. Yet he was content with small goals. Building something "successful" was not important to him.

It is the spiritual goals and the inner qualities that make a man— always have and always will.

It will be clear to you by the end of this book that I do not exalt material goals. It is the spiritual goals and the inner qualities that make a man—always have and always will. Yet we in America live in the most prosperous country in the world. And in our culture, we need finances to live. So I believe it is important that men understand that with hard work and diligence they can improve their lot in life financially—for themselves, for those who depend on them for support and to bless others. (See 2 Corinthians 9:6–11.)

So if you are not a millionaire, does that make you a failure? Of course not. If you are struggling financially, however, I have some principles to share with you later that could completely revolutionize your finances. And it may be that some of your financial struggles result from the relationship you had with your dad.

In the late seventies I came across a book about recruiting

corporate executives. The book was recommended to me by a friend, or I would not have ordinarily read it. The book devoted an entire chapter on how to evaluate a potential success when recruiting a CEO by discovering what sort of relationship the man had with his own father.

The author made an observation that made such an impression on me that I remember it twenty years later, mainly because I have quoted it so many times. Almost without exception I have found that men have never thought about this, but that they nearly always agree with his theory.

The author believed that financially, most men cannot become more successful than their fathers, other than by a factor of about 10 percent. And he measured it by the way the boy looked at his father at age five. His point was that you can predict someone's success in the workplace by knowing how successful or unsuccessful his father was.

Think about it. Many boys follow their dads into the same line of work and generally live at the same economic level. Laborers' sons often become laborers, too. But the son of a senator will often run for high political office, as we've seen with both Al Gore, whose father was a senator, and George W. Bush and Jeb Bush, whose father was president of the United States and whose grandfather, Prescott Bush, was a senator.

The book gave anecdotal information on how many men found it difficult to become "more successful" than their own dads. The author said many of these men would actually subconsciously torpedo their own financial success if they moved beyond this invisible financial ceiling dictated by the way they viewed their dad's success at age five. Stop and think. Other than the fact that the standard of living has generally improved for everyone in the last few decades, do you earn more than your dad when you were a boy? Probably not.

Remember the famous book called *The Peter Principle* by Laurence J. Peter, which said that people tend to be promoted to their level of incompetence? Well, I wonder if this is a sort of financial Peter Principle where young boys are "marked" based on how well their own fathers performed financially.

There are many things more important than just being a success financially. And there are other reasons why men may not succeed financially. But I insert this idea here just because we are evaluating the effect on men caused by their dads. To a man, his job and earning power are as important as nearly any other part of his life other than family and spiritual things.

The bottom line is this: All of us have been stunted by the limitations placed on us by our dads—simply because none of us had perfect fathers. Some of us may have been stunted more because our fathers were more imperfect than others. But none of us are doomed to failure or powerless to rise above the limitations of imperfection in our fathers.

We have access to our perfect heavenly Father and His power to succeed. We have the Word of God, which is powerful to the breaking down of strongholds. We have a new destiny—because we can be new men in Christ.

Now let us look at one of the biggest ongoing problems men face—dealing with their sexuality.

Talk about it   Think about it

Fatherlessness: The Root of the Problem

Author's note: When we had some "focus groups" before the book was published, this chapter generated the most discussion. These questions are good for personal reflection or to discuss in a group.

For more information on this topic (which we will add to as time passes) check out our www.oldmannewman.com website. Use the user id: **oldman** and the password **newman**. These are **case sensitive,** so use all lowercase letters and leave no spaces.

1. Which of these epitaphs from the clip at the beginning of this chapter most closely describes your relationship with your father?

2. What do you suppose was going on in the life of your father—good or bad—to cause this to be true?

3. Relate why you agree or disagree with this statement on page 17 of the book: "The father-wound is a wound of absence. Therefore, it's harder to recognize than other wounds—*and ultimately, more destructive"* (emphasis added)?

4. On page 22, Preston Gillham quotes: "Regardless of whether your dad fumbled the ball or handed it off to you definitively, the point remains: *Your heavenly Father has placed His capable and determined hands on the ball, and while handing it off to you, He has blessed you as a man. He is proud to call you His friend and His son."* What does it mean to us that this is true?

A clip from

New Man July/August 1998

The Masturbation Puzzle

New Man: What would you say to the man who sees masturbation as wrong for himself but can't stop?

Dr. Doug Rosenau: Let him analyze the need he is meeting through masturbation. Is he looking for intimacy? Is he masking some inner pain? He should then ask God to help him find healthy, more appropriate ways to meet these needs. He also should share his struggle with a men's group or a close friend. Being accountable to someone is crucial in changing habits and attitudes. It is also important to stop feeding the lust with television or other environmental stimuli that he can control.[1]

Analyze the need

oldmannewman.com

Chapter 3

Sexual Problems:
Are They Always an Issue?

OLD MAN Deals with habitual, enslaving hidden
        sexual sin.

NEW MAN Lives like Jesus—tempted, but without
         sin.

Sex is a wonderful gift from God that is meant to be opened on the wedding night. But what is meant to be a gift of God can become a curse if it is abused and misused. Our society is so perverted that often a man's first information about sex is pornography. As I have counseled men, I have found that a surprising number have had to deal with some sort of serious sexual issues such as being molested as little boys or having had some type of homosexual encounters.

Thankfully, I was raised in a home where none of those things took place. I was an older teenager before I even knew what the words *incest* or *homosexuality* meant. Yet many Christian men fight ghosts of the past because of terrible, shameful ways they were introduced to sex.

This is especially true if they were molested as boys. When this happens it marks a boy for years—if not a lifetime. It makes him think that sex is dirty. It makes him question if he is gay. ("Why else would he have abused me unless I'm gay?") And it makes certain aspects about sex that are OK in the bounds of marital love to appear to be dirty and lustful.

All men struggle, whether it is with pride and self-righteousness or abject perversion. Remember, all have sinned and come short of the glory of God—even those who appear most pious.

Still, within evangelical circles, there is a hierarchy of sins. An imaginary sin "bell curve" stretches from little white lies ("My golf score was 82 today"—meaning you didn't count the balls that fell in the water) to the horrible opposite end: bondage to a sexual addiction.

Of course, there are things considered even worse by evangelicals, such as heavy drug addiction or alcoholism (but men with these problems generally do not even try to serve God or attend church) or things such as murder or robbery (which are dealt with by secular authorities, not usually the church). Within the church, serious sexual problems seem the most sinful to many people.

> I have found that what we cover up,
> God will expose anyway,
> **so it is best to come clean**
> **from the inside out.**

Because of our tendency to rank sins and define ourselves out of the most heinous categories (according to our judgments), the church is often seen by the secular community as unloving and intolerant. And men who grapple with sexual addictions—to use one example—are pushed to the margins, as if their sin is terminal.

I have been astonished as I read the responses of men who write us at *New Man* magazine to learn how many Christian men grapple with sexual issues. They are not necessarily homosexuals or sexual perverts, but somewhere along the line they developed wrong sexual responses to various stimuli, often because they were molested as little boys.

This is what happened to Dale, who was nine years old when

the fifteen-year-old neighbor boy who had been paid to watch them came into Dale's room and molested him. He warned Dale, "I'll kill you if you tell anyone." Dale's younger brother found out, and although Dale begged him not to, he told their mother. The neighbor was dismissed from sitting, but no other action was taken and the damage had been done. As Dale approached his teen years, he began to ask himself questions. Why did the neighbor molest him, but not his brother?

Dale still had a tender heart toward God, and he knew that God loved him. But confused by his unresolved feelings about his own sexuality, he developed a habit of masturbating several times a day. The condemnation he felt was overwhelming.

Later in his teens he met the lady who would become his wife–a dedicated Christian *and* a virgin. He knew God had put her in his life, yet he still had deep, unresolved roots of sexual confusion. Dale and his fiancée were married, although he did not tell her of his past sexual problem and subsequent struggles. For a few years he led a normal life, but still masturbated and could never function normally in the bedroom.

Then one night he opened up to a close Christian friend, and the healing began. Dale committed himself to facing the problem, and he cut off everything that fostered sexual stimulation. He began to gain control of his thoughts. God gave him grace to meet the affliction each time he needed it. Gradually his masturbation lessened. God started putting his marriage in order.

But during the time of success, old thoughts tried to come back. For a time, thoughts of the abuse were so powerful that Dale was nearly paralyzed with fear. God suddenly seemed very far away. Dale decided to tell his wife all that had happened. This was especially difficult since their sexual relationship had been recently revitalized. Dale knew he could lose her, but felt he had to risk it.

Over the next several weeks, he told her about his past, and she agreed to walk with him through the pain. Gradually the torment lifted, and he and his wife entered a new realm of love, honesty and intimacy.

"God has restored me and my marriage," Dale explains. "The enemy had me believing for a long time that I would never be free. I am sure that many men out there need help in the sexual area just as I did. I am still free today and am always ready to reprove the works of darkness. As I tell my own testimony, it seems as if I am talking about another person. I consider myself a very blessed individual to have been given the freedom I have."

It took Dale years to open up to his wife about his sexual problems, but when he did, God put him on the road to freedom. How many men are like Dale, hiding some past sin or shameful experience, allowing it to seep poison into their thoughts, marriage and the bedroom?

Hidden sins that we carry around with us hold great power to hinder us from being the healthy, godly men that we should be. But when the darkness within is brought out into the light of God's love, it dissipates—there is no darkness in God's light.

Let me add an important disclaimer here. Many times it does help to be totally open with your wife, as it did for Dale. But while it may make *you* feel better, it may create a problem for your wife that she will never get over. In the same way you would not confide a sexual addiction to your minor children (because they can't handle it emotionally), there are some wives who cannot handle this level of "honesty" about past sexual problems.

You need to confess your sins, but go to a pastor, an older, trusted Christian friend or to a trained counselor. Talk over with them how much you should tell your wife. She probably already knows you are dealing with something pretty bad. And if you just tell her you are struggling with lust (after reminding her that all men struggle with lust) or masturbation, that may be enough without going into all the gory details.

My Experience

A preteen boy does not usually have sexual thoughts. It is not until he reaches puberty that they begin. At least that is what happened to me. My parents told me how babies are born, but they did not warn me about the onset of puberty. Around age fourteen, my mind became filled with sexual thoughts. I feared that if my interest in sex kept increasing at the same rate it had been for the last year or two, I would be in serious trouble by the time I was a senior in high school.

Thankfully, my teenage libido took a less radical trajectory. But like all men, I learned what happens when the hormones kick in.

Sex is a wonderful gift from God that is meant to be opened on the wedding night.

Science tells us a male's sexual drive is the result of testosterone. Unlike any other mammal, our sex drive is generally the same day after day. Thankfully, the sex drive continues long after the woman's childbearing years have ended, and men can sire children—and enjoy an active sex relationship—late in life. But for those whose concerns about unwholesome sexual feelings hound them day after day, it seems like more a curse than a blessing.

I had one great-grandfather who did not marry until he was forty-nine, and then he had six children. Another great-grandfather remarried (after his first wife died) and fathered four more children when he was between the ages of fifty and fifty-six. I am glad God allows us to enjoy sex more than just for the purpose of bearing offspring.

I have a fantastic wife, and we have enjoyed a wonderful marriage for more than twenty-eight years as I write this. We all approach subjects from our own perspective, but when dealing with sex, I cannot write about my own experiences without including my lover. Out of deference to her and her privacy, I will be silent about my own experience, except to say I have a lot to be thankful for in a godly and loving wife! I know for a fact that sex is a gift of God. The Bible says, "Whatever is good and perfect comes to us from God above" (James 1:17). Sex within marriage can be—and should be—very good.

As I was writing this chapter, a friend told me he had thought for years that if he had any type of sex other than the so-called "missionary position" with his wife, he was giving in to some sort of perversion, the result of a single homosexual encounter he had several decades before. When he formed a close friendship with heterosexual Christian men and learned from them that "variety is the spice of life" when it comes to foreplay and intercourse in marriage, he totally changed his self-concept.

The purpose of this book is not to be a primer on healthy or unhealthy sexuality. There are many good books on the topic (and we've recommended several in the Appendix). I believe that some things are between the Lord and a married couple. My biblical backup is, "Marriage is honourable in all, and the bed undefiled" (Heb. 13:4, KJV). This means that since God created sex to be enjoyed, a certain amount of variety is meant to be enjoyed within marriage.

This is advice that I heard a well-known Christian psychologist say many years ago. It seems hard to believe that a grown man learning this in a candid conversation among Christian men in a small group would be so impacted. The friend mentioned above learned it only because he was vulnerable enough to open up and share his heart. In a later chapter I will deal with the need to be open with close friends who help you through life and hold you accountable.

One of the other great plagues of our day is pornography, but it is not new. Ancient Indian and Chinese artwork were often pornographic. There are many examples of pornography in Western culture, and the exploits of the Roman elite during the decline of that empire are well known. But since the printing press, pornography has become more and more prevalent and available. I am told the pornographic magazine industry is as large as the entire legitimate magazine industry put together.

When I was a boy, if you wanted pornography you had to go to the corner store and buy it. In Florida where I live, it must be behind a counter with a wrapper around it, making it hard to "browse." Most boys today get their first view of sex from pornography on the Internet—often at a website they access on their father's computer. A friend of mine didn't discover pornography until he was home on break from college and discovered a stash of *Playboy* magazines his father owned. It started him down a path toward sexual addiction from which he has only recently been delivered.

Now, of course, the Internet makes available with a few clicks of a mouse that which used to be hidden in less desirable parts of town. Not only that, but every conceivable perversion is available—some of which I hardly knew existed and don't want to know about.

Another good friend was telling me that he discovered his fourteen-year-old son looking at pornography on the Internet even though the dad had blocked the son's access. Apparently the boy figured a way to log on using his dad's log-in name—and his dad's name wasn't blocked. To make matters worse, the boy was fairly naive, but he was looking at a very perverted site. Horrified, the father immediately felt immense guilt for having unknowingly contributed to his son's introduction to such perversion. He lovingly pulled his son aside and talked to him about the importance of keeping our minds free of such perversions. Rather than turn the experience into a hostile and angry situation for them both, this father was able to cry and pray with his son about this, and hopefully something good came out of it.

A lot of fathers block Internet access for their children because of situations like this. The fact is, they need to block it for themselves, too. There are several new Christian filtering services. I have one on my own computer. Most of these companies are small, and it is difficult for them to find the customers who want their services. We have made an attempt at *New Man* to keep our readers up to date on what is available because this is so important.

Recently several of the major services such as America Online have begun offering filtering services that parents can enable for their children. Men can enable these same filtering services for themselves, asking their wife or a trusted friend to put in the password so there is no temptation to go around it.

Many Christian men who would never have an affair in real life, in a moment of weakness or just out of curiosity will look at Internet porn. Tens of thousands of perverted sites—many of them free—are just a click away.

To make matters worse, the chat rooms are often on topics that are less than wholesome. Some even advertise they are set up for "cyber sex" where people talk for hours about all sorts of sexual topics, usually masturbating as they talk. Many people access pornography (including phone sex) in order to masturbate. Most pornography is funded by men and for men. The size of the industry indicates the severity of the problem. On top of that, phone sex has become a major industry.

> Lusts that once existed only in the mind are now available to otherwise **good Christian men who may have a history of sexual addiction.**

Lusts that once existed only in the mind are now available to otherwise good Christian men who may have a history of sexual addiction, sexual abuse or chronic masturbation. A vast industry exists to help men act out their sexual fantasies.

"When it comes to male sex, let's stop pretending that everything is all right," writes Archibald Hart in his excellent survey of

SEXUAL PROBLEMS: ARE THEY ALWAYS AN ISSUE?

Christian men and sexuality.[2] "The truth is that most men in our culture are in serious trouble. [M]en today are becoming more and more confused about this most primal aspect of their being. They don't have a clue about what it is to be normal, and they can't figure out why women don't understand their preoccupation with sex."

Hart says the most common question he hears from men is, "Am I oversexed?" meaning, do they think too much about it? "The average normal male thinks about sex more often than he cares to admit," Hart writes.

> Men often wake up thinking about it, and they go to bed thinking about it.
>
> Immediately after being sexually satisfied, the normal male may be able to focus elsewhere—for a while. But it is just a matter of time before his thoughts lead him back to sex. And I'm talking about the preacher as much as the truck driver.[3]

His survey found that one in four men think about sex hourly, and nearly two of three think about it daily.[4]

Hart's words are not an indictment. Notice that he uses the term "normal male" twice in that passage. Thinking about sex is normal. Remember it was God who made us male and female. Sex is God's idea, and within marriage it is pure, holy and undefiled. It is all right to have an active fantasy life—*as long as the object of your fantasies is your wife.* Make no mistake about it: It is possible—even necessary—to discipline your mind to keep your thoughts pure. I will show you how later.

Sexual Addiction

Sometimes a man's thoughts about sex go beyond "normal." They become a preoccupation, a fixation—even an addiction. My observation in counseling men is that some who think they are dealing with simple lust are actually dealing with full-blown addictive behavior. The number of men who have a sexual "addiction" ought to be a warning to all of us not to toy with sexual sin.

Far too many men have become waylaid by sin before they ever knew what hit them. Men who do not control what comes in their eye gate or who cannot control what was done to them may have created a pattern of stimulus and response that draws them ever closer into sin's deadly grip. What was designed to bond them to their wives instead superglues them to pornography or aberrant behavior.

> # Churches have done far too little to bring this problem into the open.
> ## There is almost a "don't ask, don't tell" policy in place.

I read about a woman in her twenties who was visiting an exotic animal park in Colorado recently when her day took an unwelcome turn. She reached into the cage of a Siberian tiger to pet it, and the tiger began nibbling on her hand. The woman began to panic and tried to pull her hand back, but the tiger reacted and pulled the woman's arm off at the shoulder.[5] Why would she reach her hand in to pet a tiger? She was probably lulled into a false sense of security by the cage. The tiger probably appeared cuddly and harmless, lazing about in its man-made habitat. But when she stuck her hand through the bars, the tiger's true nature came out—and she will bear the consequences of that for the rest of her life.

Men often approach sex as the woman approached the tiger. They think it is harmless, and it is—unless you put your hand within reach of its mouth.

Ted Roberts, in his book *Pure Desire: Helping People Break Free From Sexual Struggles,* tells of a recent survey he conducted for a particular denomination concerning the issue of sexual addiction. He discovered that between 21 to 29 percent (depending on the region of the country) of the pastors were sexual addicts—not just struggling with sexual issues, but actually sexually addicted themselves. It is widely believed that the number of pastors afflicted with this is greater than its occurrence in their parishioners or in the population as a whole. His conclusion is that what the church has been doing is simply not working for the people in the pews—or for those in the pulpit. "It is time for the Church to become a real place of hope and healing," Roberts affirms.[6]

This lack of solution is understandable—it's hard for a pastor to provide answers when he's enslaved by the same thing. Roberts goes on to say that clinical counselors with whom he has talked have openly scoffed at the idea that the church could be a place of hope and healing for people trapped in sexual addiction. These counselors asked Roberts:

> **Do you know how many clients I have who say they're Christians and can't find any help in their churches? They say they would be openly shamed if they dared to mention they had such a problem. Do you know how many pastors I've had to deal with who only make their clients feel more guilty? They don't get any help from the Church; in fact, sometimes the Church is part of the problem.[7]**

Sadly, I agree that churches have done far too little to bring this problem into the open. There is almost a "don't ask, don't tell" policy in place.

The result is a lack of understanding the breadth and nature of the problem, and just how many men are caught in it.

Don Crossland is a minister who at one time harbored what he calls a secret world of sexual perversion. "My life spun out of control from an addiction to sex outside of marriage," he wrote in an article for *New Man* magazine.[8] "The addiction took on a life of its own, and I found no release until my addiction cycle was interrupted by the power of God." Crossland lost his ministry, but he found freedom. He outlines seven stages of the sexual addiction cycle.

1. *Secretize:* Includes creating a fantasy world apart from reality, denying it to others, justifying it to self and blaming others and self.

2. *Fantasize:* A man grows dependent on the emotional and physical "high" the fantasy produces.

3. *Ritualize:* Some men, Crossland says, will form rituals that fall short of a sex act, including flirting, viewing pornography or cruising parts of town where prostitutes roam.

4. *Realize:* Sooner or later, the fantasy and rituals are acted out.

5. *Paralyze:* The man feels hopeless and vows not to succumb again—but does. This makes him feel he will not ever be free.

6. *Demoralize:* After trying to overcome and failing, depression and suicide beckon.

7. *Desensitize:* When a man fails to overcome, his conscience becomes seared, and he may change his world-view and theology to fit his behavior.

Maybe these sound familiar to you. Maybe they fit someone you know.

Every Man's Battle is a book every man who battles sexual temptation ought to read. It is co-authored by Fred Stoeker, Mike Yorkey and Stephen Arterburn, a friend of mine who is founder and chairman of New Life Clinics and host of the daily *New Life Live!* national radio program.

At one point in the book the authors outline three levels of addiction about which they read in a book by a secular author.

Later I talked to Arterburn about the progressive nature of sexual addictive behavior. He told me that if men realized their behavior could lead to very serious consequences, they might be motivated to change.

> ## Our goal as men, whether we struggle with addiction or not, **is to make those wise, pre-zone decisions.**

Arterburn pointed out similar levels that he believed represented the cycle of addiction from a Christian perspective. Read for yourself the levels that Arterburn developed to describe the sexual addiction cycle from his Christian perspective. Where would you fit in the cycle of addiction? Have you lived this pattern of addictive behavior? Arterburn described the levels as follows:[9]

- *Level 1:* Secret sexual behaviors that involve no one but the person who is doing them. Examples of this level would include masturbation, reading pornography or looking at pornography on the Internet.

- *Level 2:* Sexual behaviors that involve other people. Examples of these behaviors would be paying for the services of a prostitute, visiting massage parlors and strip clubs, premarital and extramarital sexual relationships.

- *Level 3:* Sexual behaviors that involve criminal activity. These would include molestation, incest, sexual abuse, rape, indecent exposure and voyeurism. Anyone engaging in these activities would be subject to criminal prosecution if arrested.

Do any of these behaviors fit you or someone you know? Can you see how easy it would be to slide from one level to the next? Is it possible that what you think is not such a serious problem is really the early stages of a problem that might land you in jail or ruin your life in some other way? Is that motivation to change, as Arterburn suggests?

Ted Roberts also writes about the progressive nature of addiction. "It is crucial that we understand we are dealing with a type of behavior that has three interlocking elements," he says. He describes these three stages of behavior.

Stage 1—The problem becomes unmanageable.

Roberts says that people in this first stage are not exhibiting behavior that has recently surfaced. They have tried over and over again to stop the behavior, but they have been unsuccessful. They even may have sought out counseling, but have found it hard to be totally honest with the counselor. Because they are so enmeshed in denial, they may indicate they just began acting out the behavior. Such men have not purposely lied to the counselor—it is just the way they have learned to look at life.

Roberts says that many men, especially Christians, create some kind of a coping response that is like a binge. They stay out of control for a day, a week or a month. Then by sheer willpower, they avoid the behavior for a long period of time. But the behavior is not gone—it will rear its ugly head again at some point.

Stage 2—The behavior becomes destructive.

It is easy to see the destruction of criminal sexual behavior or sexually transmitted diseases. But Roberts says that there is an earlier destructive pattern of emotional numbness that takes place. Often the man in this stage is using the addiction to numb the memory of painful emotions rising from his past. For that reason, as time goes by that emotional numbness invades even his soul. No longer can he honestly relate to those closest to him—or to God.

Stage 3—They act out the behavior for an extended period of time.

Roberts say that in this stage, numbness becomes a way of life.

The sexual highs that men in this stage used to feel no longer satisfy. Roberts says, "A major aspect of sexual activity is a strong release of adrenaline and endorphins, which is why sexual events become imprinted in the brain. These events are memorable because we rehearse them again and again in our minds, even affecting our very perceptions of life and how we deal with the present. This is [another] reason why the battle over sexual issues can be so severe for some people."[10]

We recently had an online chat for *New Man* readers with Doug Rosenau, clinical sex thera-  pist, author of *A Celebration of Sex* and columnist for *New Man* magazine.[11] One man made the following statement: "I get into a trance and cannot seem to break it even if I pray and read Scripture. Why is that?"

Rosenau responded by saying that part of a man's decision-making is learning to make those pre-trance, pre-zone decisions. Once you are in the zone, or trance, it is more difficult to get out of it.

First Corinthians 10:13 talks about God helping us head off temptation. Rosenau believes that by the time you are in the trance, you have already neglected several opportunities when He could have helped you! He concludes by saying that our goal as men, whether we struggle with addiction or not, is to make those wise, pre-zone decisions. When we are tempted, we can call an accountability buddy. There are many pre-trance decisions we can choose to make, one of which is choosing *not* to turn on the computer.

I believe that Rosenau's advice can help us avoid getting entrenched mentally in sexual thoughts. But I also believe that we must press on to deal with the reason we are having those thoughts in the first place. Resisting "acting out" a sexual urge is only half the battle—we must also deal with our thought life and get rid of those "ghosts."

At *New Man,* we have received dozens of letters from men who have been at any one of these stages. One man from

Alabama wrote: "As a Christian, I suffered through twenty-five years of addiction to sex and pornography. It controlled me completely, and not until four years ago did I realize I had more than a 'little problem' or 'a little sin in my life.' I got help by first admitting to my unsuspecting wife about my secret life. This was very hard on both of us, but getting the problem into the light was critical. After that we shared with trusted friends and our pastor, and then got counseling from a ministry for sex addicts. It has not been easy; it cost us a job and strained our finances. It changed our lifestyle, but it has been worth it. I am not going back to that black hole that I lived in for so long."[12]

A man from Illinois wrote this to us: "I am thirty-one years old and have been married to a wonderful woman for eight years. When I was much younger I began a life of homosexuality, pornography and occult involvement. Only through Jesus Christ and His patience, love and mercy am I here today."[13]

I have a friend named Matt who enjoys what appears to be a normal, not very dramatic life. He has never had a moral breakdown and has never been addicted to pornography. He and his wife will soon celebrate their twentieth wedding anniversary and have been Christians all of their adult lives.

But Matt still struggles, however invisibly. "No one sees what is in my heart!" he told me. "Nobody sees the battle that I have with lustful thoughts. Nobody sees this from the outside, but I am all too aware of my inner condition." Matt told me he has vowed many times not to give in to sexual thoughts and masturbation, only to go on a business trip and willingly access the pornographic movies in the hotel room.

"I know the feeling of self-condemnation that overwhelms me like a giant wave consumes someone on the beach," he wrote. "I know the guilt and remorse of feeling that I have betrayed my beloved Savior—again." But Matt claims a degree of victory.

"I believe that the Lord has shown me that we must come to the place where we see there is no hope in trusting our flesh to be good enough. There is only one source of hope and victory, and that is in the cross of Jesus. Have I mastered all of the temptations in my life? No. But little by little, the Lord has been changing my heart's desire. The sins that seemed to control me have lost their mastery over me, and the desires seem to be diminishing all the time. God has replaced these ungodly desires with contentment, peace and joy. I believe the reason for this is that through the work of the Spirit, I see my only hope is the cross."

The "M" Word

Masturbation is a subject every man knows about. I heard someone say that 90 percent of men masturbate, and the other 10 percent lie about it. Hart's survey found that 61 percent of married religious men continue to masturbate by themselves, mostly because they enjoy it or felt they had a strong sex drive. His survey found that most men start masturbating at age fourteen.[14] This man's findings have been verified through other sources.

See poll results
oldmannewman.com

> ## God designed romance and erotic arousal to be deeply connecting, including all three dimensions of our person—body, soul and spirit.

New Man magazine took a poll in 1998 asking readers what they thought about masturbation. Was it right? Wrong? Healthy? Unhealthy? Unacceptable in any circumstances? Acceptable only in some?

Seventy-eight percent of those who responded said they were strongly against masturbation.

"It is often psychologically tied to repressed anger and/or avoidance of interpersonal intimacy, so it might be a cover for not dealing with real relationship issues," wrote one marriage therapist.

"Intimacy is what men and women desire most, not sex," wrote an anonymous wife. "Masturbation reduces intimacy by providing a temporary substitute, which is the opposite of intimacy. Worse, it is extremely destructive to a wife's self-esteem."

Another woman had a different point of view. In response to one of our articles, she wrote this letter to the editor: "My husband and I are in our mid-forties, and we both have Christ at the center of our lives. We have a beautiful sexual relationship. Sometimes, however, my husband cannot reach a climax during intercourse. So what if he rolls over and calmly masturbates? Do I care? Does his Savior care? I think not."

Some people do not think masturbation is a very big deal. "It doesn't hurt anyone else," they say. Some Christians point out that the Bible is silent on the subject. I will leave this to everyone's own conscience between him or her and God. But I will point out that the Bible is also silent on child abuse. The bottom line is this: "Everything that does not come from faith is sin" (Rom. 14:23, NIV).

Doug Rosenau gave his opinion to our readers some time ago by saying that while the Bible has no direct commands against masturbation, the bottom-line principle in any sexual theology must be God's ultimate purpose for creating gender and romantic sexuality. God designed romance and erotic arousal to be deeply connecting, including all three dimensions of our person—body, soul and spirit. Ultimate sexual fulfillment is the one-flesh, intimate relationship of marriage.

A self-centered exercise
oldmannewman.com

Rosenau asserts that masturbation will always fall short because it is a self-centered exercise.[15] The most it can be is a shadow of the joyful connecting that can take place only in marriage. He teaches us that God does use righteous guilt to convict us about wrong behaviors and attitudes. Rosenau says that for most married men and those struggling with sexual addiction, there may be healthy guilt attached to masturbation.

If a man sees masturbation as wrong but cannot stop, he must analyze the need he is meeting through masturbation. Is he looking for intimacy? Is he masking some inner pain? He should ask God for a more appropriate way to meet those needs. He should also share his struggle with a men's group or close friend. Being account-able to someone is crucial in changing habits and attitudes.

> Make no mistake about it: A man's sexual issues spill over into other areas—especially the marriage.

Some couples stimulate each other's genitals as part of foreplay or sex play. But I don't consider that to be masturbation. To me, masturbation means solo sex. Women engage in it too, but appar-ently with less frequency than men do.

In Christian circles, masturbation is the quiet shame. Pastor Jack Hayford says that often it inhibits men from lifting "holy hands" before the Lord in worship because they are aware of what these hands were doing just hours before.

Unfortunately, many Christian men are habitual mastur-baters. And if single men think that the issue will go away after marriage, they are wrong. For one thing, marriage and its sexual joys only make a man more interested in regular sexual release. And if the wife is too tired, busy, uninterested or unexciting, then there is always a way a man can relieve himself.

I am told of a major denomination that was having a rather dull seminar for traveling ministers, dealing with various trivial items. One outspoken man created quite a stir when he raised his hand to ask permission to make a comment and said, "This is all well and good, but the problem is when I travel and am alone in the motel, I masturbate." Those august denominational leaders did not know how to respond to what was probably a problem with more than just that one traveling evangelist.

The subject will probably come up at some point in a men's group if the group exists long enough for the men to move beyond superficial discussion. Men will debate if it is OK or not for a Christian man to masturbate. Some will say if the wife says it is OK, then what is wrong with it? And if he doesn't "lust" or if he thinks about his wife, whom does it hurt?

> # We can take comfort that Christ was tempted, but without sin. That is how we must live.

All right, but who among us is good enough not to lust at least some of the time? And why do men almost always feel guilt or shame after having masturbated?

If nothing else, masturbation is selfish and immature. It reduces a middle-aged (or older or younger) man to acting like a teenager again. And it deprives his wife of some sexual release as well. Except for a few sexual athletes, the average man must "recharge" after having ejaculated, and he will not approach his wife for sex for at least some period of time. That cuts down on her intimacy as well.

Make no mistake about it: A man's sexual issues spill over into other areas—especially the marriage. Most wives have no idea of the pornography/masturbation/lust issues their husbands are dealing with. Even with husbands who have "victory" in this area, there is the memory—the residue—of past lovers, past sexual experiences or past perversions. This may make the husband a selfish lover because he is so used to focusing habitually on his own sexuality that he may be unconcerned about his wife's fulfillment. Or his habit may inhibit him in other ways sexually.

In a small group discussion on this subject, someone suggested that maybe Paul had some sexual issues. The lament in

Romans 7:24–"Oh, what a miserable person I am! Who will free me from this life that is dominated by sin?"–sure applies to how men feel after they have fallen sexually!

Paul seems to have been single, but he certainly seemed knowledgeable about the sexual sins of the church at Corinth and the sexual side of marriage. He was no naive celibate. Yet if that was his problem (and we can only speculate what was his thorn in the flesh), he obviously had a mature attitude and had overcome anything that he fought.

For me, the bottom line is that Scripture teaches that Jesus (who was single, yet without sin) was tempted in all ways as we are. Since we men are tempted sexually, we know He was tempted, too. He even had some women following Him. No doubt some were attractive. And He was criticized for having had dinner with prostitutes and tax collectors.

Scripture never describes the specific sources of His temptation. We can only speculate. But the Sinless One did say, "All right, stone her. But let those who have never sinned throw the first stones!" (John 8:7). And He also knew how men lust in their hearts after women, because He said that lust was the same as committing adultery. Jesus was well aware of the male human condition. He was a man, after all. We can take comfort, however, that He was tempted, but without sin.

That is how we must live. Tempted, but without sin. We cannot avoid temptation–it is all around us and within us as our brains replay images. You already know these things. But here is the good news: Jesus makes us new. Old things *have* passed away. Behold, all things *have* become new. We can become new men in the sexual area of life, too. And as you read this book, I will show the keys to victory that are making a difference in lives of men all over the world.

But first let us look at the frustration of moving forward spiritually three steps, then falling back two steps. So stay with me.

Talk about it   Think about it

Sexual Problems: Are They Always an Issue?

Author's note: This chapter is definitely written to men, NOT to women. If you are an individual reading this, take time to reflect on these study questions.

For more information on this topic (which we will add to as time passes) check out our www.oldmannewman.com website. Use the user id: **oldman** and the password **newman**. These are **case sensitive,** so use all lowercase letters and leave no spaces.

Note to leaders: This chapter directly and forthrightly addresses the sexual struggles that most men face as they seek to move forward in their relationship with Jesus Christ. Chances are that the men in your group are really going to want to discuss these issues—or they are going to make eye contact with the floor, say nothing and hope the discussion time for this issue goes away as quickly as possible. As leader, your role is crucial. For this session at least, not only pose the questions—be the first to answer them. You set the pace. If you are not vulnerable, they will not be. It is pretty much that simple. So you decide before God how real you want the group to be, and adjust the questions below accordingly.

1. This chapter begins with the following sentence: "Sex is a wonderful gift from God . . . " Do you always feel that sex is a wonderful gift—or does the struggle with temptation sometimes make you feel more like it is a terrible curse?

2. Page 48 declares that "God designed romance and erotic arousal to be deeply connecting, including all three dimensions of our person—body, soul and spirit." Do you agree with this statement? What are the implications of this idea?

3. On page 47, someone responding to a survey said this about masturbation: "It is often psychologically tied to repressed anger and/or avoidance of interpersonal intimacy, so it might be a cover for not dealing with real relational issues." What do you think is the connection between masturbation and repressed anger and loneliness?

4. How important is accountability in helping men overcome sexual addictions?

A clip from

New Man May 1997

The XXXtent of the Problem

Here are some revealing results from a three-year study assessing the frequency and impact of pornographic use among Christian men.

Thirty-three percent of men surveyed agreed with the statement, "I enjoy looking at sexually oriented material."

Seventeen percent said they had "purchased some pornographic material in the past year."

Men who had "purchased pornographic material in the past year" had significantly lower marital, fathering and family-life satisfaction when compared to those who hadn't purchased pornographic material in the past year.[1]

Revealing results
▶ oldmannewman.com

Chapter 4

Three Steps Forward:
Two Steps Back

OLD MAN — Yields to the sinful nature as it tries to reestablish control.

NEW MAN — Yields to the Holy Spirit, living life in all its fullness.

Roger sat across from me at Denny's, deeply troubled yet relieved at being able to express himself freely to a friend. I could read the sincerity on his face. He had sought me out as a mentor, and as we got to know each other he quickly opened up, asking me some important, gut-level questions.

"Why do I struggle in spite of knowing all the right answers?" he asked before pouring out his life story.

He had been a Christian since his early twenties. At times he had been active in leadership in his church, serving on the deacon's board. But lately he had backed away from leadership because he felt like such a failure as a believer.

Even though on the outside others considered him to be a strong Christian, everything was not OK. Occasionally he would purchase pornographic magazines. Masturbation continued to be his secret companion when his wife was not available sexually—something he rationalized as not as bad as an affair. He would repent each time, and his resistance would improve, if only for a while.

Slowly Roger felt himself getting pulled into the muck and

mire. He said he was tired of fighting it, and he even wondered if he should accept that he was destined to live a double lifestyle. With intense emotion he told me that he felt he was stuck for life in a pattern of failure, and that all he could hope for was that God in His mercy would forgive him before he died. If so, at least he would make it to heaven.

His question to me was simple, vulnerable and as real as it gets. It was the question of a man who was tired of playing the game, tired of appearing right instead of being right, tired of having the jackboot of sin pressed again his neck. Was there any way to change these life-disabling issues that seemed to take him two steps back every time he moved forward spiritually?

The "Old Man" Is Not Going Away on His Own

Many men find themselves in the same desperate state as Roger. His question is one we all must deal with: How can we live a Christian life that *works?*

When a man surrenders his life to Christ, he literally becomes a new man. The Bible says, "Those who become Christians become new persons. They are not the same anymore, for the old life is gone. A new life has begun!" (2 Cor. 5:17).

But as much as we would like to have all our problems solved instantly, and as much as God does heal and deliver from even besetting sins in a moment of time, the Christian life is still a process we work through day by day. We struggle. We endure. We resist. We stand firm. We overwhelmingly conquer. All Christians must strive to conform to the likeness of Christ, no matter what age, ethnic background, gender or culture.

Yet it seems somehow that men struggle more than women or youth. Maybe that is why most Christians become Christians when they are young—because it is easier to follow Christ when they are not so set in their ways. Or maybe it is why most churches are made up mostly of women—it is easier for them to follow what Christ says to do.

Meanwhile the guys are struggling with things that defeat

them spiritually. As they try to follow Christ, it may be three steps forward, two steps back. Not only do they feel the shame of failure, but they never go on to the deeper things of God or to a place of church leadership where they can minister to other hurting men from a position of spiritual maturity.

Most struggles are more common than you would think. Indeed, the Bible declares, "The temptations that come into your life are no different from what others experience. And God is faithful. He will keep the temptation from becoming so strong that you can't stand up against it. When you are tempted, he will show you a way out so that you will not give in to it" (1 Cor. 10:13).

If you feel you are the only one struggling, you are not. And this book is my humble attempt to show you "the way out" that the Father promises us. No man is immune from problems. We all need "the way out."

I recently read about a huge oak tree that had stood in Frankfort, Ohio, for many decades. Several generations of people had come and gone in that city during the lifetime of that one oak tree. It was as tall as a six-story building—indeed, one of the country's largest oak trees. During a severe thunderstorm, it was struck by lightning and split in half. Though it had been a living monument in that city for decades, yet in one moment it was utterly destroyed. Its proud history is now just a memory, and the tree is only good for firewood.[2]

If any man thinks he is immune to failure, the Bible instructs him, "Be careful when you think you stand lest you fall." (See 1 Corinthians 10:12.) Even the mightiest oaks can be felled in a single night.

But what causes a man to fail? What are the problems that threaten men? The apostle Paul outlines them in Galatians 5:19–21: "Sexual immorality, impure thoughts, eagerness for lustful pleasure, idolatry, participation in demonic activities, hostility, quarreling, jealousy, outbursts of anger, selfish ambition, divisions, the feeling that everyone is wrong except those in your own little group, envy, drunkenness, wild parties, and other kinds of sin."

Then he says, "Let me tell you again, as I have before, that anyone living that sort of life will not inherit the Kingdom of God" (v. 21).

Eugene Patterson, in his New Testament paraphrase (which reads more like an essay), gives further definition to these problems: "Repetitive, loveless, cheap sex; stinking accumulation of mental and emotional garbage; frenzied and joyless grabs for happiness; trinket gods; magic-show religion; paranoid loneliness; cutthroat competition; all-consuming-yet-never-satisfied wants; brutal tempers; impotence to love or be loved; divided homes and divided lives; small-minded and lopsided pursuits; the vicious habit of depersonalizing everyone into a rival; uncontrolled and uncontrollable addictions; ugly parodies of community" (Gal. 5:19–21, THE MESSAGE).

It is hard not to find at least one characteristic that has defined us at some point in our lives.

On the positive side, Paul says, "But when the Holy Spirit controls our lives, he will produce this kind of fruit in us: love, joy, peace, patience, kindness, goodness, faithfulness, gentleness, and self-control" (Gal. 5:22–23).

Then he concludes, "Here there is no conflict with the law. Those who belong to Christ Jesus have nailed the passions and desires of their sinful nature to his cross and crucified them there. If we are living now by the Holy Spirit, let us follow the Holy Spirit's leading in every part of our lives. Let us not become conceited, or irritate one another, or be jealous of one another" (vv. 23–26).

In the next section of this book, we will learn how to move from the negative problems that men face to the positive expressions of the fruit of the Spirit. To do that, we must learn to overcome our flesh.

Whether talking openly or sitting silently on a pew next to you in a church service, many believers are struggling with what the Bible calls "the lust of the flesh." For some it is a minor annoyance, easily dealt with, but for others it is an epochal struggle every single moment—and the result is very much in doubt.

Either way, we never really dealt with these issues at the moment of salvation. Even when delivered of these problems, if we fail to fill the vacated spot in our hears, their absence leaves the door open, as the Scriptures say, for demons to come back eight times worse than before. (See Matthew 12:43–45.)

My heart goes out to men who face these struggles. I know what it is to struggle against the flesh, wanting to do what is right, but being pulled toward what is wrong. It seems that everything in our society pulls us in directions that do not please God. If it is not toward sexual immorality, it is toward materialism or lust for control. Just having to deal with the cares of this world on a day-to-day basis seems to quench the Spirit's power in our lives.

These problems are usually hidden under the surface like a volcano about to explode. When they are not dealt with, they eventually manifest themselves. Some men have affairs; others freak out and leave their families. Some become violent and abusive to their wives and children. Others lead lives of quiet desperation, never being "too bad," but never achieving their destiny in God or overcoming what the Bible calls the "old man." Sadly, they are never really happy.

As Christians, we know these problems are the result of the sinful nature—the warring of the "old man" trying to reestablish control. The conflict between our sinful nature and our new life in the Spirit will never cease. We will be confronted constantly with the choice between right and wrong. Our natural response will often be contrary to what the Spirit desires, but we have the power in the Holy Spirit to make right choices.

A young man I counseled told me about the struggles that had hounded him since his teenaged years. As we talked, I told him what the apostle Paul tells us in Galatians 5:16: "So I advise you to live according to your new life in the Holy Spirit. Then you won't be doing what your sinful nature craves."

The King James Version of the Bible calls this kind of living our "walk in the Spirit." If we are concentrating on our new life in the Holy Spirit, we will not have to worry about fulfilling the desires of the flesh. This promise is so powerful, it is hard to grasp. Instead of focusing on what you cannot do, focus on your new life in Christ. Think of it like this: You cannot walk north while you are walking south. You can't forward and backwards at the same time. A side note in the *Holy Spirit Encounter Bible* says it well: "Doing all that the Spirit prompts you to do will leave you no time, no desire and no thought for the cravings of your old nature."

Instead of focusing on what you cannot do, focus on your new life in Christ.

Life in the Spirit doesn't remove us from the sinful environment any more than using an oxygen tank when we scuba dive keeps us from getting wet. But just as scuba gear allows us to exist in an underwater environment that ordinarily would kill us, so the Holy Spirit enables us to live in this sinful world without being ensnared by it.

Life in the Spirit is not just to make us feel good—it is about survival. It is the way God has designed for His children to live—doing what the Spirit wants and avoiding the temptations of our old sinful nature.

Jesus has come to give life in all its fullness. With His help we will become "new men" in Christ, taking the journey toward renewal one step at a time. The next section spells out how.

Talk about it   Think about it

Three Steps Forward: Two Steps Back

Author's note: This chapter will help you to balance out your Christian life and avoid those steps backward. Aim for forward motion only.

For more information on this topic (which we will add to as time passes) check out our www.oldmannewman.com website. Use the user id: **oldman** and the password **newman**. These are **case sensitive,** so use all lowercase letters and leave no spaces.

1. We are looking for "a Christian life that *works.*" Describe what that life would look like to you.

2. The chapter describes the experience of many of us when it talks about three steps forward and two steps back. What are the consequences that occur when we take those steps backward?

3. Read Matthew 12:43–45. What do you think is being described here, and how do you think it happens in the lives of men?

4. This statement appears on page 60: "Doing all that the Spirit prompts you to do will leave you no time, no desire and no thought for the cravings of your old nature." Explain why you agree or disagree with this statement.

Section II

The Solution Is Becoming a New Man in Christ

A clip from

New Man   May 1997

Object of His Love

It was not that I came upon Jesus Christ and, when I saw Him, something within me ran out to meet Him and, holding on to Him, begged Him to lift me out of myself and make me the person of my dreams. It was that He came upon me. His heart rushed out to me. He held on to me. He said He would make me the person that I wanted to be. He saw me. He loved me and chose me. I didn't find Him. He found me.[1]

—**Bob Benson**

He found me!
oldmannewman.com

Chapter 5

Salvation:
Brings New Life

OLD MAN   Feels lonely, discouraged, empty and locked into sin.

NEW MAN   Experiences a loving, forgiving, restoring relationship with Jesus.

It sounds much too simple—the way to become a new man in Christ is to stop responding as an old man. And indeed, it is not as simple as it sounds. In this section of the book we will begin to take a closer look at "new man solutions." As we learn to apply these solutions, we can become new men—fully prepared to move into the wonderful destinies God has prepared for His new men. This chapter deals with the foundational solution to the old man—crucify it through God's wonderful plan of salvation.

God has provided a way for us to experience a relationship with Him. It can be ours by receiving God's gift of salvation, a gift that is ours because God loved us so much that He gave us His only Son, Jesus, who willingly gave His life on the cross so that we could experience forgiveness and restoration to God. By accepting the gift of salvation, we also have the privilege of experiencing a personal relationship with Jesus, our Lord and Savior. His love wipes away our sin and dispels our loneliness.

Perhaps you have not yet had that experience and are still lonely, empty and lost. Maybe, like actor Dean Jones, you may be locked in a bondage that will not let you go. Jones tells us the story of his introduction to Jesus in the March/April 2000 *New Man* magazine.

Dean Jones has made some forty-five motion pictures, including ten Disney films. He will be forever remembered as Herbie's friend in *The Love Bug*. For Jones, success came quickly in life–but it came with a price. By the late sixties, Jones had attended college, married, served time in the Naval Air Corps, starred on Broadway and acted in both television and on the big screen. He also became aware that his life was out of control–and he was helpless to change it.

Although Jones had heard the story of Christ's love and forgiveness as a child, he seemed unable to apply it to his life. He says that once you have heard the truth, and once the reality of Christ is seeded in your heart, it spoils you for joyful sinning. But for Dean Jones, it was too late. "I would only grit my teeth and go forward, hell-bent for leather in spite of the truth that was lodged in my heart," he says.

> ❝ **I would only grit my teeth and go forward, hell-bent for leather in spite of the truth that was lodged in my heart.** ❞

As Dean Jones indicates, his life did go forward on the road to hell for some time. Starring in one or two Disney films a year, he fought his traditional post-picture depression by joining his motorcycle-riding friends, who for kicks raced through the Baja, Mexico, desert. Racing over rugged terrain at sixty miles per hour, he saw a ditch ahead and decided to jump it. His bike hit the other side, cartwheeling him through the air and smashing his pelvis in thirteen places. His friends eventually found him and carried him to safety.

"I lay there for a day and a half, and I came to see the emptiness of the life I was pursuing. But by that time, I could not stop. It had me in bondage," Jones says.

Finally in 1969, after he and a companion got roaring drunk, Jones detoured onto a construction site as he tried to drive home. Driving wildly up a steep hill, he nearly killed himself. Later that night he was filled with self-loathing. Stone sober, he knelt by the bed and cried, "Is anybody there?" As it turned out, there was—God was there. At that moment, Jones received his revelation of God—and it changed his life forever. He says:

> **When I surrendered everything to the Lord, the peace of Christ rolled over me like an ocean wave.**

God's miracle work of grace and forgiveness poured into Jones's life that day. Over the next few months, with God's help Jones cleaned out his life of all the bondages that had kept him from being the man God had created him to be. Even his career had to go. Being born again ended his career. For a time, he continued making two pictures a year, but then he did not work for eleven years. "But at some point you have to give up your pride and what other people think about you," Jones believes. "The fear of men's faces is a snare and a trap."

But Dean Jones has found what he always wanted. God has restored his marriage, filled him with the Holy Spirit's power to live a godly life, given him a min-istry and revived his acting career. But more important than those

Deep-down fulfillment
oldmannewman.com

external evidences of God's blessing on his life is the fulfillment he has found within where the emptiness once existed. He tells it like this:

> **You see, I'm blessed in having a measure of success and realizing the futility and emptiness of it. I see people all over this city of Hollywood who have not yet made it, but think that if they ever did they would be happy, fulfilled human beings. It ain't true. It's all an illusion. Only Christ can bring deep-down fulfillment.[2]**

In this chapter, I want to show you how you can make a radical change in your life as Dean Jones did. I want those of you who need a revelation *of* God to be able to use this book as a catalyst to introduce you to a God who loves you so much that He gave His only Son, Jesus Christ, so that you could break the bonds of sin and bondage that hinder you from experiencing that radical change to freedom. God wants to pour His forgiveness on you, redeem you and give you a fresh start toward victory.

Then I want to help those of you who desperately need a revelation *from* God to make sense of the confusion and failure of your present-day experience. You may love Jesus with all your heart, and you want to "strip off every weight that slows [you] down" (Heb. 12:1). But still you feel lonely, empty, discouraged and locked in to "the sin that so easily hinders [your] progress" (v. 1).

God wants to give you the power to live in victory. He wants you to have access to His insights and wisdom to live pure, godly lives before Him.

There are others of you whom God has been chasing since you were little boys. It is not that you are running from God; you have just never ceased from your own pursuits long enough to stand still and allow God to pursue—and catch—you in His life-transforming grip. He wants you to know the pleasure of being held tightly in His strong, protective embrace. He wants to empower you to step out in your destiny, charge right into the very camp of the enemy and defeat his purposes in your life—and in the lives of those Christ will enable you to rescue.

Receiving a Revelation of God

Like Dean Jones, when you receive a revelation of God, He will transform your life. Ask Him today to reveal Himself to you. God's only Son, Jesus, gave His life so that You could be forgiven of your sins, released from your bondages and empowered to live as a new man in Christ. Ask Him to give you a fresh start—to give you fulfillment instead of emptiness, friendship with Jesus instead of loneliness and power instead of impotence to change your life. God has a wonderful destiny for your life—right behind the revelation of who He is in your life.

Anyone who attended church as a kid—even for only a short time—probably learned this verse in Sunday school: "All have sinned, and come short of the glory of God" (Rom. 3:23, KJV).

That verse places every one of us in the group that needs a revelation of God. We have all utterly failed to live up to God's expectations for us. At some point we must face the aching loneliness in our soul for something more, something bigger and greater than what we have found in a life without God.

Remember God's Word is absolutely able to tell us now to find that something more—we do it by recognizing that God already made a plan for bringing us out of our loneliness and despair to live in peace and joy. God's Word tells us about that plan in another verse we can probably all recite: "If we confess our sins, he is faithful and just to forgive us our sins, and to cleanse us from all unrighteousness" (1 John 1:9, KJV).

However, it is two different things to recite that verse and apply it to our lives through a revelation of God that becomes a life-transforming experience.

Ted, one of my friends, has a wonderful story of how he came to Christ and received a revelation of God. Ted had lived a pretty wild lifestyle before he and his wife were introduced to Christ through a Christian friend. Ted, curious about salvation, went into a Christian bookstore and read about the gospel. One of the books contained the sinner's prayer.

The book convicted Ted deeply of his sin, and he wanted to be saved. He gave his life completely and wholeheartedly to Jesus.

> **The next two weeks were wonderful. I knew that something deep and impacting had happened to me, and I suddenly became aware of the reality of the sacrifice that Jesus made for me. It all made complete and perfect sense.**

Ted shared his experience with his wife and led her in the same prayer he had prayed. All of this happened in their home, without anyone helping them. They were uncertain of what to do with this newfound but totally transforming experience. They began attending the church they had been attending rather sporatically. But instead of the services being boring, they found they could barely contain themselves as the songs and scriptures came to life.

Some of you have never experienced that before. Like Ted, some of you need a radical change in your life. You need to see Christ differently, from a biblical, truly spiritual point of view. Some of you need a revelation *of* God. Some of you need a revelation *from* God. Others need to allow your hearts to be conquered by a God who has been chasing you since your boyhood.

Receiving a Revelation From God

You may already have had a revelation of God. You have experienced the love, forgiveness and grace of God that transformed your life anew. And you may still feel empty, lonely or powerless to be the man God wants you to be. Some of you may be like my friend Dan Kays of Chattanooga, Tennessee, who experienced God's transforming salvation—but still had to learn to live a consistent, daily, godly life by seeking a fresh revelation from God every day of his life.

> **Some of you need a revelation *of* God. Some of you need a revelation *from* God. Others need to allow your hearts to be conquered by God.**

Dan was saved from a life of moral squalor, which he describes as being full of hurt, shame, anger and unforgiveness. He felt alone, as if no one else on earth could relate to the things he had gone through. Then through a process of what he calls divine reversal, God completely turned around his life. "God took the broken pieces of my life and put them back together," Dan says.

Today, Dan's life seems very normal now. He has a wife and children, friends, a nice home and a new car. He has no chemical vices like smoking or drinking. He even avoids secular music and R-rated movies.

But all of those things were beyond his wildest imagination less than ten years ago. In 1991, just before God came into his life, he was living in a virtual pigsty—a place where the carpet was always damp and smelled like mildew and where the pests roamed unchecked. Alcohol, tobacco and drugs had a strong hold on him. He would light one cigarette off another all day long, and his cocaine habit was costing hundreds of dollars.

Dan came from a home that today we would call dysfunctional. His father would fly into a rage and beat the children. To further complicate things, Dan reached out to one of his school teachers as a father figure. After gaining his confidence, the teacher sexually molested him. The teacher introduced him to pornography and initiated him into the world of drinking, smoking and drugs. He concluded that suicide was his only way out, but he didn't want to die.

How did Dan go from this kind of life to being someone who is now highly regarded at work, church and in the community? Instead of killing himself, Dan cried out for God to save him—a God he knew was real, but whom he hated for years for letting his life become such a mess. That day the Lord instantly delivered Dan from drug addiction. For the first time in his life, he felt joy, peace and hope.

In the midst of his newfound joy, however, he discovered that he had to learn to live a godly life day by day. He needed a fresh revelation from God daily in order to learn to turn his life around and discard the habits and behaviors of the "old man." It wasn't easy.

"I don't want to disillusion anyone," Dan says. "Parts of the turnaround in my life were instantaneous, but other parts were very slow to turn around. Some things fell off painlessly, while at other times it was as if I had to lie on my heavenly Father's operating table and let Him cut things out of me. Some things I gave up freely, while other things I hung onto.

"The past nine years have been some times of incredible joy," Dan says, "while other times, the process seemed more than I could endure. But the rewards make every tear and struggle worth it."

> # He cried out for God to save him— a God he knew was real, but whom he hated for years for letting his life become such a mess. That day the Lord instantly delivered Dan.

Dan believes his testimony is one of hope for all men, whatever the circumstance, whatever the sins. "I used to think that what God did for me was unusual, abnormal. But every day I meet people who have been through similar circumstances. You would never know it by looking at them. But they are there, and they are a true testimony to the living God that we serve."

With Dan Kay's story in mind, read the following verses and let their message sink in.

> Our old sinful selves were crucified with Christ so that sin might lose its power in our lives. We are no longer slaves to sin.
>
> —Romans 6:6
>
> What this means is that those who become Christians become new persons. They are not the same anymore, for the old life is gone. A new life has begun!
>
> —2 Corinthians 5:17

> Throw off your old evil nature and your former way of life, which is rotten through and through, full of lust and deception. Instead, there must be a spiritual renewal of your thoughts and attitudes. You must display a new nature because you are a new person, created in God's likeness—righteous, holy, and true.
>
> —Ephesians 4:22–24

> Don't lie to each other, for you have stripped off your old evil nature and all its wicked deeds. In its place you have clothed yourselves with a brand-new nature that is continually being renewed as you learn more and more about Christ, who created this new nature within you.
>
> —Colossians 3:9–10

Now ask yourself, do these verses describe you?

- Are you in Christ?

- Are you putting off the old man?

- Are you determined not to serve sin?

- Are you being renewed in the spirit of your mind?

Some of you are like Patrick Morley, a self-described recovering materialist, who thought he was a pretty good Christian, while in fact, he was not.

"Though I believed in Jesus, there was nothing exceptional about my lifestyle that would recommend Him to others," Morley writes in *Second Wind for the Second Half.* "I was Jekyl on Sunday, but come Monday morning, I was Hyde. My life was shaped more by the forces of commerce than by Christ. I was reading my Bible for comfort, but *Forbes* for direction."

Simply put, Morley was living a double life. His turning point came when he learned to make a full—not partial—surrender to Christ. It involved not only adding Jesus to his life, but subtracting some other things also. He decided to stop seeking the God he wanted, and start seeking the God who is.

"Man is a rebel. I am a rebel. I did not come willingly to the cross, but Christ regenerated my heart," Morley says. "He put in me the desire to know Him: 'No one can come to Me unless the Father who sent Me draws him; and I will raise him up at the last day'" (John 6:44, NKJV).[3]

Don't be miserable.
oldmannewman.com

Bob Buford, author of the popular book *Halftime,* believes that men are afraid to yield to Christ because "they fear where it will lead."[4]

"The trouble with many men," Billy Sunday, a famous evangelist, once said, "is that they have just enough religion to make them miserable."[5]

> ## Stop seeking the God you want, and start seeking the God who is.

I have already told how as a teenager I would make a commitment to serve the Lord at a summer youth camp and then backslide by the time school started. So I know what he means.

The Need to Recommit

Salvation is a process. It can begin with a cataclysmic conversion, but it takes a lifetime to live out—as the Bible says, in fear and trembling. Eugene Peterson calls Christianity "a long obedience in the same direction." From my years of living in the family of God, I believe that Christians need to recommit to Christ at every point of transition or crisis in their lives. That is not a theological statement as much as an observation. Every morning, if you tell your wife you love her, you are in a way recommitting to her. Such a recommitment may not be dramatic, but such small, daily decisions keep us going in the right direction.

I committed my life to Christ as a five-year-old with as much spiritual understanding as I had at that tender age. But when I recommitted my life to Christ when I was in college, that commitment has stood the test of time.

I commit my life again to Christ before and after making big decisions, whether for my company or in my personal life. These are not ritualized; in fact, I may not even notice that I am "recommitting." But when I examine my thoughts, I do see that every day brings fresh challenges to my faith, and every day demands that I choose again to carry the cross and follow Christ.

Conquered by God

Even when we have had both a revelation *of* God and a revelation *from* God, we still need to be so gripped by His presence in our lives that we learn to live a life of authentic Christianity. That is one without pretense, one that is consistently godly and real, one that models a supernatural walk with a living, dynamic, speaking, personal God.

Many men fail at living this kind of a Christian life. Sometimes it is because we are so busy pursuing our own personal goals and agendas that we do not realize God has been pursuing us for years. In Francis Thompson's poem "The Hound of Heaven," we read about this tendency we have to flee from God:

> I fled Him, down the nights and down the days;
> I fled Him, down the arches of the years;
> I fled Him, down the labyrinthine ways
> Of my own mind; and in the midst of tears
> I hid from Him, and under running laughter.

We have already read testimonies of men who have been pursued by God. One of those men, Dean Jones, tells us of the impact this poem had upon his life: "I was the guy fleeing all those incidents in my life; God was pursuing me."

Jesus pursued Dean Jones as a bloodhound chases a convict. He pursued him through a motorcycle wreck that shattered his pelvis; He pursued him through a midnight joy ride in a trench-riddled construction site. Heaven's Hound finally treed him in a New Jersey hotel room.

And when God caught him, gripped him in His transforming grip of grace, Dean Jones learned to live an authentic Christian life.

Bill Hybels, pastor of Willow Creek Community Church in suburban Chicago, calls inauthentic Christianity one of the great ills of the church at large. He says that inauthentic Christianity manifests itself in many ways. Some of these ways are shown below.

Salvation is a process. It can begin with a cataclysmic conversion, but it takes a lifetime to live out in fear and trembling.

- A style of Christianity based more on external methods than on internal change, an attempt at godliness that lacks the power

- Christian men with no idea what it means to "be like Jesus," who bounce between traditional macho models and contemporary soft male versions

- Relationships marked more by deception than honest dialogue

- Misguided Christians who hide heartache and grief behind smiling masks

Hybels goes on to say that at one time he was going through the motions of Christianity, but not really connecting with God. He was working hard in ministry, but not sensing the Spirit's fruitfulness in his efforts.

"I spoke of the priority of marriage, but my relationship with Lynne was falling apart," he admits. "I loved my kids, but I spent too much time at the office to convince them of that."

In his book *Honest to God?* Hybels writes that he knew about wanting to be a new man in Christ—what he calls being godly and consistent. Instead, the "old man" was rearing its ugly head.

"Like so many people, I talked a good game. Yet beneath the impressive veneer of my life was the cheap substitute of inauthentic, artificial living." He continues:

> **Christianity is a supernatural walk with a living, dynamic, speaking, personal God. Why then do so many Christians live inconsistent, powerless lives? Authentic Christianity begins with spiritual authenticity—a vital, daily relationship with Jesus Christ. . . . Genuine spirituality starts a person on the road to a whole lifestyle of authenticity.**[6]

Like Hybels, we may hold a facade up to the rest of the world, but it is impossible to fool God about our true condition. Either we are living authentically with Him, or we are somehow faking it. That is not to say we are not sincere in our desire to be godly; it just means we may be fooling ourselves about how much we have attained.

What Hybels calls "authentic Christianity" I call being a "new man" in Christ. It shows! It's evident to those around us. It leaks into every part of our lives, and it transforms everything that we do. It permeates us—and affects those around us.

That is the way Truett Cathy, founder of Chick-fil-A, demonstrates he is a new man in Christ. From the time he opened his first restaurant in Hapeville, Georgia, Cathy was committed to doing things God's way independent of the cost. However, as a man of principle, Cathy knew that his

no-compromise approach to honoring God and living the Christian life must also apply to those times when profitability and God's will seemed mutually exclusive.

So in the midst of Chick-fil-A's 1982 crisis, he went on retreat to strategize with his top managers. It was on this retreat that

Truett Cathy rededicated his business to God and, in conjunction with his management team, crafted a new corporate mission statement: "To glorify God by being a faithful steward of all that is entrusted to us and to have a positive influence on all who come in contact with Chick-fil-A."[7]

Being a new man in Christ works through triumph or trial. And God promises us success (in His eyes) when we unalterably stand by our commitment to Him to live as a new man in Christ in today's world.

Authentic Christianity begins with spiritual authenticity— a vital, daily relationship with Jesus Christ.

Have you had a life-transforming experience with Christ that led to a day-to-day walk with Him? Do you know Him? Does He know you? Take a moment and assess your spiritual state as honestly as possible. Perhaps this is a time for a fresh revelation from Him—one that causes you to make a recommitment of your life to His plan.

Maybe you need to pause from your own efforts and goals long enough to be gripped by Jesus, the Hound of Heaven, and empowered to become a new man in Christ. Or maybe you have never known Christ. If that is the case, I have written this prayer, and I hope you will agree with the words. If you would like someone to pray with you, there are prayer counselors who are available twenty-four hours a day, seven days a week. Please call them toll free at (800) 759-0700.

Dear Lord Jesus, I know I cannot make it on my own. I know I need a Savior to free me from the grasp of sin and to give me purpose now as well as eternal life. I ask You

to forgive my sins. Help me turn from everything in my life that is not pleasing to You. Give me grace to live for You the rest of my life. Amen.

If you prayed that prayer, please write me and tell me at stevestrang@strang.com. I'll e-mail you some materials to help you in your Christian walk, and I'll rejoice that I have another brother in Christ.

If you have accepted Jesus, He will take all the junk in your life—what the Bible calls the "old man"—and make you a new man in Christ.

Keep reading, because the rest of this book is designed to help you in your Christian walk. And for those who have recently recommitted your life to Christ, or even if you have served Him for many years, I believe the following sections can help you become the new man in Christ He has destined you and purposed you to become.

Talk about it   Think about it

Salvation: Brings New Life

Author's note: God's gift of salvation to you is the most important gift you will ever receive. Open up your life and let His transforming gift come in.

For more information on this topic (which we will add to as time passes) check out our www.oldmannewman.com website. Use the user id: **oldman** and the password **newman**. These are **case sensitive,** so use all lowercase letters and leave no spaces.

The bad news about us

1. Read Romans 3:23. Why is it such a big deal to God that all of us have fallen short of His glory?

2. Read Romans 6:23. In this passage, the opposite of *death* is *eternal life*. What do you think these words mean in this passage?

The good news about God

1. Read Romans 5:8. What do you think the Father was feeling when He sent His Son, Jesus, to die on the cross in our place and for our sins?

2. Read Ephesians 2:8–9. God wants you to trust Him—and God wants to have a relationship with *you*. When did you trust Christ as your Savior? If you never have, is there anything that is keeping you from doing that right now?

Knowledge that heaven is your home

1. Read 1 John 5:11–13. According to this passage, how can we know that we have eternal life?

2. Write a prayer in the space below. If you have never asked Jesus Christ into your life as your personal Savior, do so. If He is your Savior, thank Him for His forgiveness and grace.

A clip from

New Man Free in Christ

The Ministry of Deliverance

The process of casting our demons is called deliverance. This ministry is an important part of what God does in the life of an individual and consequently in the church. Jesus integrated the ministry of deliverance and the believer's call to evangelism in the Great Commission. He entrusted this task of deliverance to His followers, according to Mark 16:15–17:

He said to them, "Go into all the world and preach the good news to all creation. Whoever believes and is baptized will be saved, but whoever does not believe will be condemned. And these signs will accompany those who believe: In my name they will drive out demons."—NIV

The ministry of deliverance must go hand in hand with the ministry of evangelism. Both are a very important part of the church's mission as the bride of Christ here on earth. When we ignore this ministry, we remove a vital part from the body of Christ. As a result, spiritually disabled Christians are raised in the church.[1]

—**Pablo Bottari**

Chapter 6

Deliverance:
Breaks Sin's Hold

OLD MAN	Is powerless to break out of demonic strongholds and bondages.
NEW MAN	Breaks free of spiritual strongholds and lives in freedom and joy.

James Robison was a firebrand, known as "the Southern Baptists' angry young man." A Texas preacher, he railed against sin from the pulpit and developed one of the country's most successful ministries. Men like Jerry Falwell and Jimmy Draper (at one time the president of the Southern Baptist Convention) were Robison's friends and colleagues. By some estimates, by the early 1980s Robison had already preached to twelve million people and seen one million people saved under his ministry.

But Robison was going through personal torment.

He was dissatisfied with the lack of permanent life changes he saw in the people to whom he preached. Even worse, he was frustrated by his own inability to live a truly Christlike life. He began overeating and gaining weight, and his mind became more plagued by lustful thoughts. As he preached, he would make inappropriate eye contact with women in the audience. He began to sense that demonic spirits were taunting him, and he would often sit on the platform of a church afraid to look up for fear of sinning in his heart.

Robison realized that much of his so-called righteous anger was really just meanness. The rage against sin that attracted so many had less to do with the Holy Spirit and more to do with Robison's own inner battles.

He was not experiencing the joy, peace and freedom he saw modeled in the New Testament, and he didn't know anyone who was. He began a quest for freedom that brought him into contact with a church layman who was known to have a deliverance ministry, meaning he prayed for people to be free of the harassment and control of demons.

> **"All traffic in your head is going to stop. All that noise is going to be silent."** **Robison says that was the day he was set free of demonic control.**

After an evangelistic crusade Robison was conducting, he invited the layman to his hotel room, and there they talked about the Word of God. Then the man looked at Robison, began to cry and said, "I have been listening to you and praying for you for six years. I feel so sorry for you. I have cast demons out of prisoners, convicts, murderers, witches, drug addicts and Hell's Angels, but I believe you are the most demonized person I have ever seen. You are so tormented I do not know how you have kept your sanity."

Robison wanted to run from the room as pride welled up in him, but he knew the man was right. He asked the man to pray for him, and the man did, praying scripture after scripture and rebuking Satan.

Then the man stopped abruptly and said, "It is all over. All traffic in your head is going to stop. All that noise is going to be silent." Though Robison felt nothing, he was hopeful and a little intrigued.

Two days later, when he arrived home, Robison woke up one

morning with scriptures he had never memorized flowing from his mouth. He felt different than he had in years. He grabbed his wife and told her, "It's gone—the claw in my brain. I have been set free."

Robison says that was the day he was set free of demonic control. That experience twenty years ago changed his life. Members of his staff said it was like working for another person. Robison began to focus on God's love, a subject he said he had neglected.

He apologized for his divisive and abrasive behavior in the ministry. He began to pray for people to be delivered at the altar at his evangelistic meetings. Thousands flocked to his meetings, even though he was criticized from many angles by people who thought (rightfully so) that he had "gone Charismatic."

From that day to this, Robison's ministry has thrived. Better yet, he has the joy, peace and free-dom he sought. He is a respected, mature Christian with keen insights  into deliverance and tearing down enemy strongholds.[2]

Weapons Not of This World

Deliverance is not readily understood. Start a conversation about confronting demons and some people will roll their eyes, saying you have gone too far out on a limb.

Some will accuse you of looking for a demon under every rock. Others will tell you how they were scarred by a horrible experience when, desperate for answers, they submitted to deliverance ministry, only to have people encourage them to "vomit up" demons and do all sorts of strange things during a grueling "deliverance" session.

Others will say they are experts in the deliverance field. Some Christians believe that raising the decibel level of their prayers will chase away more demons. They have a great desire to yell at the enemy, but they lack understanding of spiritual authority. They might scream at demons all day long with no results.

I have seen and heard much in the area of deliverance. While I know deliverance is sometimes handled poorly or even arrogantly, I do believe there is an aspect of spiritual warfare to many human problems.

Paul clearly states this. Second Corinthians 10:4–5 says, "We use God's mighty weapons, not mere worldly weapons, to knock down the Devil's strongholds. With these weapons we break down every proud argument that keeps people from knowing God. With these weapons we conquer their rebellious ideas, and we teach them to obey Christ."

> **A problem that will not go away after prayer, positive confession, fasting, strong-willed determination or medical treatment must have a demonic basis that needs a spiritual solution.**

There are Christians who do not want to believe they can have demonic problems. I personally believe that a problem that will not go away after prayer, positive confession, fasting, strong-willed determination or medical treatment must have a demonic basis that needs to be dealt with spiritually. Problems that are hard to deal with, such as rage, drug addiction and even sexual addictions or alcoholism, have, I believe, other problems at their root. There may be strongholds in the mind and soul that must be dealt with, as well as the sinful habit or behavior that is being acted out.

Let me give an important disclaimer. Some very odd behaviors are caused by some medical conditions that can be treated with medicine. I believe you should consult a doctor to rule this out as a possible cure. If the problem continues, then it may be spiritual in nature, and deliverance may help.

On this point, you may agree or disagree with me. You may feel that deliverance is not central to the gospel or is a ministry that ended in Bible times. But if you look at the ministry of Jesus, the subject of deliverance is unavoidable. You bump into it on nearly every page of the Gospels. I firmly believe that His ministry is the same today as it was then—to save, heal, deliver and preach the gospel of the kingdom. To subtract deliverance from that equation, I believe, is to diminish the gospel.

Jesus certainly understands the need to extend deliverance to those who were "bound." Many verses show us His response to the needs of the people who came to Him for help. Matthew 4:24 tells us that the sick came to him from many miles away, and "whatever their illness and pain, or if they were possessed by demons, or were epileptics, or were paralyzed—he healed them all."

Jesus instructed His disciples to drive out demons in Matthew 10:8 and Mark 16:17. In Luke 10:17, the seventy-two disciples are astonished that "even the demons obey us when we use your name." In Luke 4:36, deliverance is a sign of great authority to the people: "Amazed, the people exclaimed, 'What authority and power this man's words possess! Even evil spirits obey him and flee at his command!'"

Try to imagine the Gospels without deliverance, and you will see just how many times our Lord confronted demons and set people free. I firmly believe that it would be foolish, considering what we see in the Gospels, to exclude demonic activity entirely from the twenty-first century experience.

Free of Lust

I have a friend named Gary who is one of the most vibrant and alive Christians I have ever met. He is a successful business-man who exudes the love of Jesus. Yet when you get to know him, he will tell you that for many years he struggled with sexual purity. The answer for him was "deliverance," and he is quick to recommend it to others who seem to have life-controlling prob-lems. I first met him five years ago, not long after he received his deliverance. As I was preparing this chapter, I remembered his story and called him to get more facts.

Gary told me that during the dark years, he kept a journal that was full of confessions and failures, but he coded the language for fear that if he died, someone would find out about his sin. He tried everything to get free: reading the Word, praying, going to church, joining an accountability group, even reading a book subtitled "Pulling down the strongholds of sexual addiction," which focused on "taking captive every thought and making it obedient to Christ." Gary was always on the lookout for a solution because he genuinely wanted to please the Father and be free of the vise-like grip of sexual sin in his life, but nothing seemed to help.

Then in 1995, he heard a man testify that he had been a sexual addict (he had been caught soliciting a prostitute at one point), but that he had been set free. When Gary asked him what had set him free, the man replied that he had been delivered from the tormenting power of demons.

Gary sought out a minister who had experience in deliverance ministry—a man who had no doubt about his spiritual authority, was spiritually mature, was not out to make a show and who knew how to drive out demons in the name of Jesus. After having Gary read *Pigs in the Parlor—A Practical Guide to Deliverance,* he instructed Gary to spend a few hours confessing sins and areas of habitual sin and weakness—which we will call strongholds. Then he spent twenty minutes or so casting demons out of Gary's life. When he finished, he told Gary to rest for a number of hours.

After that, Gary was free in a way he had never experienced before. *Staying* free, he discovered, was a matter of being filled with the Holy Spirit, daily reading the Word of God and keeping a regular time of prayer and intercession.

Within a year of that first deliverance, however, Gary fell rather dramatically, which shocked him at his own behavior. He repented by again getting another "tune-up" deliverance, this time from the specific stronghold he allowed back in by his sin. Having now experienced freedom, Gary was not going to settle for less until he had total freedom from the *indwelling* work of the enemy.

To avoid a single further reoccurrence, Gary added two extra steps to his arsenal against this "insidious slavery." The first step, mentioned above, was based on the scriptural warning that "when an evil spirit comes out of a man, it goes through arid places seeking rest and does not find it. Then it says, 'I will return to the house I left.' When it arrives, it finds the house *unoccupied*, swept clean and put in order. Then it goes and takes with it seven other spirits more wicked than itself, and they go in and live there" (Matt. 12:43–45, NIV, emphasis added).

> ❝
> ## Gary never thought such a thing was possible, but it worked for him, and has for years. His desire to be free overcame his embarrassment at what the answer might be.
> ❞

The key word is *unoccupied*. By purposing to *daily* be *filled* with the Holy Spirit through quiet time and Bible study, Gary had a *guarantee* he would never again be found "unoccupied"; rather, he would be quite full of the "right stuff," with no room left over in the inn.

Secondly, Gary was given a very simple exhortation by his deliverance minister that he credits for being the difference of never having to go back: *"Fight it,* Gary. The word 'no' is an option for you when encountered by outside stimuli or thoughts. This is not cruise control; your cooperation is required."

It takes all three steps, Gary says—deliverance, staying filled with the Holy Spirit and flatly rejecting the lie "This will make you feel better" when it rears its ugly head. Gary knows better. "No, that is a noose fitted for my neck. I will pass."

Gary marvels now that he spent half his life bound up when this solution was so simple and effective. He treats his daily time with the Lord the same way a diabetic treats insulin—to not take it means death.

For those who have never experienced this type of viselike grip of the enemy, it may be difficult to realize how horrible it is to constantly be pulled down by forces you do not feel you can control. But this testimony shows that there is freedom. And for many, I believe, deliverance is the key that unlocks the door to living an overcoming Christian life—to truly becoming a new man in Christ.

At the center of any stronghold is an idea that runs contrary to the nature and character of God.

Gary never thought such a thing was possible, but it worked for him, and it has for years with absolutely no relapse. His desire to be free overcame his embarrassment at what the answer might be. Even as we went to press and I reconfirmed the details of Gary's story with him, he added, "Just this morning as I brushed my teeth, I thanked God that despite the various business pressures I am currently experiencing, I am still amazed how light they are compared with the unbearable extra weight I used to carry around—the weight of a guilty conscience. Freedom is a real place, and I am staying put. I believe Jesus was being literal when He said in John 8:34–36, 'I tell you the truth, everyone who sins is a slave to sin. Now a slave has no permanent place in the family, but a son belongs to it forever. So if the Son sets you free, you will be free indeed' (NIV). Indeed, Jesus, my Friend and my Deliverer!"

As Gary's life shows, the sexual area can become a stronghold. It is not the only area, of course. But in our sex-crazed society, it seems this problem is more and more prevalent. Through sinning, men open themselves up to demonic control that needs to be dealt with spiritually.

Charles Mylander, in the foreword to a book by Neil Anderson, wrote about his battle with lustful thoughts. He says that for years such thoughts plagued his mind and irritated his soul. He tried everything he thought a Christian should try—Bible study and memorization, new experiences with God and efforts at self-discipline—but nothing seemed to work for long.

"I prayed during those times of struggle, too—God knows I prayed," he wrote. "I repented and turned away from my sins more often than I can remember. God answered my prayer at the moment. But the lustful thoughts always came back."

Mylander did find victory, but in a different way than Gary did. And during the process he discovered a new dimension to his problem.

> As I asked Christ to bring to my mind each instance of sexual sin, three vivid memories popped into my thoughts. Each one was, I now believe, a foothold Satan and his demons used to form a stronghold in my mind. Renouncing each one led to greater freedom and joy than ever before. In the days of my greatest struggle I did not know about the activity of Satan in putting his evil thoughts in my mind.[3]

Mylander found his deliverance from the strongholds of sin by renouncing the sin. According to Webster, *renounce* means "to refuse to follow, obey or recognize any further."

Renouncing sin means simply kicking sin out of your life and not following it any further. But that simple definition requires great strength of commitment. It requires asking Christ to reveal the sin to you, calling upon His power to renounce it and then keeping that door to sin shut tightly and locked securely. In other words, it takes spiritual warfare to make it stick!

Here are two stories of victory and two different ways they

went about getting the deliverance. This is not some sort of formula that works a certain way all the time in all cases any more than one medical solution cures all instances of disease. Yet the principles are the same.

Does Mylander's struggle sound like your own? Have you asked Christ to bring to your mind each instance of sin? As He reveals those habitual sin bondages, take out your spiritual weapons and in the strength of Christ renounce each one of those sins. Renounce them aloud. Remember that Satan is not omniscient—he cannot read your mind; he does not know your thoughts. He will only know what it is you are renouncing when you speak it aloud.

Use the mighty sword of the Spirit, the Word of God, to order those sins out the door. Tell the enemy, "Get thee behind me, Satan! I renounce you and the evil you are trying to keep in my life. In the mighty name of Jesus I pronounce you gone—take a hike, get lost, get out of my life!"

Victory Has Been Won

Jesus won our redemption on Calvary. He took away the shame of our sin long before we were born. But we must appropriate that wholeness into our lives. We must take authority over Satan and renounce all control he might claim over us. This can often be done with a "self-deliverance," or taking our rightful authority over Satan in our own lives. I do this when I feel I am facing a problem that is demonically energized. If that does not work, there are ministries trained in deliverance that can help.

Now let's talk about a problem that can become a stronghold as an example of this spiritual warfare concept—masturbation. First, let me be clear that the problem areas are far more than just sexual. And this book is about spiritual victory, not just about overcoming sexual addictions. But let's face it, men can relate to this example because most men masturbate at least occasionally.

An otherwise mature man who has masturbated since early teen years and who does it several times a day has, in my opinion, a compulsion that has become a spiritual stronghold. Maybe the man has repeatedly allowed spirits of lust, and perhaps specific spirits of masturbation, to take control.

Men who battle this will testify that while they are perfectly normal most of the time, at those times they enter a "zone" where they seem unable to control their own actions. They are in this "zone" until they achieve a release. It is almost as if they are controlled by something outside of themselves. If this is the case, then prayer according to Scripture and prayed in faith will make those spirits flee in the name of Jesus.

Strongholds of insecurity and fear are supernaturally built and must be torn down by supernatural means.

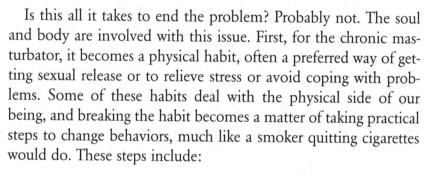

Is this all it takes to end the problem? Probably not. The soul and body are involved with this issue. First, for the chronic masturbator, it becomes a physical habit, often a preferred way of getting sexual release or to relieve stress or avoid coping with problems. Some of these habits deal with the physical side of our being, and breaking the habit becomes a matter of taking practical steps to change behaviors, much like a smoker quitting cigarettes would do. These steps include:

- Substituting a healthy activity for the unhealthy one

- Enlisting the support and encouragement of others who spur you on to the desired outcome

As we stated earlier, bad habits often have other problems at their root, involving strongholds in the mind or soul. James Robison makes the point well that strongholds are not demons. If they were, we could cast them out. A stronghold is like a beachhead from which Satan tries to attack us. Another way to see it is as a dungeon that contains unhealthy thought patterns. At the center of any stronghold is an idea that runs contrary to the nature and character of God. That idea may be:

- Fear
- Insecurity
- Lust
- Greed
- Pride

Any number of "faithless" thoughts like these can form the center chamber of a stronghold. Sometimes what appears to be a sexual problem is really a stronghold of insecurity or fear.

Then there is an inner wall of reasoning and human logic. This is built when we try to fight a stronghold on human terms with arguments, intellect and analysis. The inner wall can become a barrier to getting rid of the stronghold because no matter how much we think about it, or will it away, it will not budge. As the Bible says, "It is not by force nor by strength, but by my Spirit, says the LORD Almighty" (Zech. 4:6). Strongholds are supernaturally built and must be torn down by supernatural means.

An outer wall of pride also keeps us from victory. This pride sometimes leads to fear that others will find out about our problem. Perhaps this wall is built when we grow fond of the pet sin we have, or brag about it—the kind of thinking the Bible calls a "proud argument that keeps people from knowing God" (2 Cor. 10:5). If we are to be free, we cannot fear what others will think. We must be willing to throw down our pride and admit who we really are—to ourselves and to others. We cannot fawn over, or make excuses for, our particular area of weakness.

Free Indeed

One of my friends who comes from a church background where they don't believe in a literal deliverance was telling me to tone down this section of the book. As proof for his arguments he told me of a friend of his who was battling homosexual tendencies. In his desperation for help, the friend submitted to a deliverance ministry (even though he didn't really believe it would help). Those probably well-meaning people proceeded to exorcise all the evil spirits. But the man's mixed-up tendencies continued and even got worse. He came to resent the deliverance ministry because it "didn't work." Yet I know from the testimonies of other people whom I know and from my knowledge of the Word of God that deliverance does "work"—no matter how many times the deliverance ministry has been abused. Tens of thousands of people know freedom today because of deliverance.

> " Deliverance is a real part of the gospel package, but it is only one part, **neither something to be feared, nor a magic bullet.** "

Is deliverance a cure-all? It might appear so at times because the change is so radical. But deliverance does not negate the need for "working out our own salvation with fear and trembling," renewing the mind and changing behaviors. While I believe it is a spiritual reality (and I can testify to achieving great spiritual victories as a result of breaking spiritual strongholds), it isn't the panacea to all spiritual problems. Remember that Jesus said those demons can come back—and bring their friends.

For example, I believe in divine healing. God does heal today. I know people who have been miraculously healed, and while I have had no major sicknesses, I believe I have been healed of various ailments over the years. But is everyone who is prayed for healed? No. Just because some people are not healed, it doesn't change the fact that others are healed—*instantly and totally.* In the same way, some people continue fighting the same battles even after deliverance, but perhaps in varying degrees. Others, however, are delivered and set free—instantly and totally.

Deliverance is a real part of the gospel package, but it is only one part, neither something to be feared, nor a magic bullet.

In other countries, deliverance is often a normal part of ministry. In late 1999 Joy and I flew to Argentina to sit under the ministry of Carlos Annacondia, the evangelist who has been credited with leading more than three million to Christ in a country of thirty-five million. Obviously that many conversions indicate a real revival is taking place in this South American country.

I was met at the airport by a thirty-eight-year-old businessman named Gabriel Mendez, owner of *Aromaticos A.M.,* which wholesales fragrances for perfumes. Gabriel is a layman who is active in the deliverance ministry of *Iglesia Rey de Reyes* (King of Kings Church), the great church in Buenos Aires pastored by my friend Claudio Freidzon.

As I got to know Gabriel, I probed to find out more about the incredible success the Christians in Argentina seem to be having on discipling the hundreds of thousands of new believers who come to Christ each year. At the time I was reading Annacondia's book *Listen to Me, Satan!,* which told the stories of the vast number of people who had been set free of demonic oppression, and Claudio Freidzon's book *Treasure in Jars of Clay.*

I was pondering why some never really become the "new man" that the Bible says believers should be. Yet others are totally and instantly set free. What made the difference?

I told Gabriel about the cycle I have observed in the lives of many men—indulging in pornography, which leads to masturbation, which ultimately leads to marital dissatisfaction.

Gabriel told me that he and others who were involved with him in the deliverance ministry at their church had success in these areas. He went on to explain why. The church had scheduled weekend retreats where believers who wanted to be set free of their bondages could go and take part in a time when they "cut" with the past.

All new converts at King of Kings Church are asked to go on these *retiros* (Spanish for "retreat") after completing a "school of ministry" course. The retreats are three days long and are held a couple of hours drive outside Buenos Aires.

The first two days of the retreat deal with the person's past. Maybe the person was involved in witchcraft and never asked God for forgiveness. Maybe he or she has a problem with anger or some other sin that had developed into a stronghold. Maybe some of the women were raped, or some of the men molested as boys. Maybe some of the women had had an abortion.

A leader at the *retiro* extends an invitation to those who had merely made a mental ascent to the gospel or those who had compromised their commitment to Christ to receive Christ into their lives. There is an altar call to ask these people to open their lives to Christ. This is always the first step to true deliverance.

Then the people attending the retreat begin to focus on the trouble spots in their pasts. Prayer ministers from the church encourage the participants to repent and to ask for deliverance from the strongholds that enslaved them.

The ministers take authority over Satan. Then they pray for the people to be filled with the Holy Spirit. As a result of attending the retreat, the people have a better understanding of their place in Christ and in the church. They are much more apt to remain committed in their Christian walk.

The experience at the *retiro* is so powerful that many people come back and confess sins in front of the entire congregation. Even in normal church settings I saw how the believers there are taught to take authority over evil spirits, just as Jesus did. It is common for evil spirits to "manifest" themselves during an altar call.

When demons manifest by making the person act strangely, the demons are dealt with forthrightly. They flee in the name of Jesus, and, from what I could tell, the people are free.

One thing became very evident to me as I observed the believers in this non-American setting: The Christians were not gripped by the same fear of the devil that I have often seen in Christian circles in America. I know American Christians who are almost afraid to make Satan angry by confronting his kingdom. They believe that in his anger he will send all sorts of problems to the people who make him angry. But the Word of God says, "The Spirit who lives in you is greater than the spirit who lives in the world" (1 John 4:4).

Deliverance Today

Deliverance can take many forms. For example, I believe that when some people go to the altar for salvation, they are delivered. Sometimes it is messy, with crying and all the manifestations of a significant emotional experience. At other times it happens quietly and privately, as with James Robison.

There are three requirements for people to be set free:

1. The person must want to be set free.

In his book *Free in Christ*, Pablo Bottari asserts that people do not always want to be delivered.[4] Bottari is an internationally recognized authority on the ministry of deliverance and former overseer for the tent of deliverance in evangelistic crusades led by Carlos Annacondia. Deliverance depends on a person's free will. Bottari says that no deliverance is possible until a person consciously says, "Yes, I want to be free." Unless a person is willing to surrender to the Lord, God will not unleash His power over that person's life.

2. The person must be hungry for more of God.

If a person is not longing, hungering for a change, then that means he is satisfied with things as they are. Until people long to get rid of bondages that seem to hang on no matter how they try to overcome them, they are not ready for deliverance.

We must cry out to God and say, "Lord, I need You. I am not satisfied with what I have. I want more of You and more of Your presence. Please come and satisfy my hunger–fill me with Yourself, and take all that is not of You out of my life."

If there is no other message you get from this book than this one, it is that you must hunger for more of God if you are ever to be free.

3. The person ministering deliverance must be able to take authority over the enemy.

Carlos Annacondia reminds us that although man lost his power and authority over the earth, Jesus paid the debt. When Jesus was resurrected, He canceled the mortgage—and now He has the right to demand possession of the earth. Annacondia says, "That authority enables us to say, 'Devil, let go of that which is not yours.' We take it away from him in the name of Jesus of Nazareth." Although Satan is usurping the earth, we have the power to take things away from him with the authority that comes from God.[5]

We must be like Carlos Annacondia—confront Satan face to face and say, "Listen to me, Satan; in the name of Jesus, let him go."

When a believer calls upon the name of Jesus and snatches out of the devil's hands what he has taken away from someone he has bound to sin, that sin and the evil spirits with it will leave. The light of God's truth will shine in that person's life, and freedom from bondage will take place. We must be like Carlos Annacondia—confront Satan face to face and say, "Listen to me, Satan; in the name of Jesus, let him go. I command you to let him go in the name of Jesus."

In Argentina, prayer teams minister deliverance to those who need it, often praying for hours, if necessary, until there is total freedom. This type of "soaking" prayer is also a hallmark of the Argentine revival. It is the "personal touch" that often makes the difference.

Freidzon told me that people are tired of attending a service—even an anointed service—where they are just spectators. Instead, they want someone to minister to them. Those of us who attended their annual Breakthrough Conference certainly experienced this. We were ministered to again and again.

Pablo Bottari gives a practical theological explanation for deliverance ministry. He says that many people, after receiving the Lord, manifest the presence of barriers, difficulties and problems. When people ask him why they feel that they are going downhill even though they have been believers for some time, he asks them this question: "Have you ever been ministered to for deliverance?" He says that in most cases the answer is negative.[6]

> Deliverance moves you from spiritual death to spiritual life. It could be **a solution to the "old man" struggles you are dealing with.**

Sergio Marquet is an associate pastor at King of Kings Church. He is also the coordinator for Claudio Freidzon's crusades, which are held all over the world. But he used to live in the drug district of Belgrano, where he was known as "The Frenchman," a man addicted to drugs and the criminal activities necessary to support his drug habit.

The police blamed him for everything that had to do with drugs in Belgrano, and he was arrested regularly, sometimes as often as twice a day, for possession of narcotics, trafficking, theft and forgery.

One day Marquet stopped at a plaza where he and his friends hung out. There his life would be changed. He heard a preacher talking about Jesus. As he listened, he began to realize that the speaker—and the crowds of people standing there listening to him—had light in their lives while he had only darkness. He began returning to the park every day to listen to the messages. One day he heard God say to him, "This is your last chance."

Marquet says that although he really did not want to quit using drugs, he realized that he had a great inner need. That day when the speaker invited people to come to the front to accept Christ into their lives, he went forward. But by the next day he was high again, and he returned to the park—under the influence of drugs—and went forward again for prayer. When he finished praying, he was completely sober. Day after day the same thing happened.

One night as he listened, all at once he understood that Christ had died for *him*. Although he had been rejected by family, friends, neighbors and all of society, Jesus loved him. And not only did He love Marquet, He had given His life for him. "I felt so unworthy, so dirty, that I began to cry," Marquet says. "I cried the whole evening. I could not stop crying as I thought about Christ's love. When that day came to an end, I was no longer the same man."

Marquet never again felt the need for drugs. The passion that had driven him to drugs now drove him to the Lord. Although friends deserted him, in time they had to admit the work of Christ in him as his life spoke volumes of the mercy of God at work in him.

Claudio Freidzon says that Marquet's change was so great that nobody could believe it. In a moment of deliverance, God transformed him from the old man, consumed with sin and failure, into a new man, free from bondage and filled with a new passion to be like Christ. Marquet prayed, read the Word and became devoted to the Lord's service. Through his testimony of God's awesome deliverance, many have experienced God's power at work in their lives.[7]

God can do the same thing for you. Deliverance is not spooky, weird or bad. Deliverance is the gift of God. It enables a person to get rid of sin and bondage that may have been gripping a life for years. It moves you from spiritual death to spiritual life. It could be a solution to the "old man" struggles you are dealing with.

Do you want to be set free from that thing that keeps you from being the man you know God wants you to be? Are you hungry—starving—for more of God? Then allow His work of deliverance to take place in your life. Become the new man God wants you to be.

Allow the following words from Claudio Freidzon to move you to your moment of deliverance:

> You may think you have no great qualities or charisma that the Lord could use, but He has a purpose for your life. He watches your heart. God is interested in your life. Today the Holy Spirit invites you to make one of the most important decisions of your life, a decision that will make it possible for you to enjoy a glorious future. This decision is a commitment, a covenant of love with the Lord to lift up your eyes daily and seek Him. The Holy Spirit wants to quench your inner thirst and take you to a glorious dimension where you can speak with God as Moses did—face-to-face. He desires to hear you say passionately, sincerely and from the depths of a loving heart, "Holy Spirit, I hunger for You!"[8]

God really does want to meet you face to face in a glorious encounter of power. He will quench your inner thirst and remove any barriers to an intimate relationship with Him. His power will break off any bondages or hindrances keeping you from reaching your destiny in Christ.

Want to know more about that power? It comes from the Holy Spirit, and it is the topic of the next chapter.

Talk about it Think about it

Deliverance: Breaks Sin's Hold

Author's note: God's power to deliver is greater than any bondage or stronghold that sin can place on you. Remember, at your weakest moment, God's power is strongest at work in you.

For more information on this topic (which we will add to as time passes) check out our www.oldmannewman.com website. Use the user id: **oldman** and the password **newman**. These are **case sensitive,** so use all lowercase letters and leave no spaces.

1. What is your reaction to the following statement that appears on page 86? "I personally believe that a problem that will not go away after prayer, positive confession, fasting, strong-willed determination or medical treatment must have a demonic basis that needs to be dealt with spiritually."

2. Strongholds are described on page 94 as follows: "A stronghold is like a beachhead from which Satan tries to attack us. At the center of any stronghold is an idea that runs contrary to the nature and character of God. That idea may be fear, insecurity, lust, greed, pride." Which of these ideas could most easily become a stronghold for you if you let it?

3. A requirement for being set free is that the person must be hungry for more of God. What brings men to the place where they finally become hungry for more of God?

New Man

Charisma's Bible Handbook on the Holy Spirit

Receiving the Baptism in the Holy Spirit

Just as we receive new life in the Son of God by a definite act of personal faith, even so we receive supernatural power in the Spirit of God by an act of conscious faith. The simple acrostic "READY" can provide an aid in remembering various important steps in receiving the baptism in the Holy Spirit:

R—Repent. Those who seek to be baptized in the Spirit should first of all repent of any and all sin and accept Jesus Christ as their Savior and Lord.

E—Expect. Because the Holy Spirit is appropriated by faith (Gal. 3:2, 14), those seeking the baptism in the Spirit must have an expectant attitude, believing that God will fulfill His promise to them.

A—Ask. Candidates for this baptism should come to Jesus in prayer, asking Him and expecting Him to pour out the Spirit upon them.

D—Drink. Jesus gave His great invitation, "If any man is thirsty, let him come to Me and drink" (John 7:37, NAS).

Y—Yield. Those seeking to be baptized and filled with the Spirit must be willing to yield control of every part of their being to the Holy Spirit.[1]

—**John Rea**

Chapter 7

Receiving the Holy Spirit: Empowers Your Life

OLD MAN	Spiritually impotent, immature and unable to grow into Christlikeness.
NEW MAN	Baptized in the Holy Spirit and empowered to live a godly life.

When I was a teenager I read David Wilkerson's book *The Cross and the Switchblade*, which has sold several million copies. Wilkerson's fiery style and warnings about the dangers of drug addiction were just enough to keep me from experimenting with drugs later when I was going through my rebellious phase.

The story is well known of how a young country preacher from the Pennsylvania hills was drawn to New York by an article in *Life* magazine about young gang members who were on trial for murder. When Wilkerson arrived on their turf, he began preaching a message of miracles, renewal and God's love—and a power to get off and stay off drugs.

Drugs have a tremendous hold on the human body that could be explained in physical terms alone, he found. The young people who got off drugs told Wilkerson there were two habits they had to kick when they were on drugs—the body habit (which they kicked cold turkey in three days) and the mind habit, which was much more entrenched.

Wilkerson tells how one young addict named Joe came to their Teen Challenge center in Brooklyn to kick a habit of painkillers after a serious on-the-job injury. They put Joe in an upstairs bedroom where he went through "cold turkey" withdrawal. For four days someone was with him twenty-four hours a day, helping him through the shakes and cramps and lending prayer support.

Finally, after four days of intense pain, Joe was free. Everyone rejoiced. When he said he wanted to go home and see his parents, Wilkerson was dubious, but allowed it. But Joe did not come back. Later they discovered he had been arrested for robbery and possession of narcotics.

> ## Being baptized in the Holy Spirit adds a wonderful dimension to a Christian's walk. There is something that confers power.

Why had Joe failed? Someone suggested they ask the young drug addicts who had successfully stayed off drugs to see if there was an answer.

When Wilkerson asked Nicky Cruz, the young gang warlord whose conversion is central to the story of *The Cross and the Switchblade,* Nicky told him that real freedom came for him when he received the baptism in the Holy Spirit.[2]

Being baptized in the Holy Spirit is a subject that has long since come into the mainstream of the evangelical church. For decades it has been this doctrine that separated the Pentecostals from their evangelical brethren. Baptism in the Holy Spirit is, Pentecostals believe, a renewal of first-century Christianity in which the Holy Spirit was poured out on the church on the Day of Pentecost. This gave the disciples such power and boldness that within one generation, they had turned the known world upside down.

I grew up understanding that there was a power that came from this experience—and I experienced that power and its lasting effects for myself. I know experientially that being baptized in the Holy Spirit adds a wonderful and welcome dimension to a Christian's walk.

It gives a believer access to the power source that enables us to live pure, godly lives that are pleasing to the Father. It does not eliminate the need for any of the spiritual disciplines, nor does it immunize a person from sin. But there is something there that confers power.

In other countries, missionaries of all denominations have found that those who receive the Holy Spirit have the boldness needed to confront demons, making the spreading of the gospel more effective. The power of the Holy Spirit at work in the country of Argentina in recent years has been the catalyst to one of the fastest-spreading revivals the world has ever known. Literally thousands and thousands of individuals have been set free from sin, delivered from bondages, loosed in evangelism and soulwinning and healed from disease—all by the power of the Holy Spirit.

In only one century, beginning in 1901 when the modern Pentecostal movement began, those Christians who have come to believe in the power of the Holy Spirit have grown to more than four hundred million Christians worldwide—the fastest-growing religious movement in history. And while some wring their hands about the waning influence of Christianity, the Charismatic movement is growing 3.5 times faster than the population growth of the world.

Interestingly, the account in *The Cross and the Switchblade* about the baptism in the Holy Spirit caught the attention of several Roman Catholic nuns at Duquesne University in 1967. They prayed to receive this "baptism," and that was the spark of the Roman Catholic Charismatic Renewal, which has touched the lives of more than twenty million people worldwide.

I believe that there is a key here in learning to become a "new man in Christ." Let's look at the followers of Jesus in the first-century church. They had walked and talked with Jesus and had seen the miracles. Yet when He was taken to be crucified, they all fled, with the exception of John. They cowered behind locked doors where they received word that He had been raised from the dead. They even saw Him ascend into heaven, at which time He told them to wait in the upper room until they received power from the Holy Spirit to be His witnesses.

Can you imagine the feelings of those 120 people who gathered in that upper room for ten days? They had lost the One they thought would rise up and overthrow the evil rule of Rome in their country. And rather than dying the death of a hero—He died the death of a traitor. He left them alone, discouraged, brokenhearted—and inept to do anything about it. Rather than ruling in dignity, they were cowering in shame and fear.

But ten days later the Holy Spirit came with mighty power and transformed the life of every person in the upper room. The second chapter of Acts tells how they began to speak in other tongues as the Spirit gave utterance. That encounter with the Holy Spirit gave them power to leave that upper room and turn their city, country and world upside down for God.

They never forgot how they had felt before that day in the upper room. And they never forgot what it was that changed them. They testified to everyone they met about the Holy Spirit and what He had done in their lives. They saw every encounter with an unbeliever as an opportunity to pass on that power for godly living.

Shortly after they left the upper room, Peter and John encountered a poor, crippled man begging for food near the gate of the temple. All that man thought he needed was a little handout, a little money to buy some food. Fresh from an encounter with the Holy Spirit, Peter knew he needed much more, and he gave that man much more than he expected.

In Acts 3 we read: "Peter and John looked at him intently, and Peter said, 'Look at us!' [I imagine Peter thought what had happened to him in that upper room was written all over his face!] The lame man looked at them eagerly, expecting a gift. But Peter said, 'I don't have any money for you. But I'll give you what I have. In the name of Jesus Christ of Nazareth, get up and walk!'" (Acts 3:4–6).

Peter and John, and the rest of the 120 people who had been baptized in the Holy Spirit in the upper room, went on to pass that power out to whomever would receive it. Three thousand people received it the first time Peter spoke about it. And from that day forward, the church of Jesus Christ was born, multiplying daily, until the effects of that upper room experience were felt around the world.

That power enabled them to heal the sick, raise the dead, cast out demons, spread the gospel and establish churches. Once the Holy Spirit resided in their lives, they were fearless in life–and fearless in death.

I once heard a secular speaker tell a group of company executives that it is impossible for an adult to change unless it is accompanied by a significant emotional experience. The speaker was talking specifically about creating a significant emotional experience to cause a worker to change an unwanted behavior in the workplace.

I have not adopted his practice as an employer, but as I thought about what he had said, I realized that in the spiritual realm there was a parallel. I have observed that for adults who accept Christ, it is often difficult to change unless something significant and emotional happens. This frequently happens at the time of salvation when there is true heartfelt repentance, often with tears, sorrow for one's sin and a plea for forgiveness and eternal life. Sadly, however, when the gospel is presented on an intellectual basis and the person is asked to accept on faith alone and counseled to ignore "feelings," that sort of conversion all too often doesn't "stick," and the person later goes back on his commitment to follow Christ.

Another way to look at this is to realize that what I am identifying as an emotional experience comes only when a person comes to the "end of themselves." A person must be so tired of how he is living that he is willing to change, to turn to God and ask the Holy Spirit for help.

I know there is vast power available to help us change—it is the power that comes from the baptism in the Holy Spirit. Not only does the baptism give us the power to change, but it also gives us power in many other areas. These include:

- Power to hear God's voice
- Power to pray and see results
- Power to manifest the fruit of the Spirit
- Power to love
- Power to minister
- Power to speak beyond what you know
- Power to take authority over circumstances
- Power to take authority over the evil one
- Power to deliver people from the evil one
- Power to do miracles

The Spirit Brings Life Changes

One of my dear friends was Jamie Buckingham, a Baptist pastor who had two moral failures involving adultery. After losing his ministry and devastating his marriage, he was crushed by guilt. This experience opened him to the Holy Spirit. He received the baptism in the Holy Spirit and went on to become a well-known leader in the Charismatic movement—and he never had another moral failure.

Jamie became my mentor, and as you will read later, I witnessed firsthand how being baptized in the Spirit transformed Jamie and empowered him—not only to get past his failures in the past, but also to move into a future that was powerful and life-changing not only to Jamie, but to all who knew him.

Being baptized in the Holy Spirit doesn't guarantee that someone will live a holy life—but it does guarantee that they will have the power to live a holy life. Several well-known Charismatic leaders, and countless lesser-known ones, have fallen into sin. Being baptized in the Holy Spirit does not obliterate free will and choices—but it does make available to us the power we need to live a life of miracles—and often the greatest miracle is the transformation of our own hearts.

I received the baptism of the Holy Spirit when I was twelve at an Assemblies of God youth camp. I can remember the late-night altar services in which I felt the presence of God and cried out for this baptism experience I had heard about all my life. I see now that I understood only a little of what the baptism of the Holy Spirit is all about.

Yet I left that youth camp totally convinced that God was real and that somehow He had a plan and purpose for my life. I can see now that this experience was the bedrock foundation that brought me back to God after a rebellious time later in my life.

> **There is vast power available to help us change— it is the power that comes from the baptism in the Holy Spirit.**

Even though receiving the baptism was a very dramatic experience, I started rebelling at age fourteen and did a pretty good job of serving the devil until I was twenty. At various times I would recommit my life to serve Christ at youth camp, then backslide again after I got home.

Obviously, the experience is not a cure-all—unless we allow it to be. But I am convinced that being empowered by the Spirit in this unique way gives Christians a far greater chance of staying true to their commitments and overcoming stubborn sin habits.

The Spirit Brings Healing

Often when the baptism of the Holy Spirit takes place in a believer's life, more than sin bondages are broken. In the case of Dr. Fuchsia Pickett, best-selling author and international speaker, she received a physical healing at the same time. Dr. Pickett has become a close family friend and mentor to my wife, Joy, and has had a huge influence on my own life. I believe she is one of the most-gifted Bible teachers of our generation.

Here's her story. Afflicted by a hereditary disease and forced to wear cumbersome braces, she nevertheless had an intense longing for more of God. Despite the progression of her disease, she pastored and taught in Bible school. But finally she was hospitalized, fitted with a body brace and scheduled for surgery to fuse her back together to keep her from hemorrhaging. While waiting at home for the surgery, she convinced a friend to drive her to church in her wheelchair—a Pentecostal church that she had never attended before.

During the service she felt God nudge her and tell her to go forward for prayer. Again and again she resisted God's prodding. Finally she promised God she would go forward if the congregation sang another stanza to a hymn—one she thought was over.

When they sang, she tells us what happened:

> I pulled on the girl's dress who had taken me to the church and said, "Stand me up." She looked at me strangely, but she heard my tone and knew she dared not fail to respond. So she stood me up. Dragging my weakened body in my braces, I picked up my Bible, went up to the little man, looked in his face, and said, "Sir, I don't know why I am here. But I have a feeling that God would like these people to pray for me."

Dr. Pickett says he anointed her and prayed gently in the name of Jesus. "It changed my life—and my theology—totally," she states. The Lord spoke to her, asking, "Are you willing to be identified with these people—to be one of them?" She said, "Yes, Lord, I will be identified with these people." Then she asked to say something to the audience. "I am going to live. Jesus just told me so," she told them with tears running down her face. She tells what happened as she started back to her seat:

> Suddenly the power of God struck the base of my neck and coursed through my body. The miraculous, healing power of God put me back together instantly. It was the infinite, triune, omnipotent God who touched me that morning. I was made every whit whole inside my organs, my blood condition, and my bones. And when He turned me loose, I ran and danced and shouted. I had been struck by resurrection power, which healed me and set me free.

Fuchsia Pickett's divine "Teacher" had come to fill her with Himself and to split open the veil between her soul and her spirit. He intervened in her desperate circumstances and healed her miraculously, even though her mind did not believe the doctrine of healing. For the first time in her life she began to understand, through revelation, the same Scriptures she had studied and taught faithfully for many years. The Scriptures came alive to her, not as information, but as power that was working in her and transforming her life.[3]

66 **That experience became a "naturally supernatural" part of Hayford's everyday communion with God that allowed him to express with more liberty his love for God.** 99

The Spirit Brings a Prayer Language

Jack Hayford, who wrote the foreword to this book, was the

longtime pastor of The Church On The Way in Van Nuys, California. He now serves as chancellor of the King's College and King's Seminary. He is a man I have known and respected for many years—one who has had a mentoring role in my life for the past eight years. I have been in his home, and he has been in mine. I even have the privilege of serving on the Board of Trustees for the King's College and King's Seminary.

Hayford tells the story of how he received the baptism in the Holy Spirit as a young college student after some years of doubt and skepticism. He had heard all the warnings: Don't seek an experience for its own sake! Look out for deceiving spirits! Beware of manipulation, emotionalism and suggestiveness! Don't let sensationalism about the supernatural catch your fancy! Hayford says there were enough obstacles to block any Christian from pursuing a freely open, fully available, spiritually vulnerable moment in the presence of our precious Savior. But he was both hearing and desiring—both understanding and feeling—the truth he was being presented. When the invitation was given to come forward for prayer, he went to the designated room.

In those moments of prayer, God put a four-syllable, non-English phrase in Hayford's mind, but he did not speak it. In fact, he did not speak the phrase for three more years because of his expectation that speaking in tongues would be a supernatural seizure of the tongue rather than a voluntary cooperation with the Holy Spirit. He had to get past several blocks in his own willingness to receive the baptism.

When he did speak those four syllables, and many more, at the close of an evangelistic service, he "sensed that Jesus Christ had filled me with the Holy Spirit, but I had also experienced a release into a beautiful language of praise and prayer."

That experience did not turn out to be a one-night thrill ride as he had feared, but became a "naturally supernatural" part of Hayford's everyday communion with God that allowed him to express with more liberty his love for God.

In his excellent book *The Beauty of Spiritual Language*, Hayford goes on to say four things about the baptism in the Holy Spirit.

1. Speaking with tongues is neither unbiblical nor outdated.

You may have discovered that not all believers believe the same thing about the baptism of the Holy Spirit and its accompanying evidence of speaking in "other tongues."

Hayford tells us that never have the majority of Christian theologians or expositors argued against the timeless availability of this prayer form. A diminishing number of sincere but stubborn souls still stoutly disagree, but nothing in the New Testament Scriptures restricts or confines speaking with tongues to being only a first-century exercise.

Hayford asserts, "Only strained, laborious interpretive schemes can impose such a notion onto the text of Scripture. The idea of 'passe' or 'outdated' or 'early church only' cannot be found in God's Word."[4]

> ❝ When I do not have the words to express to God my longing to overcome circumstances in my life and bring me to victory, I can use my prayer language. ❞

Many believers call the experience of speaking in tongues unknown to them as receiving a "prayer language" from the Holy Spirit. The Bible speaks of the benefits of such a prayer language: "And the Holy Spirit helps us in our distress. For we don't even know what we should pray for, nor how we should pray. But the Holy Spirit prays for us with groanings that cannot be expressed in words" (Rom. 8:26).

What a benefit. When I do not have the words to express to God the depth of my despair or my longing for Him to overcome the circumstances in my life and bring me to victory, I can use my prayer language—a language understood by the Spirit, who speaks through me to the Father, and understood by the Father, who empowers the Spirit to work in my life to give me the victory for which I so desperately long.

2. Speaking with tongues is not a transcendental experience.

There is really nothing goofy or weird about praying in a language I have never learned. I am not falling into self-hypnosis or giving up control of my mind to some occultish mind-invading experience.

As Hayford puts it, "The ways of God in dealing with His redeemed children may be supernatural in the source of His operations, but they are not weird in their ways of working. To speak with tongues is not to resign the control of one's mind or indulge one's emotions to a point of extraction. The exercise of spiritual language does involve a conscious choice to allow God's assistance to transcend our own linguistic limits, but it does not surrender to any order of a mystical, trancelike trip beyond oneself."[5]

3. Speaking with tongues is not a status symbol.

Perhaps one of the things that turn off many men—and women—to the subject of speaking in tongues is seeing its abuses. Some take this gift as a badge of spiritual superiority, or the gift is not used correctly in all congregations. Yet can we honestly admit that other gifts are not abused? Do not some even wear their salvation as a badge of superiority when it is nothing but the grace of God that saves any of us sinners?

Hayford address this problem and gives us some good advice:

> One of the most common "uglies" concerning spiritual language is that the sole orientation many have to the subject of tongues is its presentation as a qualifier, as a required manifestation to verify that they, as Christians, have passed some initiation rite. Consequently, if devoted believers in Christ hear this, and they have not spoken with tongues as yet, they feel they're being cast in a role of second-class citizen, as slightly sub-Christian—only on the grounds of their not having yet spoken in tongues.

> Unsurprisingly, they flee the subject, since the very proposition smacks of cultishness and violates Scripture.[6]

The Bible doesn't tell us that tongues are to be used to impress other believers with the importance and spiritual maturity of the one who speaks. The Bible tells us, "Dear brothers and sisters, if I should come to you talking in an unknown language, how would that help you? But if I bring you some revelation or some special knowledge or some prophecy or some teaching—that is what will help you" (1 Cor. 14:6).

In another place, the apostle Paul says, "So you see that speaking in tongues is a sign, not for believers, but for unbelievers" (1 Cor. 14:22).

4. Speaking with tongues is not proposed as a substitute for spiritual growth.

Using our prayer language and speaking in tongues will not cause us to grow spiritually even if we do it seven days a week and twenty-four hours a day. Hayford tells us what will cause us to grow spiritually:

> As beautiful as an ongoing experience in the use of spiritual language can be at prayer, and as perfectly scriptural and desirable as it can be demonstrated to be, by itself, speaking with tongues holds no particular merit. Growth in the Christian life requires feeding on God's Word, walking in the disciplines of His Son, and fellowshiping with His family—the church.[7]

The baptism in the Holy Spirit is of immense importance to the believer. The Spirit impacts my life daily and helps me to mature and grow into Christlikeness. I thank God continually for gifting me with my prayer language, for it enables me to say things to God in prayer that I would not know how to say in my own words.

As Hayford has already said, "Growth in the Christian life requires feeding on God's Word, walking in the disciplines of His Son, and fellowshipping with His family—the church."

The Holy Spirit gives a man the power to live the overcoming life. I, for one, need all the power I can get to live for Christ. I believe we all do! But His power in my life has helped me to step confidently into the destiny God has for me. I do not have to wonder every moment of the day if I am really going to make it or be afraid that right around the corner is the big temptation that will be too hard for me to withstand.

God's power has taken away the fear of failure, and replaced it with "power, love, and self-discipline" (2 Tim. 1:7). He can do the same for you.

Now that we have covered salvation, deliverance from evil strongholds and receiving the power of the Holy Spirit, what is next? Accountability to other brothers.

Talk about it Think about it

Receiving the Holy Spirit: Empowers Your Life

Author's note: If you have ever been to the point of wanting desperately to make some life-transforming changes, but lacked the strength to make the changes, this chapter is for you. God's strength—the power of the Holy Spirit—is yours for the asking.

For more information on this topic (which we will add to as time passes) check out our www.oldmannewman.com website. Use the user id: **oldman** and the password **newman**. These are **case sensitive,** so use all lowercase letters and leave no spaces.

1. On page 110, we read about the transforming power of the Holy Spirit. The author lists a number of areas where the baptism in the Holy Spirit brings power. Which of these areas of power could you use *right now,* and why?

2. Pages 112–113 contain Dr. Fuchsia Pickett's account of being healed of sickness by the power of the Holy Spirit. Why do you suppose that some Christian people believe that God is not working supernaturally in the world today—and secretly hope that He does not start any time soon?

3. The baptism in the Holy Spirit is described on page 114 as a "'naturally supernatural' part of . . . everyday communion with God that allows [us] to express with more liberty [our] love for God." Is there anything that is keeping you from receiving the baptism in the Holy Spirit right now?

A clip from

New Man September/October 1999

For New Surfers: The Top Ten for Men

Check out these great websites for men:[1]

1. www.theromantic.com The RoMANtic inspires men and women to enrich their relationships.

2. men.crosswalk.com Your source for meaningful, lively dialogue and practical resources.

3. www.newmanmagazine.com Official website of *New Man* magazine.

4. www.edcole.org Official website for Dr. Edwin Louis Cole and the Christian Men's Network.

5. www.fathers.com National Center for Fathering (NCF) inspires and equips men to be better fathers.

6. www.marriagebuilders.com You will be introduced to the best ways to overcome marital conflicts and restore love.

7. www.smallgroups.org Resources to help sharpen your focus, intensify your leadership skills. . . .

8. www.militaryministry.com A civilian-run ministry to empower your life with the Holy Spirit.

9. www.newlifeministry.org Online sex addiction support group with a Christian perspective.

10. www.greatdads.org Seminars to motivate and train fathers to be great dads.

Great websites
oldmannewman.com

Chapter 8

Accountability: Keeps You in Touch

OLD MAN **Has no support system of relationships to hold him accountable.**

NEW MAN **Develops meaningful male relationships that provide richness and stability.**

As we move ahead to become new men in Christ, there are two important aspects that follow our salvation, getting free of spiritual strongholds and receiving the power of the Holy Spirit to live a holy life. The first is discipleship—learning to be a disciple of Jesus. The other is accountability. That is having someone with whom you can be—and are—totally honest, someone who will confront you when you get off course.

Life is like driving a car. First you must be taught how; you must practice those skills under the watchful eye of an instructor. That is because the stakes are high—if you make a huge mistake driving, you may end up getting killed.

Then, as you drive, you learn to make constant course corrections. In fact, we do it so automatically, it becomes subconscious. However, without that small, changing direction of the wheel every few feet, we would end up in a ditch or worse—heading toward oncoming traffic in the opposite lane.

In life, discipleship helps us to learn to follow Jesus. We need a spiritual instructor—a pastor, a Sunday school teacher, an older Christian—to help us get grounded as new believers. Over the years I have been impressed with the way Campus Crusade for Christ and the Navigators each disciple the young people they lead to Christ. Studying their materials is a good source of discipleship materials.

As we develop patterns of daily prayer and Bible study, we begin to develop that intimacy with Jesus necessary for living an overcoming Christian life.

Bob Weiner, my long-time friend, founded Maranatha Ministries in the early 1970s. Today he travels the world leading thousands of people to Christ. He has learned how to disciple.

When a person comes to faith in Christ, Bob tells the person who led him to make the decision to meet with him daily for two weeks to study the Bible and to pray. He also gets the new convert to write out his testimony, and within a week, he or the person who led him to Christ goes with the new convert to visit a friend who needs Jesus so the person can give that friend his testimony. In this way, during those first few crucial days (like the first few days or months of life) this new believer is cared for and taught how to study the Bible. He is also taught to reach out to others. There is nothing that will cause you to grow quicker in Christ than to verbalize your Christian commitment to others.

I believe this is a key. Many men who struggle year after year have never been discipled themselves. They never learn good habits of studying the Bible or how to develop a prayer life. And they are so self-absorbed with their own problems that they never tell anyone else about Jesus.

Yet the Book of Revelation tells us this: "And they have defeated him [Satan, the accuser] because of the blood of the Lamb and *because of their testimony*" (Rev. 12:11, emphasis added).

This verse tells us that we overcome the devil by the blood of the Lamb (which is what happens at salvation) and by the word of our testimony. That can mean different things. But one of them is clear—we should testify to others about the change in our own lives.

As we develop patterns of daily prayer and Bible study, we begin to develop that intimacy with Jesus necessary for living an overcoming Christian life.

Become Accountable

What about the areas of our lives where we need to steer in a different direction to stay on course? That is where accountability comes in.

President Clinton's marital problems a few years ago show how easily one's life can spin out of control. While a number of other U.S. presidents are said to have had extramarital affairs while in the White House, almost no one knew. This time, however, the whole world was privy to Clinton's affair with an intern half his age.

One thing seems obvious to me: God allowed that to become public, just as He allowed Nebuchadnezzar to lose his throne and to eat grass due to the pride in his heart. Right after President Clinton admitted to the nation he had lied about his relationship with Monica Lewinsky, the men in my men's group had an interesting discussion about how easily one's life can get off course and how important it is to have constant course corrections.

This was the point I tried to make in a recent article in *New Man* magazine about the importance for men to have close personal friendships that can hold them accountable. I described my own close relationship to Jamie Buckingham and how I learned the importance of being open and staying on course spiritually. In the article, I told how a group of men rallied around me when Jamie died, and from that grew an accountability group that has been invaluable to me personally.[2]

I think the foundation of any relationship is trust. You can't have a relationship without trust, so you must exercise trust and

Develop friendships

oldmannewman.com

be trustworthy. Vulnerability fits into this because you are *trusting* another with who you really are—or with more of who you are than is generally available to the public or to casual acquaintances. Similarly, you show trustworthiness by keeping the secrets of another. But underneath all of this is trust.

Life is a series of course corrections and decision-making. We decide, hopefully through the guidance of the Holy Spirit, to live in a certain place or do a certain kind of work. That affects whom we know and whom we marry.

Along the way it is easy to get off course. But who will help us make those course corrections? Maybe a pastor, maybe a spouse.

Pastoral counsel alone is not the answer. And it is hard for wives to help husbands, especially when the course correction involves secret sin or an ungodly thought life.

Relationships are built through vulnerability. When vulnerability is held in confidence, intimacy builds. Over time, intimacy develops into trust.

I have known men at church who seemed strong Christians on the surface. But I did not really know the struggles they faced, and I had no relationship to speak into their lives. Suddenly their lives seem to have spun out of control, they left their wives, and they turned their backs on God. At that point, it is almost too late to try to get them back on course. How much better had they been able to make course corrections before their lives crashed and burned.

As I have worked with ministers through *Ministries Today* magazine, I have learned that pastors are often the loneliest people in a church; they rarely have the kind of close friendships where they can open up and share their frustrations or hurts. I believe many pastors whose ministries get off base, who get into greed or abuse of power or sexual sin, do so because they made small decisions to think certain thoughts or harbor certain offenses.

Suddenly the door was open for Satan to attack them, and little by little their lives—and ministries—got off course.

I believe in risk management. There are things I do on a practical basis to reduce my risk, whether it is buying insurance to cover calamities or even buying certain types of investments that are a hedge against a down market.

In our spiritual lives it is necessary to manage risk, too.

Friends are a hedge against calamity. As we study the Scriptures we learn that the Christian life is about living in community. When we get into trouble, we are to confess our sins to each other that we may be healed.

There is a place for tenderness and forgiveness, and a place for getting in a man's face if he begins to get off course. This is the accountability I find with my GOLF (Group of Loyal Friends) group.

One day I was having dinner with a close friend, and we were talking about this subject. He had opened up only once with a pastor about the most hurtful event in his life—a moral shortcoming more than two decades before that he repented of long ago. The pastor repeated this man's secret to the pastor's wife, who proceeded to spread it around the church. Not only was this man humiliated, but he was also betrayed by what should have been a professionally confidential conversation.

This friend was interested in starting a small group. He had gone to some men's fellowship breakfasts at his church, but few relationships were started. Someone got up and preached at the men about what they should be doing, but there was no time for relationships to form.

We can only speculate that if in his early political career Bill Clinton had had godly friends who could have held him accountable, his life would have taken a very different course, not only by his avoiding extramarital affairs, but also by challenging him to have a biblical view on the issues of abortion and homosexuality.

Relationships are built through vulnerability. When that vulnerability is held in confidence, intimacy builds. And over time this intimacy develops into trust. It is like your personal finances. Before you can make a withdrawal from the bank, you must first make a deposit. Otherwise, when you write a check, the check is going to bounce.

But the first step is opening the account and putting some deposits in. That's vulnerability. And unless that happens, no withdrawals can ever be made.

> ## The best way to disarm critics is to confess everything **before they have an opportunity to accuse you of wrongdoing.**

What Is Really Inside

I watched a television documentary recently about four teenage boys who went on a crime spree that included arson, robbery and finally the murder of a band teacher at their high school in Fort Myers, Florida. These were, by all appearances, "normal" teenage boys with curfews and part-time jobs at a fast-food restaurant. The night they were arrested, they were on the way to rob their own place of employment, but only after calling to let the manager know they would not be at work that night.

People were astonished that no one could tell the evil that was in these boys' hearts until after their deeds were done.

In a similar way, I have known many Christian men who also had deep dark secrets. Their inner evil tormentors led them first to abandon their families, then to plunge into all sorts of perversion (much of which society overlooks unless it leads to violence) and finally to abandon their relationship with the Lord altogether.

A wise poet said no man is an island. Men veer off course if there are no friends to keep them on course. If no one knows the truth about us, and if no one knows us well enough to tell us the truth about ourselves, we are living a disconnected and volatile life.

A few years ago a respected pastor of a successful church in my state was sent to jail for dealing drugs and pistol-whipping a man who owed him money from a drug deal. I knew the man and would have never imagined him to have a problem with drugs, let alone dealing drugs. Apparently he lived this double life while continuing to preach on Sunday morning with what others perceived as power and anointing, all the while rotting away inside.

Today he is rotting away in prison. His family and his life are totally devastated. Thankfully the church has survived this horrible scandal.

One of the reasons my men's group has stuck together for eight years is so each of us has someone to reach out to in those moments when we are tempted. Otherwise, with no accountability, it is too easy to make small decisions to do what is wrong—to entertain lustful thoughts when we look at other women, to enjoy wrong secret sexual fantasies or to glance for a few seconds at the "free" preview on the X-rated channel in the hotel room when we are lonely. Step by step we can make ourselves vulnerable to Satan's attacks until we find ourselves head over heels in sin.

One of the best ways to avoid this is to be open and vulnerable with close friends. First, it is best to have an open relationship with our wives—who ought to be our closest friends. However, there are some temptations—especially of a sexual nature—that may be better shared with a male friend. There are some things wives do not understand, and it is not fair to always burden them, especially if you are just grappling with the temptation.

A wife might not understand the temptation a man might have to look at pornography. She might wrongly feel that the few extra pounds she has put on makes her unappealing to her husband, when that may not be the reason he is turned to pornography at all. It may be that her husband is struggling with lust issues from his teenage years or some other sort of problem. He may still love his wife and find her attractive. In this example, it is better for the husband to confide in another man—a man who understands the struggle because he has been there.

In my own life, I have found that it is a good policy to never have any secrets. I'm talking about those things I'm so embarrassed about I wish no one knew. I believe that provides a measure of protection that I feel I need.

Secret sins hold a certain power. The fact that I have admitted my sins means that a lot of the power they might have over me has been broken.

And if for any reason I'm tempted to go back to something from my past, I have someone whom I can call, and who won't be shocked, because he already knows that about me.

I consider this investment of myself in other men "insurance" against backsliding.

> ## I want you to know that I have experienced the power of being **open to Christian brothers who have made a difference in my life.**

I remember the advice of Jamie Buckingham. He believed the best way to disarm critics is to confess everything before they have an opportunity to accuse you of wrongdoing. Some men can live that way; others do not want to be that open with the world.

In his book *Radical Honesty,* Brad Blanton, a psychotherapist from Washington, D.C., puts forth his idea that lying is the major source of all human stress. "Healing is possible only with the freedom that comes from not hiding anymore," he writes. "Withholding from other people, not telling them about what we feel or think, keeps us locked in the jail. The longer we remain in that jail, the quicker we decline. We either escape, or we go dead. The way out is to get good at telling the truth."[3] Blanton differentiates three levels of truth-telling:

- Revealing the facts and allowing others to know the truth about us, even if it makes us look bad

- Being honest about current thoughts and feelings instead of spending energy to convince others we are more saintly than we are

- Admitting that whom we have pretended to be for so long is not who we really are[4]

One advantage of being open with a brother is that you learn that his struggles are similar to yours. A bond forms, and you gain a certain energy knowing you are not alone in times of weakness and sin. This makes it more difficult for Satan to tempt you.

Time of Storms

Last year I found myself overwhelmed with a cloud of temptations and sinful thoughts that had to come from an all-out attack of Satan. I found myself thinking things and having wrong desires that I had assumed had been "crucified" years before. Since I firmly believe we move in the direction of our dominant thoughts, I knew it was only a matter of time before I would act out on what was going through my mind.

In desperation I called a man I had known for many years—a respected Christian leader with whom I had more or less lost touch. At the time I felt as if I had no one to turn to—itself an irrational thought since I have several close friends who are always "there for me."

Why did I not call them? Circumstances, I suppose, or the fact they knew I sometimes struggled with these temptations and I was too proud to admit the temptations continued in spite of my sincere prayers and efforts.

As I was struggling, this man's name kept coming to mind. So when business took me to his city, I called him. I was desperate enough to humble myself because I knew I needed help. I told him on the phone I was struggling, and I asked him not to let me off the hook. I wanted to meet him for dinner and talk about the struggle, and I made him pledge not to let me skate through the meal without addressing it.

He didn't let me forget what I had said on the phone, and I was open with him—not about every detail of every temptation, but enough to let him know the severity of the problem.

Instead of condemning me, he encouraged me, even giving me a small gift and writing "Philippians 1:6" on it. When I read the verse, I choked up: "And I am sure that God, who began the good work within you, will continue his work until it is finally finished on that day when Christ Jesus comes back again." In fact, he said he was glad that what I was struggling with at the time "wasn't worse." My temptation had not turned into actions, but I was afraid it would if I did not get help.

Something happened that night as we talked and as I humbled myself. Something broke that set me free. I wish I could put my finger on what it was so I could offer it as a solution to readers who may be coping with similar issues. I just know that something broke in the spiritual realm.

For several weeks after that, my friend called me to see how I was doing. I remember telling him I had not felt so free in a long time. It was wonderful. I know this man's love, understanding and prayers (and checking on me) helped make the difference.

I have been on the other side of the table countless times for other men. I mentor several men who have told me that my talking and praying with them has helped them find similar freedom. Whenever this happens I am awed by God's mercy and grace that He would use me in such a way. I am also confused because the counsel I give is pretty standard—counsel they have heard before. It is counsel I have also given to men who decided not to take it and received no help from me.

Later, it is hard for me to remember the impact they say I made in their lives. But last year when I found myself in a similar need of a friend, I had no trouble remembering it. I will be eternally grateful to my friend who was there for me when I needed him. Who knows how different the course of my life would have been had we not talked that evening for several hours.

Why do I tell you this? It is not that I am proud to admit I sometimes struggle with temptation. It is because I want you to know that I have experienced the power of being open to Christian brothers who have made a difference in my life.

Taking Off the Mask

When I spend time talking with men in a small group setting, I usually ask if the men with whom I am speaking have close accountability relationships either with peers or with older, wiser men.

Most of the time men say they do not. In fact, just mentioning topics such as "accountability" or "mentoring" will cause some men to pour out their pent-up hurts and repressed feelings. They long to talk with other men, both at a peer level and a mentoring level.

One of the greatest examples of accountability and discipleship in the Bible is that of the apostle Paul and his relationships with other men. Paul had close relationships with several men. Some of them were peers with whom he held himself accountable. Barnabas was a fellow traveler as Paul visited the Gentiles and established new churches. Silas also accompanied him on several trips and stepped into an accountability relationship with Paul about the time Paul parted from his traveling companionship with Barnabas.

There were other young men whom Paul mentored and led into spiritual maturity. John Mark accompanied Paul on a few trips. At one point, John Mark and Paul came to a parting of the ways. The Bible does not tell us clearly what happened, but perhaps John Mark was unwilling to respond as Paul expected him to respond. Or perhaps Paul had difficulties being vulnerable and patient enough with John Mark, who was not as mature spiritually as Paul.

Later Paul established a close discipleship relationship with Timothy. He looked on Timothy as a spiritual son. He taught him the disciplines of Christian living, mentored him as Timothy took his first steps into ministry and commended Timothy for his maturity. His words to Timothy illustrate the effectiveness of good discipleship—and should inspire each of us to spiritual maturity:

> And so I solemnly urge you before God and before Christ Jesus—who will someday judge the living and the dead when he appears to set up his Kingdom: Preach the word of God. Be persistent, whether the time is favorable or not. Patiently correct, rebuke, and encourage your people with good teaching. For a time is coming when people will no longer listen to right teaching. They will follow their own desires and will look for teachers who will tell them whatever they want to hear. They will reject the truth and follow strange myths. But you should keep a clear mind in every situation. Don't be afraid of suffering for the Lord. Work at bringing others to Christ. Complete the ministry God has given you.
>
> —2 Timothy 4:1–5

Perhaps the greatest evidence of Paul's example of accountability and discipleship can be found in his willingness to have others examine his life and his confidence that when they did examine it, they would find a model for how they should live their own lives. He said, "I don't mean to say that I have already achieved these things or that I have already reached perfection! But I keep working toward that day when I will finally be all that Christ Jesus saved me for and wants me to be. . . . Dear friends, pattern your lives after mine" (Phil. 3:12, 17).

Good advice for all of us!

GOLF Group

Thankfully I have men I can talk to as I navigate the tumultuous waters called midlife. I've been in a small group for the last eight years with men who offer me spiritual accountability and mutual mentoring. They confront me when I am wrong and rally around me when I am hurting. I do the same for them.

> **I wondered what a group of Christian men could do if they motivated each other not for financial success alone, but to be all they could be in Christ.**

The support the group has given me over the years has been priceless. When my dad died unexpectedly in 1997, the first two people I called were men in my small group. They were willing to talk long hours as I worked through my grief.

In fact, it was a grieving process that provided the impetus for the group.

My long-term mentor and friend Jamie Buckingham died of cancer in 1992. I had not accepted that Jamie would die until seven days beforehand, so his death hit me harder than normal. He was my closest confidant and probably the most open person I have ever known. In books such as *Risky Living*, he talked frankly about how God was removing the junk in his life and conforming him into the image of Christ.

Before I ever met Jamie, I had read several of his books and admired him from afar. (In all, he wrote forty-five books during his life.) I met him in 1978 and could barely believe I was meeting the "great Jamie Buckingham."

I did not know it, but in my mid-twenties I was desperate for a mentor. I reached out to Jamie, we hit it off and he agreed to have lunch with me once a month. I gladly drove the eighty miles from my home in Orlando to his in Melbourne on the East Coast of Florida. It began a mentoring relationship that lasted thirteen years until he died. I wonder if *Charisma* magazine would have succeeded had it not been for his help. Jamie fulfilled a "father-figure" role to me. Yet he was also a colleague and coworker. He took me on my first trip outside the United States. We climbed Mount Sinai together, and he introduced me to Christian leaders in the Spirit-led community. I saw him relate to others, handle conflicts, deal with disappointments. All the while he was my friend and confidant.

So when he died, I was at a loss. Where would I replace that special relationship?

In my grief, I turned to several friends who offered to let me talk about how I felt. I had heard that talking through your feelings helped you cope with the grief. In the process, a bond formed, and I began wondering if maybe we should start some kind of small group.

I had already been thinking about forming a group of Christian businessmen who would meet monthly, a little like a secular group of businessmen that I had been in for a couple of years. That experience motivated me as I was getting my fledgling company off the ground, but it did nothing for me spiritually. If anything, it would have pulled me down had I allowed it to.

But the concept was good, and I wondered what a group of Christian men could do if they motivated each other not for financial success alone, but to be all they could be in Christ.

I posed this question to the Christian friends who had rallied around me. I suggested we meet once a month for a year, and then decide whether or not to continue. I even organized the topics we would discuss on different months: finances, marriage, spirituality, accountability and so forth. This was in 1992—before I had ever attended a Promise Keepers event and heard anyone talk about small groups. My primary motivation was to form meaningful relationships that would keep us strong in times of trouble.

Staying on Track

But I also had another motivation. I had seen men who claimed to be Christians turn their backs on their wives, families and God. I often wondered why someone did not reach out to them and help them stay on course. Sadly this has been reinforced to me even in recent months. A Christian man I knew pretty well in the 1970s, but with whom I had lost touch, recently went back to a drinking habit and ended up taking his own life at age fifty-one.

Not long ago one of the men with whom I had attended church for several years found a new girlfriend and left his wife and family, turning his back on the Lord. This is a man with whom I went to one of the earlier Promise Keepers meetings. He, his wife, Joy and I have attended many social functions together. At one time I helped him start a small men's group, but that group never jelled. I have asked myself "what if" I had taken a more active role in discipling this man? Would the results have been different?

Staying on track has become the focus of my men's group. In fact, we joke that we have only two goals: to help each of the guys stay saved and to help each other through midlife crisis. I am happy to say that eight years later, all the men who are in the group are still serving God. (And even the ones who have moved on are still in church, although I do not know how they are doing personally.)

I want to add that our goal is much more than just staying saved. Later I discuss how we try to encourage each other to become all we can become in Christ. But we joke about "staying saved" in the same way a businessman might joke how not going bankrupt is better than going bankrupt if given the option.

To me, the relationships were the main reason I wanted to invest the time and effort in a men's group. I had grown up in a family that moved every few years. I wanted to put down some roots and form some friendships that would endure for the long haul.

Even the name we picked reflected this. It is an acronym—Group of Loyal Friends, or GOLF for short. Over the years I have found that other men are very interested in my group—partly because it has lasted so long and partly because they are envious for the type of relationships we have.

> # Being in a small group is like steering a ship with a small rudder. You make many small turns that keep the ship on course.

A Cure for Backsliding

Not long ago we held a focus group with randomly selected readers of *New Man* magazine. Of the nine people in the room, most had been in a small group at one time. Only one of the men still was. Most of the groups fizzled after about three months.

This statistic was confirmed by leaders of national men's ministries that met recently to discuss the future of men's ministry in this country. They said it was easier to get men to a large gathering of men—like a Promise Keepers' conference—than it was to get them into small groups.

I met with a businessman whose church was trying to start a men's ministry, which would add an additional service each week, just for men, following a detailed curriculum. But they couldn't get anyone to attend. (In the meantime, the leadership team that met to try to get something going formed close relationships!)

Since I travel a lot and network with Christian men of all backgrounds, I have talked about relationships and the small group dynamic several times. One such man with whom I talked was Jim Wagner from Gainesville, Florida. Jim is typical of many men I meet—a bright young businessman with a growing family.

When I met him, he had three kids and one on the way. He had been a Christian for sixteen years and had been to Promise Keepers once. I consider Jim a strong, mature Christian.

But as we talked late one evening while drinking some sodas, Jim expressed a deep need to relate to other godly Christian men. He had tried being a part of a men's ministry. But it did not meet his needs. He had trouble getting up in time to attend the 6 A.M. breakfast meetings, and while he got acquainted with a few men, none of the contacts turned into anything meaningful.

Jim was fascinated by the relationships I described that had developed out of my GOLF group. He asked so many questions that I finally heard myself asking him why he did not do what I did—just start his own men's group. I suggested he pray about inviting men he knew who also hungered for the type of relationships that this type of group allows.

Within a week I got an e-mail from Jim saying he was taking my advice. He had talked to eight men, and seven of them enthusiastically agreed to join the group. He set the first meeting for later that month. It turned out that my travel plans made it convenient for me to be in his city the same day as his meeting, so Jim invited me to attend to give a perspective of how a group can last a long time. He asked me to talk about what the group meant to me personally.

I told the men that I believe being in a small group is like steering a ship with a small rudder. You make many small turns that keep the ship on course. Each one seems so small at the time it seems inconsequential. But without each course correction, the ship would stray off course.

In my men's group, there are times we urge one of the men to take his wife away for a honeymoon weekend to help relieve some of the stress in their marriage. A small thing, to be sure. But it is these small things that keep bigger problems from developing that might lead to divorce court.

Or, the accountability might cause a man to repent of slipping into looking at pornography on the Internet, rather than allowing it to become an ingrained habit that ruins his marriage and his walk with God.

My friend Scott Nelson told our men's group that he believes any man who stays in a small group won't backslide. That is because if a man insists on backsliding, he will quit the small group to avoid the accountability. So if he just stays in the group, that means he is not in immediate danger of backsliding. Not a bad philosophy.

The men in Jim's group came from a variety of backgrounds and attended several different churches. The one thing they shared in common is they wanted to become stronger Christians. They all seemed to hunger for deeper, more meaningful relationships. The men were surprisingly candid for their first meeting.

They confessed the type of problems that confront most Christian men and asked the other men to keep them accountable. As in my men's group, we had an extended time of prayer over each man that night.

Ideas That Work

As I drove home from that meeting, it hit me that many men are like the men in Jim's group and the men in my GOLF group. They have a deep need for fellowship, relationships and mentoring that most often goes unfulfilled.

When offered the chance to be in a small men's group, they jumped at the chance.

At the same time, many of the men had tried being in small groups, but they had failed. Why had mine lasted so long? I concluded that inadvertently we had hit on some principles that work. Let us look at some of these principles.

1. Each man desired to form deeper friendships.

We had a group of men who deeply desired to form deeper friendships that would help them in their Christian walk. Because that need was fulfilled, the group has succeeded.

Sometimes I am asked how our group manages to form close relationships when we meet only once a month. I answer that by pointing out that close relationships often exist when you see a person infrequently.

I have a number of really meaningful relationships with men such as Edwin Louis Cole or Jack Hayford with whom I spend time only a few times a year. I have relatives whom I love dearly, including my brother, Paul Strang from Kentucky, and sister, Karen Whittington from California. I see them less frequently since we live so many miles apart.

> # Being a man of God is a team sport. Men need more than just a casual buddy or a golfing partner.

2. We kept everything very simple.

On a practical level, my men's group worked because we kept everything very simple. We met only once a month instead of every week. But we blocked off the evening when we met—from 6 P.M. to 9 P.M.—which is long enough to really get a "group dynamic" going. The meeting often continues for another hour or so as we stand around our cars before we drive home. So we spend some quality time together.

Sometimes I am asked why we meet monthly instead of weekly. The reason is that our schedules are such that meeting weekly for breakfast isn't feasible. We have actually had some morning meetings, and we spent much of our time just ordering and eating breakfast before it was time to rush off to work. And it is difficult to pray together in a public setting, which we do when we meet in a more private setting.

The group means enough to us that the men attend most meetings. I have only missed two meetings in eight years. I mark off the third Sunday night of each month and schedule my extensive travel around it.

For us the goal of the group is not so much close relationships (although that is a wonderful by-product). The main benefits are the accountability that the group gives and the consistency of meeting month after month. We meet often enough that we really enjoy each other's company. But it is infrequent enough that we do not get on each other's nerves.

Two of us work together—Bob Minotti and I. (Bob is vice president of advertising and has worked with me since 1988). Scott Nelson, who is a CPA, now works with Brian Walsh, a successful builder who has been my friend for more than fifteen years. Scott Plakon, who is president of a publishing company, and Gene Koziara, a medical doctor, were good friends before the group began. We also get together outside the group setting. And at least once a year we do something special with all of our wives as a group.

We do not have a perfect formula for a successful men's group. But since 1992 it has "worked." There has been relatively little turnover in the group, and each of us is a much stronger Christian as a result of the group. It is also good to have some guys I can depend on no matter what.

To keep things simple, we have focused on relationships, rather than on a certain curriculum or some fancy program. Another thing that is important to any group is to have at least one person who is the glue that makes the group stick together. In my group I am the one. I provide the meeting place and call the meetings.

3. We learned to multiply ourselves.

About two years ago, I was aware that there were men locally who wanted to join our group. But knowing that a group of more than about seven or eight was too big (and aware that it's hard to form meaningful relationships if there are always strangers joining the group), I suggested the men in my GOLF group start several other groups.

I told the men we needed to give as well as to receive in a small group setting. I also told them it is important to develop their leading and mentoring skills. So we paired up and started three other groups. One has since fizzled. The other two have continued for the same reason my group succeeded—the men in the group get something out of it.

Gary Rosberg, an author and counselor, says that being a man of God is a team sport. He believes that men need more than just a casual buddy or a golfing partner.  They need men who will "go to war" with them.

"If you wish to shield yourself from Satan's poison-tipped arrows," he writes, "you should cling to the truths of God's Word—and link up with other men of God."[5]

I believe there are thousands of Christian men who want to be more like Jesus, but they have no one to guide them or feel no one cares if they succeed or fail. I wonder if there aren't men out there like Jim Wagner whose own desire for this type of relationship would prompt them to do what Jim and I did—start our own groups.

A Strategy

There are a few more basic ideas that I have found helpful in bringing longevity and authenticity to small groups. Rosberg has outlined these principles in his article:

Acceptance
This should be the atmosphere of any men's group. Without this, the whole thing is just a religious exercise.

Authenticity
Without this, a group will evaporate as one man after another leaves to find real relationships. Rosberg tells how he initially feared that too much honesty would cause  the other men to reject him. In one of his previous groups, he had skated through without opening up.

He says the men in the group had met for Bible study and fellowship for years, but they rarely got to the heart of how they really lived life. He was not totally honest with the three men in the group. When they would ask how he was doing, he would say, "Things are a little rugged, but we are OK." But his answer was wrong!

"It wasn't so much that I was intending to lie," he says. "I was just pulling them into my own rationalization and self-deception. Deep down I knew I wasn't leading my family well. I was just too scared to admit it."[6]

Like Rosberg, anyone who tries to mask their way through a men's group will only frustrate themselves and waste time.

Confidentiality

Men fear exposure that would lead to ridicule or cause other people to respect them less. There must be high walls of safety built before a man will bare his soul.

> **We are better men because we are secure in Christ and secure with each other— and our wives are the beneficiaries of this masculine security.**

Encouragement

Perhaps the worst thing that can happen is when a man shares a deeply felt struggle or sin, and other men pounce on him, quoting Scripture and berating him for not being "stronger in the Lord." The need for acceptance is far greater than the need for another sermon, especially from someone who is a peer. Instead of always giving advice, add a good dose of encouragement.

Accountability

Don't let your group become a meeting of yes-men. God has not called us to passively watch other men sink into sin.

Encouragement and accountability should be two edges of the same sword, and that sword should be wielded in an environment of trust and confidentiality. Holding other men accountable means asking hard questions, pointing out blind spots and not pulling punches when you sense they are ready to hear the truth.[7]

Expectation

Plan realistic expectations for each member of the group. People respond to the level of expectation. If you challenge men at a low level, that is how they will respond. So set high requirements right up front: attendance (the  meeting is your top priority in that time slot—you schedule everything else around it, not vice versa), accountability, confidentiality and others. Do not beg men to come in. Say things like, "This group isn't for everybody."

Some general principles apply to the format of a small group:

- Men must be personally invited.

- The group should have shared leadership.

- The group needs an outreach mind-set.

- The group should meet for a specific period of time in a comfortable place.

- Homework should not be assigned. (However, the men may decide from time to time to study a book together such as this book. Obviously everyone must read the book to discuss it. But that is different from assigned homework.)

- The men should be allowed to discover Bible truths for themselves.

- Men should not be asked to do or share something for which they are unprepared.[8]

Rosberg affirms that you will notice the benefits of a men's group as soon as you start one, but the greater benefits come over the months and years as the trust level grows. Other areas of your life will begin to reflect the richness and stability that come from meaningful male relationships.

Preston Gillham adds this humorous anecdote in his book: "How vividly I remember the Wednesday morning one of my SWAT team buddies came into the kitchen of the sixth-floor office where we meet with a message to deliver. As he kissed his wife good-bye and headed for the garage, she said, 'Tell all the guys I love them.' Of course, we laughed and carried on, but each of us knew what she meant, and we knew each of our wives would say exactly the same thing. We are better men because we are secure in Christ and secure with each other. And it has not escaped the notice of our wives that they are the beneficiaries of this masculine security."[9]

I think you will find—as I have—that once you make the effort to break the ice, you will see other men long for close relationships so they can share openly about their concerns. You will find out other people's problems are often worse than your own, which makes you realize your problems are not so bad. And as you "sow" seeds of friendship, you will reap a "harvest" of meaningful relationships.

Having looked at some of the areas that will help us become new men in Christ, we now turn to the final step—putting these into practice. This final section is crucial if we are to move forward and make lasting changes.

Talk about it Think about it

Accountability: Keeps You in Touch

Author's note: It is good to think about these issues, but even better to discuss them, since in doing so you are beginning the process of accountability.

For more information on this topic (which we will add to as time passes) check out our www.oldmannewman.com website. Use the user id: **oldman** and the password **newman**. These are **case sensitive,** so use all lowercase letters and leave no spaces.

1. Page 126 contains this powerful principle: "Relationships are built through vulnerability. When that vulnerability is held in confidence, intimacy builds. And over time, when intimacy develops into trust." Talk about a time when you built a relationship following these principles. Talk about a time when a relationship was stressed—or even destroyed—because these principles were violated.

   Share why you agree or disagree with this statement.

2. On pages 141–143, Gary Rosberg identifies these ingredients for a successful men's group: acceptance, authenticity, confidentiality, encouragement, accountability and expectation. What is the one area which you think the group is doing the best at? If you could improve one thing about the group, what would it be?

Section III

Getting Your Act Together

A clip from

New Man   January/February 2000

The Making of a GREAT MAN

What makes a man great? Above all else, great men are visionaries. What makes these men tick?

1. Vision More than anything else, great men are propelled by great dreams.

2. Innovation Great men give the world "ideas" that change the existing order.

3. Sacrifice Great men deny themselves for a greater good.

4. Integrity At their core, great men have unwavering character.

5. Optimism Great men possess a passion that touches that noble impulse in each of us.

6. Never Give Up Great men display unwavering belief in their mission.

7. Ability Great men possess special abilities.

8. Relate to Others Great men have empathy and love for people.

9. Yahweh Great men are first godly men. Great men do what they do to bring glory to God.[1]

Making a great man
oldmannewman.com

Chapter 9

Getting a Life Vision:
Finding Your Purpose

OLD MAN **Lacks vision and a life purpose for becoming a man of God.**

NEW MAN **Has a God-birthed vision and goals for reaching his destiny.**

This is it—the moment we turn "new man" ideas into action. From here on we need not just to read, but to do. The value of this book to you will be determined by how you respond to the next few chapters. I am confident that having come this far you are ready for the life changes we have talked about, and in this final section we will look at the practical things we can do to get on track and stay there.

The first question is basic: What is your life purpose?

Why were you created?

What is your task on this planet? Is it large or small? Risky? Safe?

My mentor, Jamie Buckingham, had a printed sign in a large frame that hung above his desk. It read: "Attempt something so big that unless God intervenes it is bound to fail."

Jamie lived that kind of life. After two devastating moral failures that would have ruined most ministers, the experience instead left Jamie empty and open to the infilling of the Holy Spirit and a new life of what he called "Risky Living."

He did not begin writing books until he was thirty-five years old—

a time in life many men are giving up on their dreams. Yet he wrote or co-wrote forty-five books before his untimely death in 1997.

In the late 1970s, Jamie asked me a question that was pivotal in my life:

"What would you attempt for God if you knew you could not fail?"

Jamie was the most open person I knew. He lived a life that vulnerable and transparent. He was a great man in my eyes, even though I saw his weaknesses as well as his strengths.

> ## Jamie asked me a question that was pivotal in my life: What would you attempt for God if you knew you could not fail?

Vine Books has recently published a wonderful devotional called *The Promise of Power* in their Life Messages of Great Christians series. Jamie Buckingham is in the series with other greats such as Dwight L. Moody, Andrew Murray, Oswald Chambers, Charles Spurgeon, Smith Wigglesworth and Corrie ten Boom, with whom he wrote *Tramp for the Lord.* The devotional tells us that there is a place in the Christian community for the dreamers. The book quotes Jamie from his book *Where Eagles Soar.*

> **Most of us dream dreams, however, then put them aside as impossible. Yet God never puts a desire in our heart, or beckons us to walk on water, unless He intends for us to step out on faith and at least make the attempt. Whether we achieve or not is almost immaterial; the passing of the test lies in whether we try, in whether we're willing to be obedient to the inner call to greatness—the onward call to spiritual adventure.[2]**

Unfortunately, most Christians never learn this. Or, after one attempt, they give up. They never learn that there is a price to be paid.

Having a vision is a crucial beginning to becoming the men of God that we should be. We should all pray for God to give us a vision that will transform our lives and motivate us to move forward toward out destinies.

Rick Godwin is a man much like Jamie. A former Baptist who experienced the baptism in the Holy Spirit, he pastors Eagles Nest Christian Fellowship in San Antonio, Texas. He is also in great demand as a speaker. He talks straight, and no one knows what he'll say next. My pastor, Sam Hinn, says that Godwin comforts the afflicted and afflicts the comfortable.

Godwin says the reason most Christians quit growing and most churches plateau is that people are not willing to pay the price.

"God gives you a vision," Godwin said when we spoke at my church not long ago. "But what is that vision worth? Is it worth the pain and frustration? Is it worth the risk? Or is it easier to stay in the comfort zone—that boring place of mediocrity where most Christians live."

This is such an important point. We do not imagine up a vision of what we should be doing. We do not read a book titled *101 Visions to Choose From,* and then close our eyes, hold up our finger and slowly place our finger on a page in the book hoping that will be just the right vision for us. We let God birth the vision in our spirits. You must know, beyond the shadow of a doubt, that the vision you have bought into for your life is the unique, divinely ordained vision God gave you.

Then we must get ready to act upon the vision.

Jerry Horner writes that people "generally fall into one of three groups:

1. The few who make things happen,

2. The many who watch things happen, and

3. The overwhelming majority who have no notion of what happens.[3]

Know what the vision is that God has given to you, and then know how to implement it in your life. Author Myles Munroe says that the wealthiest spot on this planet is in your local cemetery or graveyard where "buried beneath the soil are dreams that never came to pass, songs that were never sung, books that were never written, paintings that never filled a canvas, ideas that were never shared, visions that never became reality, inventions that were never designed, plans that never went beyond the drawing board of the mind and purposes that were never fulfilled." He asserts, "Our graveyards are filled with potential that remained potential."[4]

So what is the answer? People aren't willing to pay the price for a vision to be accomplished. Too many are comfortable, wanting to avoid pain that comes with risk. The irony is they can't avoid pain.

"Every person will experience pain," Godwin says.

"Either it's the pain of discipline, which weighs only a few ounces, or the pain of regret, which weighs a ton."

Godwin also teaches that:

- Every level of growth requires a new level of sacrifice. When you quit sacrificing, you quit growing.

- When you're wrestling with compulsive addictions, you have a lack of vision. Because you do not have the *big picture* vision, you will also lack the *little picture* visions—who you are and what God wants you to do.

Whether it's because they struggle with compulsive addictions or because they are merely complacent, the idea of sacrificing for a life purpose is not easy for most Christians to hear. They'd rather focus on the blessing of serving the Lord or of being in a good church service than to admit they are stuck in comfort zones, impacting nothing.

Far too many Christians think they are having an impact when really, they are wasting potential. Some think they are spiritual superheroes just because they have begun some program or taught a class at church, when in fact, God has given them much greater gifts for much greater tasks that, unfortunately, go undone.

Don't allow yourself to become comfortable with small programs, ideas and goals. Reach out for the "brass ring" or vision. Like the weightlifter who pushes up those heavy weights day after day even though every muscle in his body is crying out in protest, push past the protesting pain of complacency and comfort to move up to the next level spiritually in your life. Be willing to take a risk for God.

> ## Far too many Christians think they are having an impact when really, they are wasting potential.

Often the most successful and fulfilled men are those who are not afraid to put everything on the line. Is God calling you to a great, but *risky* adventure? *New Man* magazine interviewed some "divine daredevils" to see what drives the heart of a risk taker. Let's take a look at some of their answers:

> Everybody, all my friends that snowboard who aren't Christians, know that I am a Christian. A lot of times, they won't do something when I'm there. I think my example shows them that "I can do all things through Christ who strengthens me."
>
> —JEREMY BAYE, X-TREME ATHLETE

> I am consistently good at failure, but the key for me is to succeed to a greater degree than I fail. If I climb a mountain twenty feet tall and slip ten feet, but then climb another twenty, I consider that a success.
>
> —TRENT GAITES, RISKY BUSINESSMAN

> I'm thankful every day for the opportunity I have to help

people who are not able to help themselves. I realize that my job is a high calling, a part of a greater plan to serve others.

—CHARLES MOOSE, LAWMAN

We must ask ourselves, What pleases God? It all depends on the motive. Why did I do that? To impress people? As an act of penance? Or to honor God and advance His kingdom?

—STEVE MURRELL, MANILA MISSIONARY

Risk is a primary component of faith, and the Bible teaches that without faith it is impossible to please God. In Matthew 25:14–30, Jesus condemned the unfaithful servant who wouldn't risk his talent, but hid it to be safe. Jesus called him "wicked and lazy" and took the talent he had and gave it to the one who had invested his five talents and doubled them.

No matter what level each of us is at—whether a young person full of the excitement of just following Christ, or one who has enjoyed a measure of success in following your dreams, or one who has followed God for many years and is tempted to coast— God wants us to move into risky living: *faith living.*

 But goals are so much more than making a lot of New Year resolutions. They are dreams—*with a deadline.*

We should believe Him for new mountains to climb, new visions to pursue. That is how we grow and develop our faith and move from "glory to glory." As Jamie Buckingham put it so well, each of us should "attempt something so big that without God it's bound to fail."

Many times Jamie and I sat over lunch, and he spoke directly into my life. Here are the kinds of things he told me:

- When you have a clear vision, you can risk your own life.

- What is your vision worth?

- Great athletes train hard for a gold medal. People who run to win are willing to pay the price.

- The reason most people quit growing is that they are not willing to pay the price.

- Faith equals risk. Without faith (not without spirituality or without Scripture memorization) it's impossible to please God.

- God has big plans for you. Don't take what God meant for you and ruin it with mediocre living.

- What are you willing to give up to get what you want?

Goal-Setting

Once we have had God birth the vision into our spirits and have determined that, at all cost, we will implement His vision in our lives, then we must decide how we are going to do that. Over the years I have learned what it is to see God's plan and purpose unfold in my life. Much of it, for me, was learning to set goals.

The closest most people get to goal-setting is making a list of New Year's resolutions, which last only a short time. But goals are so much more. They are dreams—*with a deadline.*

In all honesty, I was not raised to be a goal setter. I grew up in a Pentecostal environment where spirituality was measured by a sincere desire to remain in God's will, resulting in what I see in my mind's eye as a group of people in suspended animation. In an attempt to stay in the bull's-eye of God's will, they remained in neutral. If you had any ambitious goals, they were thought to be your own desires, not God's.

Those folks never accomplished a lot, but they were certain they were in God's will. Perhaps they were. I don't want to judge them. But my mind always ached for big things, big challenges and partnering with God for great things. And I do believe that many Pentecostals are frozen by fear of leaving God's will, much like the man who was afraid of his master and buried his talent.

It wasn't until the 1970s that I even discovered books that taught about the necessity of setting goals to accomplish anything meaningful. It was just what I needed as I was starting a small church magazine called *Charisma*. I set a goal for it to be a national publication with 100,000 circulation—a seemingly impossible goal. But with God's grace it became a reality within five years, and it set me on a life-long course of goal-setting and achieving.

For those who know me well, such as the men in my men's group or those who work with me at Strang Communications, it has become something of a joke because I am so predictable about talking about goals. People know I'll work something about goal-setting (when appropriate) into the conversation.

If asked to speak extemporaneously, I'll talk about setting and meeting goals. I do that because it's something I know well, and I have found most people—men especially—know little about it. They drift through life because no one has shown them how to move ahead.

Setting a goal is like focusing sunlight with a magnifying glass. When your life energy is shining on a pinpoint, you can start a fire. A goal poorly set is better than no goal. In a simplistic way, going somewhere is better than going nowhere. Writing down spiritual, family, professional, self-improvement or fitness goals often will set in motion the habits necessary to achieve them. The mind moves in the direction of its dominant thoughts, and what you measure and monitor improves.

Our goals should not be self-focused or small. Setting a goal to spend time with your children every day or buy a bigger home for your growing family is worthwhile, but those still are not life goals and not worthy of people who profess to be led by the Spirit of God. I learned that from Jamie Buckingham. Jamie challenged me to do what I would do if I knew I could not fail.

That challenge became a defining principle in my life. I realized how small my dreams had been and how much I was limiting

God. I made a decision to change. Now I consciously try not to limit God, even though I am sure His plan for my life goes further than I imagine.

A few years ago I read a book by James Collins and Jerry Porras called *Built to Last,* in which they document how great companies have unattainable goals that propel their organizations to greatness even after the founders die.

For example, not long after World War II, a small Japanese company set a goal of making the phrase "Made in Japan" synonymous with *quality.* At that time, "Made in Japan" meant only one thing: cheap. The name of that small company: Sony.

Another small company set this goal in the late 1970s: "A computer on every desk; a computer in every home." That company: Microsoft.

Or consider Oral Roberts' goal of combining the healing power of God and medicine. It was radical when first set; today many are working on it, and prayer for healing is commonly accepted in churches around the world.

Or David Yonggi Cho's goal of one million church members in Seoul, Korea. Impossible? Visit his Yoido Full Gospel Church with nearly 800,000 members to see it coming to pass.

Or the late Dr. Lester Sumrall's goal of reaching one million souls with the gospel by the end of his lifetime. Impossible? Seemingly. But it propelled him to get onto Christian television and to work at a pace that would have tired ten average men. I believe more than a million people will be in heaven because of his goal.

How to Set Goals

Myles Munroe believes that God wants us to become people who have plans. He believes that plans are documented imaginations. If we can document an imagination, we've developed a plan for action.

"If you are having real problems in your life, you probably don't have a piece of paper on which you have documented your plans for the next five years," he says. "You're just living from day to day in the absence of a concrete, documented plan. You've been dealing with the same issues and habits and struggles for years. You slide forward a little only to slide backward again. Whenever things get hard, you start reminiscing about 'the good old days' and fall back into habits you had conquered. Progress requires a plan of action. Ideas must be put down if they are to influence the way you live."[5]

It's important to know how to set goals.

Are your goals written down? Do other people know about them? Does your wife? Do your friends?

Begin with general goals.

I set written goals every day. In my day-planner I have goals for the year: spiritual, family, physical, professional. For example, as I thumb through this recent month I see these long-term goals:

- Spend an hour with God every day.
- Read through the Bible.
- Live a holy life.
- Be a righteous leader in the body of Christ through publications.
- Help the poor in a nearby city.
- Take care of my [widowed] mother.
- Help Chandler to learn to enjoy schoolwork.
- Spend time communicating with Joy, being sure our priorities are in sync.
- Go on a family vacation to England.
- Improve my racquetball and golf games in measurable ways.

Break your general goals down into specific daily tasks.

These are typewritten and in my day-planner so that I have them with me wherever I go. Each month I make the general goals specific and break them down to daily tasks:

- Finalize dates for men's conference.

- Finish *Old Man New Man* manuscript.

- Set strategies for next year for sales and marketing.

- Fund-raise for homeless mission.

- Personal: Set golf game with Bob by month's end.

> # The times I get away from fulfilling my goals are the times when I drift. Goals give me a sense of direction, boundaries, priorities.

I cross them off once they are accomplished. I probably only finish 80 percent of them, because as I complete them, I set more.

The times I get away from fulfilling my goals are the times when I drift. Goals give me a sense of direction, boundaries, priorities.

Set some life goals.

I like to talk with people about their life goals. One of my favorite ways to relax is to play a hard game of racquetball with one of my staff or with a new friend, then get a bite to eat after cleaning up. Sometimes I'll get the conversation going by asking them what their goals are. I might ask how much money they want to make in five years, or what career path they want to be on. I'll ask what they want people to say in their obituary.

Most people have an opinion about these things, but few actually have a plan.

Establish a personal mission statement.

Many men go through a difficult midlife period, which may rob them of goals, or make them feel as if what they have achieved is ephemeral. Patrick Morley, author of *The Man in the Mirror*, says that midlife is like a lake.

"Early in our lives we run swift like a river, but shallow. As we put years behind us, though, we deepen. Then one day, we enter the opened jaws of midlife," Morley says. "Where once we felt direction and velocity, suddenly we find ourselves swirling about, sometimes aimlessly, or so it seems. Each of us, like individual droplets of water, will take a different path through this part of the journey. For some of us it will only be a slowdown. Others will feel forgotten and abandoned by the father of the river. Some, unable to see where the waters converge and on again grow strong, will despair."

Morley's crisis started at age thirty-six. He says that it can occur well into your mid-fifties. (Remember, in our diverse culture there is no singular midlife experience anymore). "You come to a point that you feel somehow imbalanced—like something is missing," he says, "like it's not enough. All the years of pressure deadlines have taken a toll. You have discovered a vacuum in your soul for meaning, beauty, and quiet."[6]

He recommends writing a life mission statement that includes four elements:

1. A life purpose: why you exist

2. A calling: what you do

3. A vision or mental picture of what you want to happen

4. A mission: how you will go about it

Morley takes us full cycle through the birth of one vision, the implementing of that vision, the setting of goals to attain it, the commitment to a personal mission statement *and on to the birth of a new vision—greater than the first.*

"A new vision must spring up from a foundation of gratitude for what God has already done to use us and make us useful. The motivation cannot merely be wanderlust; not more for the sake of more. Rather, one chapter has closed and another beckons to be opened. A vision is a goal—a big one. Visions are not the work of today or tomorrow or even next month," Morley says. "Rather, a vision has a longer term."

He reminds us that visions rarely turn out exactly as planned. The apostle Paul had the vision of going to Jerusalem and then on to Rome. He didn't consider that he would make those visits as a prisoner, but that's how it came about. Often, God must delay the fulfilling of a vision or desire until He has prepared us to be people who can handle it with grace and humility. It is not God's nature to give us greater visions and accomplishments if they will work to our destruction. Instead, God allows us to be hammered into the shape of a vessel that can gracefully contain the vision.[7]

> # When we stand before the Lord He will hold us accountable for the talents, resources and dreams He bestowed upon us.

What God-inspired goals do you have for your life? Are you a scientist or doctor who can set a goal of finding a cure for a disease? Are you an entrepreneur who can pledge to give several million dollars to a credible missions organization? Are you a board member or pastor who can start a program for the poor in your city, or network churches to meet the need?

What is it you would do if there were no boundaries on your imagination or budget?

If you haven't had big goals and dreams before now, I pray you will learn to set goals and give them deadlines. Keep in mind that when you stand before the Lord He will hold you accountable for the talents, resources and dreams He bestowed upon you. You stand to lose nothing by going for God's highest plan for you, and on that day when He says to you, "Well done, you good and faithful servant," you will know that you attempted and accomplished much for your Savior.

Is determing God's vision difficult for you? Maybe you need to renew your mind first. Read on.

Talk about it   Think about it

Getting a Life Vision: Finding Your Purpose

Author's note: Not everyone in the group may have a clearly formulated life vision yet—in fact most will not. The important thing is that the men in the group help each other discern their unique vision and then encourage each other in the realization of this vision.

For more information on this topic (which we will add to as time passes) check out our www.oldmannewman.com website. Use the user id: **oldman** and the password **newman**. These are **case sensitive,** so use all lowercase letters and leave no spaces.

1. Page 151 contains this powerful statement: "We do not imagine a vision of what we should be doing. . . . We let God birth the vision in our spirits." Talk about a time when God birthed a vision in your spirit.

2. What would you attempt for God if you knew you could not fail?

3. Pages 157–160 describe the process of setting goals: begin with general goals, break your general goals into specific daily tasks, set some life goals and establish a personal mission statement. Share with the group your experience with doing this. Then, decide as a group how you can go through this process together, first by establishing general goals and then sharing them with the group, next by breaking those goals into specific daily tasks and so on.

A clip from

New Man   January/February 1999

Hollywood, Hip-Hop and Heaven

Deezer D. isn't a nurse, but he plays one on TV. In fact, he plays nurse Malik McGrath on *ER*, NBC's hit drama series. Deezer gave us the lowdown on his faith and career.

On his early years: "I grew up in South Central L.A. Most of my relatives were drinkers. It was dysfunctional. [So] when I started doing it, it wasn't really a big deal. Everything was acceptable. After I moved out, I looked back on it and said, 'My house was like *The Jerry Springer Show.*'"

On becoming a Christian: "When I first started going to church, I thought, 'This is boring. This is weak.' I never looked for the positive. But then I started hooking up with some guys who were fun and crazy like me—but they loved the Lord. Now, I do everything that I used to do. Except I'm not out there chasing the females. I'm not out there drinking. I'm not looking to fill the void like I used to. I have a personal relationship with Jesus."[1]

The void is filled

oldmannewman.com

Chapter 10

Renewing Your Mind: Changing the Way You Think

OLD MAN Finds his mind invaded continually by impure thoughts.

NEW MAN Discovers God's thoughts flowing into his mind to stop impure thoughts.

The New Testament is a book about fresh starts. I think of the words of Jesus on so many occasions: "Neither do I condemn you . . . Go now and leave your life of sin" (John 8:11, NIV). In Luke 17:19, He says, "Go. Your faith has made you well."

With these commands, and many others, Jesus set free those who came to Him in faith. A major part of His work on earth was teaching people to renew their minds. What does this mean? *Renewing your mind* means replacing old, dysfunctional ideas with life-giving ideas from God.

Why, for example, did Jesus spend three years with the disciples rather than simply pray for them one time and send them out? It's because God has given us minds that, for the most part, cannot be instantly, totally reprogrammed to accept everything He has said.

Think of how many times Jesus said to His disciples, "Are you still so dull?" or "Do you still not understand?" or "You of little faith!" Life is about walking with Jesus and letting Him renew our minds bit by bit. Like it or not, that is how our human minds work. Jesus said the Kingdom is like a little bit of yeast that is kneaded into a large batch of dough (Matt. 13:33). The yeast will have great effect, but only after it has been laboriously worked into the dough.

God wants Christian men to be consistent in their walk. He isn't looking for superstars, necessarily, but for people who will go the distance with integrity and finish strong. Renewing the mind—or learning to think differently—is the only way to produce consistency in our lives.

Henry Cisneros, mayor of San Antonio from 1981 to 1989 and Secretary of Housing and Urban Development, said this recently to a graduating college class:

> Over the years I have learned that the people who are the most successful, the people I have admired the most, are not necessarily those who are the most brilliant, or witty, or have mastered a particular discipline, but those who had the stamina to stay the course over a long period of time. . . . It's like the difference between the shooting star that flashes across the sky and is gone—you're not even sure it was there—and the North Star that is there every night, night after night.[2]

Even unbelievers have noticed that the mind can be an organ of change if fed the right information. There is a lot of secular material—some of it good, some of it rather New Age—which talks about changing your thoughts. How much more should we who are followers of Jesus believe this! We have the promises of God, many of which pertain to renewing the mind.

One of the best-known scriptures in Romans says: "Don't copy the behavior and customs of this world, but let God transform you into a new person by changing the way you think" (Rom. 12:2).

I learned this technique in my late twenties—a particularly stressful time as I tried to get *Charisma* magazine off the ground and felt overwhelmed by problems I didn't know how to solve.

Someone gave me some "faith confessions" by Don Gossett that I repeated so often I memorized them and still repeat when I want to keep my mind on the Lord. The Word of God is true, and how better can we get those concepts in our heart than to memorize God's Word and then repeat it? I pasted these "confessions" on my mirror so I saw them every morning, and I wrote them on index cards so I could carry them in my pocket and read them at traffic lights.

God's Word is a powerful tool for renewing your mind. Let me share these verses with you so that you can have them ready to help you in moments of temptation:

- "Run away from sexual sin!"–1 Corinthians 6:18

- "Run from anything that stimulates youthful lust. Follow anything that makes you want to do right. Pursue faith and love and peace, and enjoy the companionship of those who call on the Lord with pure hearts."–2 Timothy 2:22

- "Humble yourselves before God. Resist the Devil, and he will flee from you."–James 4:7

- "Our bodies were not made for sexual immorality. They were made for the Lord, and the Lord cares about our bodies."–1 Corinthians 6:13

- "Get rid of your evil deeds. Shed them like dirty clothes. Clothe yourselves with the armor of right living, as those who live in the light."–Romans 13:12

- "If your sinful nature controls your mind, there is death. But if the Holy Spirit controls your mind, there is life and peace."–Romans 8:6

- "Jesus replied, 'I assure you that everyone who sins is a slave of sin. . . . So if the Son sets you free, you will indeed be free.'"–John 8:34, 36

- "Try to find out what is pleasing to the Lord. Take no part in the worthless deeds of evil and darkness; instead, rebuke and expose them."–Ephesians 5:10–11

■ "So I run straight to the goal with purpose in every step. I am not like a boxer who misses his punches. I discipline my body like an athlete, training it to do what it should. Otherwise, I fear that after preaching to others I myself might be disqualified."—1 Corinthians 9:26–27

This became one way I renewed my mind. Though it may seem high schoolish to write reminders on index cards, sometimes that's what it takes! Victory is rarely won in moments of great circumstance; rather, victory is won by thousands of small steps taken in the right direction. And if using index cards to get your mind on the Word of God helps direct your steps, I suggest you get past your pride and do it.

> ## Victory is rarely won in moments of great circumstance; rather, victory is won **by thousands of small steps taken in the right direction.**

The Key to Change

Renewing the mind is so important that I believe it is the difference between Christian men living in the past, with chains around their minds, and being free.

John Paulk, a former homosexual who gained national attention after his autobiography was published, says that his freedom

No magic formula
oldmannewman.com

from the old lifestyle has been real, but incremental. Read what he told *New Man*: "The so-called 'instant deliverance' stories do happen, but they are few and far between. God is into the developmental process. He works through our experiences. There is no magic formula. It is knowing Christ and the fellowship of His sufferings."[3]

We must reprogram ourselves to know what is wrong, and then develop a taste for what is right. This is never easy, because change is inherently uncomfortable, but it is absolutely necessary if we are to be new men in Christ. We must want it with a burning desire and be willing to pay the price to get it.

Almost every single thing we do in life, consciously or subconsiously, is a habit we have learned—walking, feeding ourselves, waking up, speaking in a certain manner and so on. Our lives are made up of thousands of learned behaviors, which we call habits. Even our personalities are essentially large buildings made up of many bricks or habits.

Some habits are not good for us. During college I developed a smoking habit that lasted several years. The smoking was both a habit and addiction. Jesus broke the addiction. I had to break the habit.

We must reprogram ourselves to know what is wrong, **and then develop a taste for what is right.**

I quit cold turkey, but I also backslid a time or two or three, and actually didn't have the last cigarette until seven years later. Now I don't smoke at all, and have no desire even to smell cigarette smoke. That brick was removed from my building and replaced with something better—a workout routine that keeps me in shape.

Getting up early to exercise or meditate on the Word of God is a habit. Habits only become habits by practice. Think of habits you have had. Perhaps in college you formed a habit of staying up late and sleeping in. You had to stay up late and sleep in several times by choice before it became a habit by instinct. We have all heard the concept that you must do something for three weeks for it to become a habit.

I'm sure the number of weeks or days varies with the person and the habit in question, but the core idea is correct: Life changes occur when a determined person says day after day, "I will do this differently." There is no other way.

Renewing the Mind and Sex

A lot of men have habits of lovemaking that are counter-productive. It is too easy to think of our own sexual fulfillment first, leaving our wives frustrated. Perhaps during sex we visualize other women or certain sex acts we have seen portrayed in pornographic literature or movies.

This kind of admission doesn't shock God. He addressed it many times in the Old and New Testaments, including in the Ten Commandments and the Sermon on the Mount.

> **I learned to take captive my impure thoughts and to think the thoughts God would be pleased with. I thought about God's love for me and His idea of what a man was.**

I know that many men, like me, also desire purity and freedom from lust. We respond to teaching that helps us overcome sexual sin or selfish behavior. Our minds are incredible. We can think about God one second and hell the next—without batting an eye. Real maturity comes when we begin to take those transient thoughts captive rather than letting them flit through our minds. Someone once said we can't keep the birds from landing on our heads, but we can keep them from building a nest in our hair!

Charlie, an acquaintance of mine, told me of the horrible struggles he had been having to keep impure thoughts from flooding into his mind. Although he had taken many steps to eliminate temptations, it seemed as though just one quick glance at a good-looking woman could open the floodgates to impure thoughts and sexual fantasies.

Charlie had been a Christian for many years. He found great support in his local church, and had been able to find mentors, men who made him feel safe and with whom he could share his struggles.

What really helped Charlie was what we have been discussing in this chapter. He told me that what set him free was the process of renewing his mind.

"It wasn't easy," he says. "But I learned to take captive my impure thoughts when they first began to come into my mind, and to think instead the thoughts I knew God would be pleased with. I thought about God's love for me and His idea of what a man was."

It took Charlie a long time—a very long time—before the impure thoughts no longer came in like a flood, but it did happen.

"I do occasionally have a bout of momentary fear when an impure thought knocks on the door of my mind, but I refuse to let it stop me from being what God has made me to be. Once we get started, the fear dissipates. My wife is aware of my past struggles and my desire to have a renewed mind and is always patient and supportive."

Dan Kays, who in an earlier chapter told his experience of transforming salvation, also had to go through the process of renewing his mind. He recognized that salvation was just the first step—a very important and very necessary first step, but a first step nonetheless. When Dan realized that God loved him so much that He would deliver him from drugs, it made Dan excited to learn more about Him. So he began to study God's Word.

"This is so important," Dan says. "As you begin to read and study God's Word, His thoughts begin to flow through you. You can't have God's thoughts flowing through you without causing change. I found myself spontaneously praising and worshiping Him as He began to reveal His nature to me through His Word. One by one things started coming off of me. First the foul language, then anger and rage."

We can't defeat the dragon alone, and we can't defeat him simply by trying harder intellectually. It is, in the final analysis, a spiritual battle.

God has promised us that the task of renewing our mind is one at which we can be successful. He gives us clear direction on how to stop an impure thought as soon as it appears and to keep from yielding to the temptation to sin.

In 1 Corinthians 10:13 we read, "But remember that the temptations that come into your life are no different from what others experience. And God is faithful. He will keep the temptation from becoming so strong that you can't stand up against it. When you are tempted, he will show you a way out so that you will not give in to it."

Second Corinthians 10:5 instructs us, "Casting down imaginations, and every high thing that exalteth itself against the knowledge of God, and bringing into captivity every thought to the obedience of Christ" (KJV).

How do we do that? We do it by reading the Word every day, for it is filled with God's thoughts—thoughts that flow through my mind and push those lustful thoughts out of the way. Read the Word, and His thoughts will become your thoughts, and when the attack of the enemy comes against your mind, God will provide that way of escape.

Sound too simple? So was salvation—too simple to believe.

But you believed, and He saved you. What have you got to lose now?

Ted Roberts shares his insights on renewing the mind specifically in the area of sexuality, but his advice can go a lot further than that. Ted believes that sexual addiction is both demonically energized and a learned behavior that needs to be unlearned.

"For some reason," he writes, "when it comes to sexual addiction issues, we seem to completely forget that Scripture admonishes us to renew our minds."

When Ted explains to the men he counsels that a single prayer is not going to be the solution to their inner conflicts, he also strongly encourages them to get involved in a For Men Only group in the church so they can be held accountable and start dealing with the way they think. "No one can win this battle alone," he says. "Finally, I pray for them, because this is not just a battle of the mind; it is also a profound struggle with the demonic forces of hell. We can't defeat the dragon alone, and we can't defeat him simply by trying harder intellectually. It is, in the final analysis, a spiritual battle."[4]

Cry From a Motel Room

Recently an anonymous letter arrived on my desk, with CON-FIDENTIAL printed on it in big block letters. It was from another state and contained a poem written on a post card from a national hotel chain. Usually I don't pay attention to unsigned letters, but this was different. It was a man's lament, written from a lonely motel room. I'm guessing he related to what I have written about in some of my columns for *New Man*. Here's what he wrote:

Just a few days on the road;
The wife and kids sitting at home.
Temptations seem to come from everywhere—
Porno movies, needy women, a six-pack of beer.
Many things deserve contemplation;
Even thoughts of masturbation.
Not tonight though; I've had enough.

It's time to pray and give God my stuff.
With Jesus I walk, my body is His.
In Gideon's I read what the real truth is.
No more of Satan's trick here;
By God's power, the Holy Spirit is near.
In a way this place is the perfect test–
Once obedient, a room for good rest.
Can't wait for hugs from the wife and kids.
Protect me, Father, as I leave again.
It's my ol' home again–the motel room.

This man seems to understand the struggle and the victory. I want to thank him–whoever he is–for sharing this poem.

> ## The first way God usually leads us is out of anything that keeps us in a perpetual cycle of defeat.

How Do We Do It?

Over the years since I made a radical commitment to Christ, I have also had to struggle to learn how to walk in faith. I've had to learn the importance of forgiveness. I've struggled to renew my mind in many areas.

I've had to learn that the Christian life is a constant process of "working out our salvation with fear and trembling." There's never a time that we *arrive* spiritually. The world around us is ready and willing to be a handmaiden to our lusts, and our inner sinful nature propels us in the wrong direction at every new turn.

Even the apostle Paul seemed to understand this struggle in his own life. He wrote, "What a wretched man I am! There is a bent toward sin loosed in my members, and the more I try to serve God the more it wars against my mind. There is nothing in me to battle it. Even though God gave me the law and I try to keep it, this lust for sin persistently wages war inside me. I can't seem to stop it" (Rom. 7:24, AUTHOR'S PARAPHRASE).

Then Paul gives us the answer two verses later in Romans 8:1–2: "So now there is no condemnation for those who belong to Christ Jesus. For the power of the life-giving Spirit has freed you through Christ Jesus from the power of sin that leads to death."

The Bible answer to renewing the mind is very easy. In Galatians 5:16 we are told, "So I advise you to live according to your new life in the Holy Spirit. Then you won't be doing what your sinful nature craves." Romans 8:14 says, "For all who are led by the Spirit of God are children of God."

But how can we do this? Sometimes people think that when God leads us, He always leads in the direction of a new ministry or a new job. *But the first way God usually leads us is out of anything that keeps us in a perpetual cycle of defeat.* He leads us on the path of renewal.

The Bible talks about having a thirtyfold and sixtyfold return, and many Christians live in that realm. But what about that last 40 percent we need to have a hundredfold return? It's that last 40 percent that is the hardest to get. I believe that is because so many Christians have many significant unrenewed areas in their minds.

Mark 4:20–22 gives us a key: "'But the good soil represents those who hear and accept God's message and produce a huge harvest—thirty, sixty, or even a hundred times as much as had been planted.' Then Jesus asked them, 'Would anyone light a lamp and then put it under a basket or under a bed to shut out the light? Of course not! A lamp is placed on a stand, where its light will shine. Everything that is now hidden or secret will eventually be brought to light.'"

The Holy Spirit casts a brilliant light on spiritual roadblocks that are hidden in darkness—those sins, faults and shortcomings that keep you from producing a hundredfold harvest of God's plan for your life. The flesh doesn't like to have its deeds revealed by the Holy Spirit. The Holy Spirit is the only one who can search the heart and find the root of the problem—and sometimes His spotlight hurts. But when the problem is diagnosed, He helps us to put it to death and replace it with life.

Romans 8:13 says if we don't purge ourselves of sin, we will die. This is another way of saying we must renew our minds. Paul gives us the next key in Romans 8:13: "For if you keep on following it [sinful nature], you will perish. But if through the power of the Holy Spirit you turn from it and its evil deeds, you will live."

It isn't until we find how to release the power of the Holy Spirit that we are able to put to death that old man's fleshly deeds. The natural mind thinks it can "will" to change. "I will not sin anymore," you say with gritted teeth. But sometimes you just can't break a fleshly habit using the strength of your own will.

In his book *The Walk of the Spirit—The Walk of Power,* Dave Roberson talks about the usefulness of our willpower to over-come our flesh. "Relying on sheer willpower to change your fleshly weakness will take you only so far," he says. "It is only through the Spirit that you mortify the deeds of the body."

On the other hand, "mortification" through the Spirit is the process by which the Holy Spirit rises up on the inside of you to destroy the hold that the flesh has had over you. *Instead of the sin having dominion over you, you gain dominion over it.*[5]

It's no accident that immediately after Paul talks about morti-fying the deeds of the flesh in Romans 8:13 that he says in verse 14: "For all who are led by the Spirit of God are children of God."

The term *children of God* refers to mature believers who have been nurtured by the Holy Spirit to the point that they can now walk by their new nature rather than the dictates of the flesh. This is a state of spiritual maturity where carnal patterns and systems of thought no longer dominate you because you are now walking after your new nature instead of according to the flesh.

That's what Romans 8:13 is talking about: As many as will allow their reborn human spirits to be nurtured and taught by the Holy Spirit, they are the mature children of God. For it is through the spirit–through the new nature within them–that they mortify the deeds of the flesh.

The Holy Spirit will lead us out of patterns and systems of thought that enslave us. Paul describes this battle to mortify or kill the works of the flesh in 2 Corinthians 10: 4, "We use God's mighty weapons, not mere worldly weapons, to knock down the Devil's strongholds."

We don't wage this war with fleshly or carnal means. Instead our weapons are mighty through God to pull down the invisible strongholds or fortresses that are erected in our lives. Some Christians think the word *strongholds* refers to spiritual forces that keep people in their city from accepting Christ. Often we hear about Christians praying against these strongholds.

Paul is referring, however, to strongholds on the personal level. The very next verse says: "With these weapons we break down every proud argument that keeps people from knowing God. With these weapons we conquer their rebellious ideas, and we teach them to obey Christ."

These strongholds exist in the realm of the soul, and we must bring every disobedient thought and deed into captivity, because these strongholds will hinder us greatly if they aren't broken. We will actually die defeated as Christians if they aren't broken.

In my own life, I've come to points where the Holy Spirit reveals a truth in a way that it becomes personal to me.

I see it like Jesus approached the sick man lying by the side of the pool of Bethesda (John 5:1–8). When He confronted the sick man, Jesus said, "Would you like to get well?"

To change, we must believe that we can change. Mark 9:23 says, "Anything is possible if a person believes." In Hebrews 11:1 we discover that faith is "the confident assurance that what we hope for is going to happen. It is the evidence of things we cannot yet see."

The sick man at Bethesda had to believe in more than the rippled waters that he could see–he had to believe in the healthy legs that he could not yet see. We must believe in the unseen also. That's what faith is all about. Does this happen overnight? No, it's a process.

So, what is God saying to you? Are there areas in which you struggle? The Bible tells us how we can be new men in Christ—all the time, not just part of the time. If we truly want to be, we can be free of the bondages that hold us back. This doesn't mean we're perfect. But we don't have to be enslaved to the lusts of the past. We can change through the renewing of the mind.

Talk about it   Think about it

Renewing Your Mind: Changing the Way You Think

Author's note: Implementing the principles described in this chapter is crucial to renewing the mind. If you are reading this alone, reflect on the questions.

To the group leader: Before beginning, determine as a group your comfort in discussing the questions below. If the group is not comfortable as a whole with discussing these issues, have each man commit then and there to discuss these issues with the man in the group with whom they feel most comfortable. The point is to get busy renewing the mind and not put this off.

For more information on this topic (which we will add to as time passes) check out our www.oldmannewman.com website. Use the user id: **oldman** and the password **newman**. These are **case sensitive,** so use all lowercase letters and leave no spaces.

1. What types of situations cause your mind to move in the wrong direction?

2. What practical things have you found that help you keep your mind from being captured by temptation and sin?

3. Often when we are in the grip of temptation, we completely lose sight of the consequences of failing to renew our minds. What are the consequences of yielding to sin in our personal lives, in our spiritual lives, in our families, in our ministries, in our professions and in our reputations?

4. How honest should we be with our wives about our areas of struggle?

A clip from

New Man January/February 2000

Keys to Becoming Debt-Free

Get out of debt! Seem like a pipe dream? It isn't, says financial expert Larry Burkett. Here are some of his suggestions for getting out of debt.

1. Have a written plan. "Use a written plan of all expenditures and their order of importance. The order of importance is crucial because we have lost the point of reference between needs, wants and desires."

2. Determine essentials for living. "Begin to eliminate expenditures that are not essential, remembering that many expenditures are assumed to be essential only because of our society."

3. Think before buying. "Every purchase should be evaluated: Have I assessed whether it is a need, a want or a desire?"

4. Discontinue credit buying. "If you are in debt from the misuse of credit, stop—totally stop—using it."

5. Practice saving. "This includes those who are in debt. Even if it is only $5 a month, develop a discipline of saving."[1]

Become debt-free
oldmannewman.com

Chapter 11

Ordering Your Finances: Gaining Freedom to Soar

OLD MAN Locked into dead-end financial situations and circumstances.

NEW MAN Has a godly, mature, wise attitude toward earning money and spending it.

It seems to me that men are usually free to talk about anything but money. They'll talk about sports, work, family—even their own sexuality—but never their salary. How many people beyond your boss, the payroll people and your spouse know your salary? And why is that? The reason we keep it to ourselves is because wealth is the ultimate measure in our consumeristic, money-mad culture.

I have found that men will be open about a lot of things—their opinion on politics, Scripture, doctrine or other people—before they'll be open about sex or finances. Every man wants others to think he's more macho than he really is, and every man wants people to think he's more financially prosperous than he is. I believe these are two major areas that stand in the way of a man being all he can be in Christ. I've dealt with male sexuality earlier in the book. Here I deal with finances.

Patrick Morley, author of *Man in the Mirror*, knows money can be a hindrance in our walk with Christ. He says he was a "materialist" even after becoming a follower of Jesus.

"Materialism is an addiction just like alcohol, pornography, sex or drugs," he writes. "It has power to destroy completely and finally. An addiction is any desire so strong that it overly controls actions."

About his own struggles with materialism, he says: "I was never a crass materialist. I was a refined materialist. I didn't flaunt it. I would buy things and experiences that didn't shout too loudly. But it inflated my ego to take 'Fantasy Island' trips, even if no one knew."

I've known Pat Morley for more than twenty years. For three years we were in a group of business executives who met for a full day once a month to exchange ideas and to motivate each other to be better businessmen. I've found Pat to be a very open type of man. His weekly "TGIF Bible studies" in Orlando have helped thousands of men to become new men in Christ. They also provided for the material Pat later used in his best-selling book *The Man in the Mirror.*

The old man says, "Whoever dies with the most toys wins." The new man says, "Whoever lays down his life wins."

I never had occasion to talk to Pat specifically about materialism, so I was surprised to read in his book that he had four leather briefcases—two of them that cost five hundred dollars each. Imagine Pat Morley, godly man that he is, admitting in print that he would walk by a luggage store in the mall and be mesmerized by that delicious aroma wafting out of the store! He jokingly admitted he thought the store manager put fans blowing the aroma into the concourse to lure in materialists like himself.

"For me, however, materialism was merely the symptom. The root problem was that I was not building the kingdom of God. I was building a kingdom of my own," he wrote in *Second Wind for the Second Half.* He goes on to say:

> The Living Bible puts it this way: "Happiness or sadness or wealth should not keep anyone from doing God's work" (1 Cor. 7:30). My ambitions didn't focus on "Thy kingdom come. Thy will be done in earth, as it is in heaven" (Matt. 6:10, KJV). Oh, I did things for the king-dom—taught Bible studies, sponsored evangelistic events, read the Bible, prayed regularly, and attended church—but deep down in that secret place where motives lurk, my top priority was achieving my personal ambition, not loving God.[2]

The old man says, "Whoever dies with the most toys wins." The new man, following Jesus, says that whoever lays down his life wins. There is a clear choice here.

I recently thumbed through a magazine published for wealthy tycoons. In it were advertisements for golf balls made of gold, exquisite watches, luxury helicopter rentals, $200 pens and $22 cigars. An article, complete with dazzling beach and mountain range photos, discussed the pros and cons of buying private, uninhabited islands for use as vacation retreats. Another article told how to become a professional race car driver—a popular sport for rich people who can't find a competitive thrill in the business arena anymore.[3]

I don't think the life goal of a Christian should be to aim for a tycoon's lifestyle or to amass cash for the sake of buying entire islands. Indeed, the Bible warns that the *love* of money is the root of all kinds of evil. We're also aware of the rich young man who rejected an invitation to follow Jesus, apparently because he didn't want to part with his wealth. But the opposite extreme is also dangerous: seeing money as the enemy, something dirty and altogether worldly. I believe it is every Christian's responsibility to learn to handle money effectively and wisely, and to allow the Lord to bring the increase as He wills. For some of us, that means changing the way we think about money.

Though we are not to be slaves to our bank accounts, we as

Christians are to be wise and to use money in such a way that God is honored. In my observation, that can mean prospering in business, running a tight ship and gaining efficiency and effectiveness in whatever field we are in. I am not talking about growing rich for the sake of having lots of money. I am talking about becoming a good, faithful steward with finances and allowing God to bless us in whatever measure He sees fit.

I believe it is every Christian's responsibility to learn to handle money **effectively and wisely, and to allow the Lord to bring the increase as He wills.**

My observation is that most Christians buy into the biblical concepts of money without a lot of debate, but they are clueless on how to put those principles into practice. Or they are so preoccupied by the cares of this world that they are no different than anyone else in our society—no planning, no vision, no learning how to handle money. The financial challenges Christian men face are no different than anyone else. Some men are underemployed; they have no vision on how they can prosper financially, or they struggle under a great deal of debt. Over the years Christian men seem to fall prey to financial "schemes" as much as anyone else. They are locked into dead-end financial situations.

How do we start to get on track financially?

Growing a Vision

I grew up in very modest circumstances. We weren't poor; we just didn't have any extra money. Vacations involved driving all night (to save money on a motel room) to visit relatives in distant states (the cheapest of all vacations). When my dad was in graduate school, money was so tight I wanted to drop out of band rather than pay the $40 yearly rental fee on the oboe I played. A kindly teacher got a "scholarship" for that fee to keep me in band.

My dad was a hardworking man, but because he pastored small churches and later taught in small denominational Bible colleges, he was paid small salaries. He was careful with his money, but he didn't teach me much about getting ahead financially. We were faithful to attend Wednesday night services, pray for the missionaries and try to live holy lives—those things were of paramount importance. Building a successful business, writing a best-selling book, creating a television network—those things were not considered important and were even considered worldly.

I was in my early twenties before it dawned on me that my training as a newspaper reporter didn't prepare me to earn a good income. I was making less than $10,000 a year back then, and my wife had to work to help us make ends meet. One of my motivations to start a small church magazine, which became *Charisma* (and the foundation of our communications company, which publishes *New Man*), was to earn extra income. Reason: I needed to moonlight so Joy could afford to quit her job at a bank and finish her last two years of college. I needed $75 a week more to make our household budget work.

Isn't it amazing that God used financial necessity to propel me into my life's work and the opportunity to touch the lives of literally millions of readers around the world? He may be doing the same to you, if you are willing to sincerely listen to His voice and take the financial risks necessary to make His dream for your life come true.

When I started *Charisma* (and later Strang Communications), I was ill-equipped to run a magazine or a publishing house. My college degree was in journalism, not business. We struggled, as many young couples do, with more bills than income. I had no savings and no real way to get ahead other than by earning more money.

Seek out successful mentors.

I needed to renew my mind in the area of finances. I did it by seeking out successful people as mentors for advice on business issues. For more than a year I made it a point to take to lunch local businessmen whom I had met through church or my work at the newspaper. The criteria was they had to be (in my estimation) a millionaire. It was for only an hour or two at a time, and it usually didn't go much beyond one lunch. But as I talked to them, I began to see that it was possible for me to build financial stability for myself.

For me, Pat Morley was a mentor in business—a godly man who had been very successful financially. I mentioned earlier that Pat and I were in a small group of other businessmen, a couple of whom were Christians. That was a great learning experience for me. My company was one-tenth the size it is today. But I was able to learn that the business problems I had weren't much different from the ones other men had who ran huge companies. It also gave me a vision of how to lead a much bigger organization.

In that setting I learned things I still use today such as a method for keeping track of cash flow on a weekly basis. I also learned some concepts that I still quote today, such as "what you measure and monitor improves."

> **Have a clear vision for what you want to achieve. Pursue those goals and vision with a burning desire, never giving up in the face of adversity.**

This principle seems to work for reasons I don't fully understand other than you tend to move in the direction of thoughts you focus on. So if I focus on improving subscription renewals by carefully monitoring them, or if I check on the weekly registrations to an upcoming conference, and so forth, the results seem to improve. I even began to carefully monitor my golf scores and found that my golf game gradually improved. Later I learned that at least one of the golf "greats" had also used this technique to analyze his shots in order to improve.

Carefully monitor where you stand monthly.

So here's a hint: Try this idea. If you're trying to get out of debt, take some sort of spreadsheet or handwritten chart, and carefully monitor where you stand each month. Or, keep careful track of your income by month (or whatever you find a need to improve in). What do you have to lose? Measuring and monitoring might even work! I think you'll find that it will work for you just as it does in so many areas for me.

Have a clear vision for what you want to achieve.

In my late twenties, I also discovered "self-help" books. I read Robert Schuller's *Move Ahead Through Possibility Thinking* at least four times. I have read *How I Raised Myself From Failure to Success in Selling* by Frank Bettger half a dozen times over the years. (I've listed some of the books that have meant a lot to me personally in the appendix at the end of this book.)

I noticed a pattern in the self-help books. It was to have a clear vision for what you want to achieve. This involved researching and writing down very specific goals. Then you had to pursue your vision and goals with a burning desire, never giving up in the face of adversity.

That was an important lesson for me to learn early. *Charisma* was so small and full of problems that I would have given up many times had I not had a burning desire to see my  vision to publish a great Christian magazine come to pass. You can read about my vision, and how God has allowed me to implement it during the last twenty-five years, in the August 2000 issue of *Charisma* magazine.[4]

Start small and grow to the next level.

For me, building a financial base also involved renewing my

mind. I learned the principle of starting small and having enough success that it allowed me to grow to the next level. Most great companies are built this way. I began to learn that in capitalism you must have capital, or savings from profits. So I focused on making some profits and plowing it all back into the business. Slowly our organization grew, and it allowed me to have the sort of financial independence most people only dream about.

How does this apply to you? First, if I can do it, so can you. I'm nobody special. You probably are not called to serve God as I am by publishing books and magazines. You may not have a gift for writing or journalism. But you can learn to believe God as I did to move out of whatever financial rut you are in to a new level of prosperity. For those of us who live in the United States, we have a financial system that rewards hard work, savings and investment. It almost doesn't matter what field you are in. There is always room for someone to do a job better. Maybe you can start the next Chick-fil-A success story. Or maybe there is a huge idea like Microsoft that needs to be thought of. I believe that there are God-sized ideas out there that have not been tried.

Learn the principles of free enterprise.

Renewing my mind in the area of finances meant believing that I could do more than just eke out a living. I had to believe that my dreams could come true and that God would supply my financial needs. Then I learned the principles of business and free enterprise, like making a profit.

I learned that for any organization (profit or nonprofit) having profit is as necessary to life as having oxygen is to the life of any animal. (In nonprofits it's not called *profit;* it's called *surplus income*). This extra money is invested in growth and things like hiring workers, buying inventory and being able to pay your bills before your customers pay you (that's called *receivables*).

I tell my staff members that we don't come to work to make profit any more than we wake up in the morning with the goal of breathing oxygen all day long. However, if oxygen is cut off, then suddenly getting oxygen is priority number one. It's the same way if there is no profit; becoming profitable is the main priority before you can move on to more important long-range goals.

Get out of debt.

Next came getting out of debt. Joy and I have never been head over heels in debt, and we have never had a major financial meltdown like a bankruptcy or losing a house to foreclosure. But we did live from paycheck to paycheck. Car repairs, Christmas presents or major household needs were funded with credit cards. I had to come to a point where I got control of my own finances.

It was obvious to me that the finances of our organization began taking off when I got my private house in order financially. The Word of God explains to us that if we are faithful in little things, more shall be given to us. Before God can trust us to be successful at business, I believe He must be able to trust us to be successful at home.

Learning to Give

Charles Ross, host of the national radio program *Your Personal Finances*, says there are five financial life cycles:

- Young single's cycle
- Young married couple's cycle
- Childbearing cycle
- Mid-career cycle
- Retirement cycle

Each stage carries a unique set of responsibilities. A young single person sets patterns for budgeting and investing that will be echoed throughout his or her life. A young married couple is forced to combine spending patterns and

> Five life cycles
> ▶ oldmannewman.com

habits. Smart ones start saving for retirement right away. Once they have children, the couple must save for college educations and clothing expenses–to name just two. As they get into their mid-career, more money goes into savings and investments, and it becomes important to avoid high-risk and high-debt budgets. In retirement, of course, they enjoy the fruit of their diligence.[5]

Patrick Morley lists his top ten uses for money:

1. Give 10 percent or more to the work of the church.

2. Purchase catastrophic health insurance (to prevent wiping out savings after a life of toil).

3. Pay off all consumer debts.

4. Purchase a home (or retire the mortgage as soon as possible).

5. Save and invest 10 percent of income for retirement (this can and should include life insurance).

6. Save for emergencies (e.g., a washing machine or major car repairs).

7. Provide college educations for your children.

8. Purchase the safest possible transportation for your family (after careful examination of consumer reports about cars within budget range).

9. Acquire and maintain marketable job skills (seminars, courses, etc.)

10. Purchase a few occasional nice things that will bring pleasure (e.g., a work of art, an antique, a nice piece of furniture, a fishing boat or new golf clubs).[6]

I agree with these priorities, especially the first one. One of the paradoxes of money is that giving it away will increase what God gives to you. Of course, this is a universal principle, and one that Christians especially ought to recognize.

In a recent column, Maureen D. Eha, associate editor of *SpiritLed Woman* magazine, talked about the paradoxes of dying in order to live, giving in order to get and sowing in order to reap. She recognized that for more than six years God had been teaching her to understand these paradoxes and giving her the grace to embrace them. Through the process she had learned to sow the kinds of crops He wanted her to harvest.[7] We must all do that.

An important principle is learning to give back when you have been given so much. I was taught early the principles of giving to others less fortunate. One year at Christmas, my parents did something that is permanently etched into my memory. There was a family in our church who was poor. Probably by today's standards my family was barely above the poverty line, but this family was even poorer. The dad was out of work, and we were told the kids would get no presents for Christmas—a thought my five-year-old mind couldn't fathom.

> **" One of the paradoxes of money is that giving it away will increase what God gives to you. This is a universal principle. One that Christians should recognize. "**

After we opened our presents on Christmas morning and cleared away all the wrapping paper, my parents asked my sister Karen, my brother Paul and I to pick one of our gifts to give to the children in this family. We took these cherished gifts that we were giving away before we could even play with them and gave them to someone less fortunate. I don't remember much more than that, but it impressed on me the idea of giving at Christmas—not just taking.

At another church when I was a little older, everyone brought wrapped gifts to distribute to the poor through World Vision.

My parents always emphasized that this was Jesus' birthday—and giving was vastly more important than getting. Those childhood Christmases were probably simple by today's standards, with the orgy of buying and gift giving. In some homes, the pile of presents seems to rise as high as the Christmas tree!

Jesus commanded us to help the poor. Christians fulfill this command in many ways. I've made it a point to reach out to the poor by going on mission trips to Guatemala or visiting the homeless on the streets of New York with Bill Wilson. It isn't so much to help them (although that's an element), but to help me.

I can get my focus back on what Jesus considers important: "Pure and lasting religion in the sight of God our Father means that we must care for orphans and widows in their troubles, and refuse to let the world corrupt us" (James 1:27).

Helping others was the focus of Jesus' life. Of Him it was prophesied: "The Spirit of the Sovereign LORD is upon me, because the LORD has appointed me to bring good news to the poor. He has sent me to comfort the brokenhearted and to announce that captives will be released and prisoners will be freed" (Isa. 61:1).

When we are busy developing our own financial base, we must never forget that millions live in poverty without much hope, let alone the comfort of knowing their sins are forgiven by a Savior. At Christmas our family always reaches out to others. We pack special bags full of goodies and toiletries for the men at the nearby Teen Challenge who can't go home for Christmas. Or, we wrap dozens of gifts to hand out at Mother Blanche Weaver's mission in Sanford, Florida, amid some of the worst rural poverty you'll find anywhere in the South—only five miles from our new multimillion-dollar headquarters building. Jesus came to bring the good news to the poor.

The gospel was never meant to be given only to those who can become good tithers. Jesus told us that we would always have the poor with us, and He charged us with the responsibility of looking out for them—both spiritually and financially. For several years I've tried to motivate the 600,000 readers of *Charisma* to reach out to the poor at Christmas. We've sponsored Operation Holiday Hope and raised tens of thousands of dollars to give gifts to the poorest of the poor in New York through Bill Wilson's ministry.

For two years we sponsored the Convoy of Hope by raising $20,000 among the staff of our company and volunteering to hand out groceries and gifts in a poor section of Orlando.

Dan Kays of Chattanooga, Tennessee, whose testimony you read earlier in this book, is a man I first met in 1999 at one of our conferences. Since then we've become good friends, getting together several times when I'm in his area. I admire the way God has totally revolutionized Dan's life. I told his story in chapter five. His is one of the most exciting stories I know of overcoming the old man to become a new man in Christ.

Dan is not content to just get over his own problems and to lead a happy fulfilled life. He has learned the joy of giving. Recently he spent his fortieth birthday ministering in Georgia's worst prison. He jokingly told me that if ten years ago someone had told him he'd spend his fortieth birthday in jail, he would have believed that he'd be an inmate. He wouldn't have believed that he would be ministering to other broken men.

When Hurricane Andrew devastated South Florida in 1992, Dan took it upon himself to organize a relief effort in Chattanooga, especially among the employees of the huge company for which he works. There was so much food and materials it filled two semitrailers. Dan and his team of seventeen volunteers delivered and distributed more than forty thousand pounds of food and clothing to help hundreds of families who had been left destitute. This is just one example of where Dan has learned it is more blessed to give than to receive! And I believe it is one reason his life has been so blessed in recent years—in sharp contrast to the horrible life he lived for many years in his teens and twenties.

I urge you to get involved in your own area. There are poor near where you live who need your help. You may mark positively your kids for life—as my parents marked me. And you'll be fulfilling

Jesus' command that "when you did it to one of the least of these my brothers and sisters, you were doing it to me!" (Matt. 25:40).

What does all this mean?

If you were to move to Orlando and God led you to be in my men's group, I might have the opportunity to mentor you in the area of finances as I have many men. I'm not the most successful man financially. Yet I have been blessed "infinitely more that we would ever dare to ask or hope" (Eph. 3:20).

> ## If you are not willing to honor God with your finances, how can you ask His help financially?

I'm sure there are some who would say that I am living the American dream. In some ways that may be true, but I know that anything I've accomplished is due to the mercy and grace of God.

Principles That Worked for Me

Over the years I've learned some principles both through my own life and also in giving advice to others. So I hope you will find these five hints useful to help you get ahead financially. This is not an exhaustive list by any means. But it's my attempt to give you some handles to hold on to—something you can do to improve your lot in life.

1. Understand that God is your source.

First, understand that God is your source and that what you have belongs to Him. There are principles of sowing and reaping that exist in life—including in the financial realm. If you are not willing to honor God in your finances, how can you ask His help financially? There are many good books you can read by financial experts like Larry Burkett or accountants like Ron Blue. Our appendix lists books I have read over the years that I have found helpful.

There is a spiritual aspect to this financial side of our lives. It involves believing God and seeing in faith what you hope to accomplish. For example, I remember a time when I was believing God to earn $200 a week.

To show my faith, I began tithing on that amount, as if I already made it. I don't believe my tithing on $200 forced God to act, but it released my faith to believe. I was doing what Hebrews 11:1 said—I was looking at the future victory, not the present circumstance. It wasn't long until I was making $200 a week, and God has continued to increase my financial blessing to this day.

2. Tear down mind barriers.

In the chapter on fatherlessness, I told about the man who had a theory that most men have a subconscious barrier on what they can earn. He believed that barrier was about 10 percent more (adjusted for inflation) than what their dads were making when the boys were five years old. I've had some interesting conversations over the years with men about this theory, and I have found it's true most of the time. Each of us limits ourselves by our environment and those around us. Most of us will live a comparable lifestyle to what our parents lived. Is this bad? No, not necessarily. But it can limit you if you come from a low-income background. If so, you've really got your work cut out for you financially *unless you renew your mind in this area.* You must understand this phenomenon and do something to get beyond it. Otherwise you will just gravitate toward the income level of your family. There are many ways to renew the mind. Reading books about goal-setting and positive thinking are two ways I broke out of this.

For me it came down to three things:

- Reading books on goal-setting and positive thinking. Start by reading books such as Robert Schuller's *Move Ahead Through Possibility Thinking* or Zig Ziglar's *See You at the Top.* (I've included a much longer list in the Appendix and on our website.)

- Actually setting goals—and monitoring my progress.

■ Interviewing successful people.

Anybody can do these things.

3. Understand the financial realities of life.

Begin to understand the financial realities of life. If you are a farmer and want a bountiful harvest, you need to be in a good climate, with good soil. You also need to plant the right kind of crops at the right time, tend them well and harvest when the crop is ripe. Most of us understand these basic agrarian principles even if we didn't grow up on a farm.

Well, in our capitalisitic society, there are similar principles. Even if you live in the richest country in the world, you must do something that will bring an economic value to someone.

I've counseled men who had some idea for a business they were sure would catapult them to wealth, but the fact was it was a hare-brained idea that had no economic value to anyone but them. The "market" ultimately decides who makes it and who doesn't in a capitalistic economy. Even if you work for someone else, what you do must have a lot more value to them than it does to you, or they may never give you a raise. If what you do is only of value to you, your employer may even decide that since you have no value to him, he might as well let you go.

In our company, we must have an income of nearly three times the sum total of all the employees' salaries for everything to work. So if we pay someone $33,000 a year, if the person only brings in $33,000 worth of income, we are in trouble. We have nothing to pay all the other expenses such as printing cost, postage or taxes. For purposes of illustration, that staff member needs to generate $100,000 in income (this is on the average, not each employee individually). So if the employee asks for a $2,000 raise, we want to know what that person will do to generate about $6,000 more in income.

Speaking of asking for a raise, my mentor at the newspaper in Orlando, George Clouse, gave me wise advice on how to successfully ask for a raise. I actually used this, and it works.

He said never go in and tell the boss you need more money. He said everyone needs more money whether you make minimum wage or earn $100,000 a year. (Often the high-income people need it more because they run up such huge debts supporting a fancy lifestyle.) Instead, be sure you've done something really noteworthy the year before that goes beyond what your job description demands that you do. Then go in and remind your boss of what you have done for the company that year. Explain that you think you're worth more to the company and therefore ought to earn a larger salary.

4. Get a handle on your expenses.

The next point is to get a handle on your expenses. This probably means getting out of debt because you can only get out of debt by spending less than you bring in. It doesn't take a rocket scientist to figure out that a man who makes $50,000 a year and lives on $40,000 a year is better off than a man who makes $100,000 a year and spends $110,000 a year to live.

5. Learn to invest.

If you bring in more than you spend, you have something to invest. I suggest giving 10 percent of your income to the Lord and giving 10 percent to yourself through a savings and investment plan. If your company has a retirement program, stock options or 401K program, you should take advantage of it. Even a modest investment, added to by your company and invested properly, will grow quickly.

I was thirty-five before I was ahead financially enough to begin saving and later investing. Now I put money away and basically leave it untouched.

A financial advisor helps me pick investments that make sense for me. Occasionally we'll sell a poorly performing stock. But I don't try to play the stock market. I don't have time, and neither do you.

Besides, there are players in the stock market much smarter than us who can't make lots of money buying and selling. You can never predict the ups and downs of the stock market. But it's known that over time, the stock market outperforms any other sort of investment.

One time while traveling on an airplane home from Europe, I read an interesting news report showing that if a person would save three dollars per day and invest it at a consistent 10 percent per year beginning at age twenty, by age seventy (fifty years later) those savings would have grown to $1.4 million. To accomplish the same goal in only forty years you must save six dollars per day. This is only $1000 or $2000 per year, which is very doable for most people.

John Maxwell's book *The 21 Irrefutable Laws of Leadership* tells a story of a lady who worked for the IRS and retired in 1943 with a savings of $5,000.[8] She lived to a ripe old age. When she died, she left the $22 million in her estate to Yeshiva University in New York. How did she do it? Her original $5,000 had doubled to $10,000 by 1950. When she bought one thousand shares of Schering-Plough Corporation stock it doubled and tripled and split, and is now worth $7.5 million dollars. The idea was that she saved money, invested and left it there through the ups and downs. This is the secret of saving.

She saved money, invested and left it there through the ups and downs. This is the secret of saving.

I know a minister who has worked for years at an average salary that would impress no one. Yet through careful saving and investing, first in real estate and later in the stock market, he has built up a portfolio of more than two million dollars. I say this to encourage you that regular savings properly invested can amass to a sizeable estate for your retirement years and to leave to your family and to the Lord's work.

Get the counsel of some financially successful people whom you know and trust. Study some books that are written to help you learn more about creating a sound financial base for your personal finances. Take the advice you get in seminars, conferences and tapes. Then carefully develop a consistently sound plan for handling your finances—including the money coming in, the money going out and the money you are saving and investing.

Suddenly the idea of becoming a "millionaire" seems more possible than just winning money on a TV game show. Yet the point here isn't to become a millionaire. In fact, the goal is to merely provide well for your family and to have enough to do the things God calls you to do. Is it right to be so poor you can never take time off work to go on a missions trip? Do you have so many bills you can never respond generously to a need you see? Does being poor really glorify God? I think not, even though being rich doesn't glorify God either. It's not money that's evil, *but the love of money.*

I hope as we become new men in Christ that we can have a mature, wise attitude toward earning money and spending it. I hope my ideas have motivated you to believe that no matter where you are on the financial spectrum, you can probably do better than what you're doing now. If we're growing and improving, then I believe that is pleasing to God.

Now let's focus on making your marriage great!

Talk about it   Think about it

Ordering Your Finances: Gaining Freedom to Soar

Author's note: Reflect on these questions if you are wanting to get ahead financially. Use the practical guidelines and tips to make specific goals for how you will better manage your finances.

For more information on this topic (which we will add to as time passes) check out our www.oldmannewman.com website. Use the user id: **oldman** and the password **newman**. These are **case sensitive,** so use all lowercase letters and leave no spaces.

1. This chapter contains a wealth of practical tips for turning the corner on your personal finances. Which ones are you the most excited to try out, and why? Which one seems to be the most difficult for you to master? Why do you suppose that it is especially challenging for you?

2. Tithing is a watershed issue for Christians. You either do not know how you can tithe and survive financially—or you do not know how you could survive financially if you *did not tithe.*

   What is your experience with giving and God's blessing on your finances?

   (Note: The purpose of this question is not to encourage bragging or to heap condemnation; it is to build faith and inspire new levels of trust in God. So please approach it accordingly).

3. Page 189 says this about debt: "Next came getting out of debt. Joy and I have never been head over heels in debt . . . But we did live from paycheck to paycheck. Car repairs, Christmas presents or major household needs were funded with credit cards. I had to come to a point where I got control of my own finances." In your opinion, what—if any—are the appropriate uses of debt?

A clip from

New Man July/August 2000

10 Ways to Sabotage Your Marriage

Here are some "grains of sand" that can sabotage your marriage.

1. Be a flirt.
2. Undermine your spouse in public.
3. Use negative body language when your spouse is talking to you.
4. Fail to communicate on a daily basis.
5. Stop caring about your appearance.
6. Have children in order to bring your marriage together.
7. **Men:** Enjoy playing golf (or whatever takes your time) more than you enjoy your wife.
8. **Women:** Spend more time with your friends (or whatever takes your time) than you spend with your husband.
9. Find your self-esteem outside the marriage.
10. Conceal your expectations.[1]

Avoid sabotage

▶ **oldmannewman.com**

Chapter 12

Working on Your Marriage: Making It Great

OLD MAN   Grapples with unfulfillment, discord and
           division in marriage.

NEW MAN   Experiences great peace and restful-
           ness in a marriage based on unity.

A few years ago I met a woman who was in the middle of a very difficult time. She had gone through two failed marriages and was emotionally destitute. Her parents and siblings were also divorced.

Over time she developed a friendship with Joy and joined our home fellowship group, which ministered to singles. She came to see Joy as a mentor.

Soon she met and fell in love with a man in the church. Before the wedding, she told Joy that our marriage was the first happy marriage she had seen up close.

At that point Joy and I had been married only six or seven years, but it was apparent to this woman that we had something special. Today, Joy and I have been happily married twenty-eight years, and I believe our marriage is more solid than ever before. It is not perfect, and we have things to work through and spiritual battles to fight. But we have a relationship that is more precious to me than any other in my life. I love her, and I try to treat her right. In fact I have a motto I adopted after I heard Bud Paxson of Paxnet say it: "Happy wife–happy life!"

In spite of my attempts to be a good husband, much of the credit for our successful marriage must go to Joy. She is patient and understanding, and she prods me to be the husband I need to be.

As I was working on this chapter, Joy spent the weekend in the mountains with two close friends. As they drove and talked, they opened up about their lives and marriages. Joy came home saying how thankful she is for our marriage. That is the kind of friendships I like her to have!

> **There is great peace and restfulness when a marriage hums along in unity. When there is discord, everything else in life seems to break down as well.**

Marrying Joy was the best decision I ever made, aside from salvation. I can remember the day I met her as if it were last month. It was at the home of her brother Jim Ferrell in Lakeland, Florida, in 1972. She was living there to save on expenses while she attended Southeastern College.

During my spring break from the University of Florida, I got a one-week reporting job at *The Ledger* in Lakeland to earn extra income. That led to a summer internship later that year. In need of housing, I asked if I could stay with Jim and his wife, who were long-time friends of my family.

That week Joy and I spent hours talking and debating late into the evening. We discussed politics and religion, and had radically different views. Joy told me later I was the first man she had met who could hold his own with her in a conversation and not be intimidated. I did not know I was on trial!

Without consciously knowing what was happening, we were falling in love. By the end of the week I told a friend that I had met the woman I wanted to marry. I proposed to Joy less than two months later, and we were married right before I started my senior year at the university.

During the months we were dating, Joy and I corresponded every day. I have saved all those letters, and when I reread them, I am amazed to see how open I was with her. Apparently I could be more vulnerable in writing than I could be in person. Joy tells me now she fell in love with me through those letters.

Today I would not want either of my sons to marry as quickly as Joy and I did. But for us there were circumstances that prompted us to move up the wedding date. It has proven to be the right decision for us in the long run. We did not have much money when we started, but we got by. We were in love, and we were very, very happy.

Today we strive for unity in the Spirit as part of our routine. There is great peace and restfulness when a marriage hums along in unity. When there is discord, everything else in life seems to break down as well.

Joy and I married for love, period! But people get married for many different reasons:

- Some people are lonely and fear being alone for life.

- Some (as we will see later in this chapter) just want to have sex.

- Some want their mate to fill a need (or two or three) in their lives.

- Some want to have children—or *want to have children before it is too late* (tick, tock).

- Some feel it is the normal thing to do.

- Some want to thumb their noses at a parent.

- Some have fallen head over heels in love, as Joy and I did.

- Some, especially women, dream of having a really nice wedding.

In 1996, a fifty-five-year-old Florida man was arrested for fraud and theft when he "married" a comatose woman and spent almost $20,000 on her credit cards. His motive, obviously, was not love.[2]

As much fun as a wedding can be, married people know that good marriages require a great deal of work. In my marriage, we especially have to work at communicating. Even though we work in the same building—in a business devoted, no less, to communicating with readers and viewers—Joy and I must schedule weekly meetings just to have time together. On days when we do not meet, we talk via e-mail.

We work at not drifting apart. We are both headstrong, independent people who could easily live separate lives under the same roof. She is such a strong woman that I have no choice but to be strong, too! But we are committed to each other and to the marriage, and we work at it to make it as great as possible.

Of course, we both saw commitment in the lives of our parents. Joy's parents were married fifty-five years and my parents forty-eight years when our fathers passed away. Joy was also influenced by the good marriage she saw between Howard and Rosella Ridings, her sister and brother-in-law who were influential in raising Joy.

We are committed to each other and to the marriage, and we work at it to make it as great as possible.

Rosella was sixteen years old when Joy was born, and because Joy's mom was busy rearing five other children, Rosella took a special interest in Joy. When she was four years old, Joy went on some of Rosella's dates with Howard! Today the Ridings have a wonderful, solid marriage. Howard is such a good husband that he has provided the standard to which Joy expects me to live up.

After a successful career as missionaries to the Orient and pastors in various states, today Howard and Rosella minister alongside us at Strang Communications. Their lives and marriage continue to be an inspiration to us.

At times it is hard for a husband to overcome the pull of the "old man" and to follow the biblical command to "love your wife as Christ loved the church and gave himself for it." (See Ephesians 5:25.) He may find himself periodically wanting out of the relationship, seeing the marriage as something that holds him back from the life he wants to lead.

That is what happened to Alvin and Gloria Slaughter. In the February 1996 issue of *Charisma,* we read about a marriage that almost ended. Alvin and Gloria first met at a prayer meeting when they were teenagers. Both had grown up in the church, but their relationship was far from godly. By the time they were twenty-one, they had two children outside of marriage.

Once Alvin took Gloria to a work-related function. The next day Alvin's manager, a non-Christian to whom Alvin had been witnessing, called him into his office.

"You painted this picture of Gloria as if she were a monster!" his manager said. "But she is a really nice girl. You have two children with her, but you say you don't want anything else to do with her. It sounds like you want the cookies, but you don't want to pay for them."

Then the manager put in the dagger: "Don't tell me anything about your God again. You are no Christian; you are a liar and a hypocrite."

Alvin remembers going to the rest room and crying like a baby. He says, "I never had anyone talk to me like that. I walked back to my cubicle, called Gloria and asked her to marry me."

Two weeks later they married—and things got progressively worse. Their third child was born, and Alvin recalls feeling overwhelmed; he was barely a child himself, he says, trying to raise three kids. At one point the family's utilities were turned off, and they were evicted from their apartment.

Returning home one day, his little girl met him outside. "Daddy!" she said. "Mommy threw all your clothes out!"

He ran upstairs and found Gloria in the middle of a nervous breakdown. "I hate you!" she yelled at him.

They split up. Alvin went to live with his parents, and Gloria and the kids moved into a small basement apartment with her sister.

"I would cry all the time and go to sleep holding my Bible to my chest," Gloria remembers. "I knew that this was not God's plan for me."

Meanwhile, Alvin fell apart. He stopped showing up for work and wore the same clothes every day.

> I truly hit rock bottom. I would walk down the streets of Manhattan and yell at God: "I have given You my whole life, and You have done nothing for me!"

But God was not mad at Alvin—and He was listening to Gloria's prayers. Through God's miraculous intervention, Alvin met Ralph Byrd, a pastor at Brooklyn Tabernacle. Byrd asked Alvin to come to the church to pray.

As they prayed and talked about Alvin's situation, Byrd asked Alvin two very important questions: "Do you believe that Jesus died on the cross, was placed in a tomb and resurrected?" Of course, Alvin asserted that he did believe those things. Then the pastor asked, "Then how come you can't believe He can restore your love for your wife?" Alvin tells us his response:

> I knew he was right. Pastor Byrd talked to me that day about love being a decision. I did not fully understand all that he told me. But I knew that I had made an awful mess of my life, and following his advice was one of my last chances at fixing the mess.

The Slaughters got back together and started going through

counseling. Within a year, Alvin and Gloria realized a miracle had occurred—they had fallen in love with each other all over again. Today Alvin sings around the world and shares his testimony. Gloria is positive about what God can do for other troubled relationships. "Remember, nothing is instant, nothing happens overnight," she says. "People give up too soon. It takes time to build relationship. In marriage you have to commit, and you can't give up."[3]

Don't give up
oldmannewman.com

> "He reminded himself constantly that God is the God of the impossible. He knew God was the restorer of the breach."

God and Marriage

Marriage is an institution ordered by the Lord Himself. It is holy. It is the joining of two people in the most sacred and intimate of all human relationships with the added joys and responsibilities of sexual union, bringing children into the world and rearing them in the admonition of God.

There are about 2.4 million marriages every year in the United States. There are also 1.15 million divorces every year.[4] The likelihood of marriage ending in divorce has hovered around 43 percent in the last decade or so. There are currently about 20 million divorced people in the United States, and around 111 million married people.

The median duration of a marriage is only 7.2 years. (If you have gone beyond that, give yourself a hand.) The median age of women at their first marriage is twenty-four; men, twenty-six.

How different these statistics could be if men and women

placed the same importance on the marriage covenant that God does. But for many, divorce seems to be the first option.

It seemed that way for Gary and Faye Whetstone. In fact, divorce seemed to be everyone's goal for their marriage. When they separated, Gary's Christian friends were convinced that Gary should pursue the dissolution of the marriage, and they always had scriptures to bolster their opinion. Even church leaders usually counseled Gary to let Faye go. "After all," they said, "she is the one who wants out."

But Gary was undaunted. He knew it could work. He reminded himself constantly that God is the God of the impossible. He knew God was the restorer of the breach. He knew that what God had joined together, no man or woman could separate, despite what either he or Faye might have done to destroy the marriage. When divorce seemed to be the final act of separation, God miraculously softened the hearts of Gary and Faye Whetstone and brought them back together.

By the time Faye blurted out to Gary, "I don't love you anymore, Gary," a whole lot of things had entered their marriage to destroy it. Gary had driven himself so hard at work that he consistently neglected Faye and their two toddlers.

The final straw seemed to happen one night at a party where, under the influence of marijuana, Gary had given her plenty of reason to believe that he was once more slipping into the mental illness he had experienced as a teenager. She threw Gary out of the house and even secured a court order to keep him away from their children, Eric and Laurie.

From that point on, everything went from bad to worse. Faye was deliberate about her lack of affection for him; she flaunted the fact that other men were sleeping in the bed that he once called his own, and she even attacked his manhood, telling him that he no longer satisfied her.

But Gary says that an unusual grace rested on his life at that point that seemed to shield him from her berating. Although she did everything she could to make Gary angry, he was too intent on seeing their relationship healed to react to her emotional outbursts. It was during the intensity of those days that Gary learned about spiritual warfare.

"The Holy Spirit taught me how to pray for Faye, and He constantly encouraged me that the love of God—which was dwelling in me—would overcome my wife's bitterness," Gary says. As he continued to pray and meditate on various scriptural promises of victory, an overcoming faith began to grow inside him. Even when his circumstances looked absolutely irreversible, he refused to accept defeat. He knew the Lord would change Faye's heart.

But Faye wanted a divorce—and she wanted Gary to pay for it. In 1976 they were divorced. But as they strolled out of the courtroom that day, Gary asked Faye to go to lunch with him. "After all," he said, "we're not married now. We're free to date." Gary tells what happened over the new few weeks.

> **Faye was actually bewildered by the way I treated her. As hard as she tried to resist, the love of God continued to melt her heart and short-circuit all her excuses. I would send flowers and notes, and shower her with affectionate remarks that, for all practical purposes, shouldn't have originated with a man who had been through so much pain with his wife. But I had forgiven her, and I was praying she would forgive me as well.**

Gary visited Faye and the children as often as possible after the divorce, always offering to vacuum or fold laundry or baby-sit. He could tell that she was beginning to warm up to his calculated advances. At some point during that spring, Faye began a period of deep soul-searching. "God's love was finally touching the most sensitive places of her broken heart," Gary  writes, "and she wasn't rejecting me as quickly or reacting as harshly. In time, remarriage actually became a clear option for Faye—finally!"

Faye and Gary remarried in July 1976. This time they knew it was different. They considered their marriage commitment irrevocable, and wouldn't even allow the word *divorce* to be spoken in their home. Many marriages have been restored as a result of their testimony.[5]

Love Takes Effort

Author and psychologist John Powell makes a powerful point:

> **Love works for people who work at it. In rendering to love its required "work" or effort, it is important that we seek unity, not happiness. Those who set out upon the journey of love must strive for that transparency, that sharing and community of life which is the heart of love. The work of love is to achieve a total honesty and transparency.[6]**

Love takes effort that is not always immediately rewarded with happiness. An example of this is my friend Ray Mossholder, the founder of Marriage Plus seminars, whose book on marriage I published several years ago, along with those on singleness and children.

> # Love takes effort that is not always immediately rewarded with happiness. Love works for people who work at it.

Ray testifies that he hated his wife Arlyne for the first twelve years of their marriage. He had rushed her into marriage because he wanted to have sex with her. She was a committed Christian; he wasn't. Two weeks after their wedding, he realized he didn't love her, and immediately began thinking about divorce. He had no foundation of love to go back to, only lust and loneliness. By the time their son turned four, the boy was developing ulcers because of Ray and Arlyne's constant fighting.

Ray trusted Christ as his Savior and became a committed Christian, but the problems in his marriage persisted. He stayed away from home doing "ministry" as much as he could. He worked at everything but his marriage, and even prayed for his wife to die. At one particularly low point, he decided to leave Arlyne for a young woman in his youth group–that is, until his pastor and the church elders confronted him and helped him decide against divorce.

Still, the marriage was nightmarish because Ray felt no love for Arlyne. He even diligently read through Scripture for a verse that would tell him divorce was an option, but he found nothing.

Finally, while speaking at a conference in Switzerland, Ray broke through in his understanding of what it meant to be a godly husband. He began to search the Scriptures to find out why God had instituted marriage and what a husband's responsibilities were. What he discovered eventually led the Mossholders to found a ministry that has touched literally thousands of lives around the world.

God was working for Ray's marriage, even when Ray was working against it.

And when Ray finally decided to work for his marriage, God began to bless it dramatically. I am sure if you asked Ray today, he would say that staying together and working for the marriage was worth the years of trial.[7]

Stages of Marriage

All marriages have stages, some more welcome than others. Joy and I have passed through many stages of our marriage–probably most of them in the first few years. We have moved from the romantic love of newlyweds, through the joys and struggles of an evolving relationship based on commitment. We have built our marriage on deep respect and appreciation of one another as unique and separate individuals. We've arrived at real, lasting love.

We have worked closely together, which has forced us to keep a strong relationship. We cannot take any pressures from home to work, and we sure cannot bring work-related stresses home! We have had to learn to compartmentalize our lives so that there are times we relate to each other (in the office) as professionals, yet at home we are husband and wife.

Now we are both midway through life, and we too are reaping the rewards of staying together, even through the rough periods and transitions. But we are finding that we must work to keep the marriage fresh and alive in all the ways that matter—communication, spirituality, companionship, passion and intimacy.

In life, there are plenty of transitions, and you must expect these transitions. You will not always be young. If you have children, they grow up. Interests and hobbies change.

Someone joked that women marry thinking the man they marry will change (for the better), and men marry thinking this wonderful, perfect woman will never change. Both are wrong.

In his book *The Seven Seasons of a Man's Life*, Patrick Morley writes:

> One day during midlife you will look at your spouse and think, *There's been a mistake! I can't be married to a person that old!* On the day one man hit this stage he said, "When I hugged my wife today I felt like I was hugging my mother. This can't be happening."[8]

Morley says that you may resent that your mate is getting older, especially if you think you are not. "I have got news for you," he tells us. "You are, too." Morley says that one of the biggest problems in reaching the middle years is the perception that your mate is getting older, while you have not changed that much.

When these things overtake you and your wife, Morley advises doing what Joy and I have done—reinvent your ideal of marriage as you move into the later stages of marriage. He says this may take time—maybe a couple of years. He writes that when he went through this stage, he started putting pressure on his wife, Patsy, to "recover" her youth. But just as we men cannot do it, neither can our wives.

Morley says that after going that direction for a year, he slowly began to accept his wife for whom she had become—as God had accepted him for whom he had become. We will go through periods when little black clouds (or towering thunderheads) of negative thoughts, anger and withdrawal will put us in conflict. But those times too shall pass.

"Give yourselves time to catch up emotionally to what you know to be true intellectually," Morley writes. "Remember, the ultimate objective of our marriages: To grow old with a friend, satisfied with the past."[9]

Intimacy in Marriage

Not long ago I was in a small group discussion where the discussion turned toward sex. I used the normal Christian euphemism for sex—"intimacy." One of the men present sent me an e-mail later chiding me for using "intimacy" in place of "sex," saying they were not always equivalent. This is true. Sometimes sex is cheap and sinful. Even in a marriage, sex can be more forgettable than intimate.

> Remember, the ultimate objective of our marriages: **To grow old with a friend, satisfied with the past.**

And yet good sex will always have intimacy at its core. How much more intimate can you get to totally disrobe and to enjoy sexual intercourse? If you are also close emotionally and are communicating at a deep level, then that sex is intimacy at its most pure, wonderful and holy level.

Marriage is the best thing that ever happened to sex, at least according to surveys. A university study found that 88 percent of married couples report having emotionally satisfying sex lives.

New Man magazine reported in 1995 that 94 percent said they were faithful in the past year. [10]

My friend Ted Roberts includes in his book *Pure Desire* the results of a 1992 survey called "Sex in America: A Definitive Survey," which found that married women had a significantly higher rate of orgasm than single women. "The marriage effect is so dramatic that it swamps all other data," said State University of New York sociology professor John H. Gagnon, one of the study's authors. [11]

Most married men know what good sex can do for a marriage. It enriches the relationship exponentially, allows for emotional intimacy and gives a man the chance to let down his guard and relax. Good sex is not just a perquisite of healthy marriage; it is a foundational requirement for having a healthy marriage. Without a good sex life, a marriage will be crippled, incomplete, stagnant, disjointed. Sex forces couples to confront and work through their deepest fears of rejection and shame. The bedroom can be a forum for conversations of the deepest order where closely held hurts and desires come to light.

In the same way that unhealthy signs in the economy might foreshadow a recession or depression, problems with a married couple's sexual relationship foreshadow other problems down the road. Anything that detracts from healthy sex hurts a marriage. Pornography, visualizing other women or any act done out of control or anger rather than love will pull a marriage apart.

Helpful Hints

A friend in Atlanta told me an interesting story about how his men's group helped each other focus on having a strong marriage. Apparently one of the men had learned through the "wife grapevine" that one of the men was so tight with money that he would not let his wife buy the things she felt she needed.

On top of that, he gave her a measly "allowance," as if she were a teenager. If she needed more money than that, he considered it a loan and docked it from the next week's "allowance." At the same time, he expected her to turn over to him the income from her part-time job, even though he made a very good salary as a professional.

One of the guys confronted him about this, and he admitted it was true; he felt his wife would spend the family into debt if he did not control the spending.

That was all the group needed. The men lit into him for the next hour, challenging him to love his wife and care for her rather than act like a cranky banker more interested in money than in her as a woman. The fact is, he was a control freak. He would rather have a surplus in the bank even if it meant his family going without. Yet his wife needed to feel loved, and his demeaning behavior did not show her love. No wonder they seemed to quarrel all the time.

This is an example of how a men's group functioned the way it should! The stingy husband took this correction to heart and loosened the purse strings with his wife. He bought her a brand-new car (and sold the old one for only $100, which tells you how bad it was!) and allowed her to keep the income from her part-time job to spend as she saw fit.

Amazingly she felt more loved, and much of the squabbling over money ended. Thankfully these men had good enough relationships within their men's group to be able to confront when they needed to. Who knows, their marriage may avoid much worse problems in the future than had the disagreements over money continued.

Advice About Marriage

Let's say you were in my men's group and were getting married. What kind of advice could you expect from me and the other guys in the group?

1. Put God first in the relationship.

If you are pursuing God with all your heart, and your wife is also, then Satan is not able to put a wedge between you. And if you are both moving toward God, you will be moving toward each other.

I am blessed to have a godly wife. She has an intimate relationship with God; she spends time with Him every day, and she prays for me and prods me spiritually when I need it. But I cannot rely on her relationship; I must pursue God on my own.

I believe the husband should also provide spiritual leadership in the home. This includes taking time to pray with your wife and to read the Bible and to talk about how it applies to your life and marriage. Joy and I find it fits our schedule best to do this in the evening before bedtime.

It can also be a powerful bonding experience to be intimate spiritually as well as just physically in the marriage!

2. Make a 100 percent commitment to the marriage.

It takes a 100 percent level of commitment to overcome the ups and downs that any marriage relationship endures. For Joy and me, when we said "'til death do us part," we meant it. And with God's help, our marriage will survive until one of us dies.

Every stage in life can be fulfilling if you start with that commitment.

I think it is important to talk about this with your wife. Ask what 100 percent commitment means to her. Discuss how you will handle various types of problems as they come up. Talk about the fact you are going to enjoy going through the various stages of a marriage—and that you will not stop until you reach real love.

Learn to recognize the growth that is taking place in your marriage, and enjoy each step of the way.

Joy and I have learned to do this.

In our twenties we did not have much money, but we were young and madly in love.

In our thirties, we had all the challenges of raising a young family, buying a home (and for us) starting a new business. But they were exciting go-go years.

In our forties, we are a little more comfortable financially, but we have the changes midlife brings, plus raising teenagers. Since our sons are eleven years apart, not long after one finished his teen years, we are just starting with the other one.

With God's help, in our fifties we look forward to the "empty nest" when we will be a little more free to come and go as we please. And we hope to continue to have good health as our relationship matures. It will also be a time to help our sons get settled into their careers and families.

In our sixties we hope we will feel it is a time of accomplishment as we begin to slow down a little and enjoy the fruits of years of hard work. It will also be a time for us to enjoy grandchildren.

In our seventies, eighties and beyond, we will have time of enjoying the rewards of a long-term relationship where we can pursue hobbies, minister to each other spiritually, travel and pass along to the next generation much of what God has given to us. We also plan to continue to be madly in love, even if it is a more "mature" love.

My long-time mentor Robert Walker, the former editor of *Christian Life* magazine, remarried at age eighty-three a couple years after his wife of fifty-seven years passed away. It's exciting to see the way he and his wife, Barbara, are so much in love as newlyweds! Joy and I hope to be that much in love, too.

Yes, every stage in life can be fulfilling if you start with that commitment.

3. Make each other a priority in the relationship.

Joy knows she is my number one priority over my work and even more than my sons. Understand that Cameron and Chandler are top priority. But I have only eighteen to twenty-two years of input in their lives, and then they are on their own with careers and families of their own. Joy is my wife for life. So she must be my top priority.

We try to communicate (although we have much to learn in this area, too), and we take time for each other with regular "dates" and just focusing time on the relationship. This includes having a getaway for just the two of us at least once a quarter. And we celebrate not only our wedding anniversary, but the anniversary of the day we met, along with Valentine's Day, our birthdays and other special days during the year. While we are not religious about a date night every week, we do fit it in as often as we can. That is because we just need time for each other.

4. Make the intimate part of the marriage fun for both of you.

Take time to learn to be thoughtful lovers. Since few of us have been "mentored" in this area of life, you can learn by reading excellent marriage books such as *The Act of Marriage* by Tim and Beverly LaHaye. (I met them at a convention recently and told them how much this book helped when Joy and I were first married. With a glimmer in her eye, Beverly told me if I enjoyed that book, I should read their new book about having a good marriage for those over age sixty!)

Doug Roseneau, who writes a column for *New Man* magazine, has an excellent book called *Celebration of Marriage,* which I have recommended to many men I have counseled who needed a little help in this area.

The fact is that the sexual relationship is the one thing that separates a marriage from the man and woman just "being friends." It is not the only reason to get married, of course. There are many other reasons, such as the need for companionship.

Sex is actually only a small part of marriage. Even the most sexually active couple relates far more in all the other areas of life than they do in this area (if you figure the small percentage of time in a 168-hour week). But it is one of the most pleasurable parts of marriage. And if it is good for both of you, it can provide a powerful bonding that will make all the other problems in the marriage easier to handle.

5. Work out ahead of time things you both want and need to lessen the chance for conflict later.

If you are communicating with each other, you can discuss ahead of time how you will handle finances or settle fights. Some couples even decide how much time is reasonable for the husband to spend "with the guys" either in sports or just hanging out, and the same with the wife. Then, if it is understood by both of you, it will not become a matter of conflict. Other couples I know have an understanding of how often they will make love, and even make appointments (such as every Saturday night). That way there is no misunderstanding.

Joy and I also have a division of labor that helps us. It is not what every couple would do, but it works for us. I take care of the outside of the house, and she takes care of the inside. Years ago when we did all our own painting and wallpapering, I did the painting, and she did the wallpapering. Today she gets the groceries, and I take out the trash and recyclables.

This is not rocket science. But you would be surprised at how many couples have fights over such trivial things because they have never worked out who does what.

Then, if you do not know how to resolve conflicts, that can be a problem, too. Joy and I try to talk through any problem before bedtime (don't let the sun go down on your wrath). If that does not work, we have close friends we go to for help before some small problem turns into World War III and threatens our happiness and our marriage. I encourage you to come up with your own version of what to do to lessen the chance for misunderstanding.

Remember, the Bible commands us to love our wives as Christ loved the church and gave Himself for it. That is a pretty high standard. Yet as new men in Christ, we can have wonderful, happy marriages. That is following the advice of God's Word: "The man who finds a wife finds a treasure and receives favor from the Lord" (Prov. 18:22).

Now let's talk about impacting your children's lives.

Talk about it Think about it

Working on Your Marriage: Making It Great

Author's note: This chapter helps you understand how to prevent conflict in your marriage and to move to a relationship based on unity, trust and commitment.

For more information on this topic (which we will add to as time passes) check out our www.oldmannewman.com website. Use the user id: **oldman** and the password **newman**. These are **case sensitive,** so use all lowercase letters and leave no spaces.

1. An often quoted expression about marriage is: "Happy wife—happy life!" Share why you agree or disagree with this.

2. The clip from *New Man* that launched this chapter lists ten ways people sabotage their marriages. These include:

   1) Be a flirt.

   2) Undermine your spouse in public.

   3) Use negative body language when your spouse is talking to you.

   4) Fail to communicate on a daily basis.

   5) Stop caring about your appearance.

   6) Having children in order to bring your marriage together.

   7) Men: Enjoy playing golf (or whatever takes your time) more than you enjoy your wife.

   8) Women: Spend more time with your friends (or whatever takes your time) than you spend with your husband.

   9) Find your self-esteem outside the marriage.

   10) Conceal your expectations.

Excluding way number eight, which one of these is most like you, and which one is least like you?

3. Is it hard or easy for you to pray with your wife? Why?

4. Share with the group things you have done to create special surprises for your wife—as well as favorite getaways and vacation spots that you enjoy.

5. What are the dreams, visions and goals of your wife? What are you doing to further them?

A clip from

New Man   July/August 1998

Bullish on Fathers

"I think about the fact that Grant [Hill], Kobe [Bryant], and I had strong fathers. I know people are concerned about the behavior of some young players, but it starts at home. I wish some of the other guys in the [NBA] could have had fathers at home, just to see what it's like, just to see how much better people they could be."[1]

**—Former Chicago Bulls
Superstar Michael Jordan**

Quality Time
Average daily time a parent spends communicating with each child: 14.5 minutes. Of that time, the amount spent in parental criticism or correction: 12.5 minutes.[2]

Fathers at home
▶ oldmannewman.com

Chapter 13

Impacting Your Children: Speaking the Father's Blessing

OLD MAN
Lacks wisdom to establish a close relationship with his children.

NEW MAN
Honors his father and speaks blessings into the lives of his children.

There is something very unique and special about a father and son relationship. Sons who had a good relationship with their fathers never forget it. It shapes their destiny. That is exactly what it does too for sons who did *not* have a good relationship with their fathers. It shapes it, but not in a positive direction.

One of the most important things a father can do for his sons is to help affirm when they become men. The problem is that in our society there is no point at which a boy becomes a man—in sharp contrast to the custom in Latin America where the most important day in a girl's life is her fifteenth birthday, called *quinceañera*. At that time she is considered to be a woman. Interestingly, nothing in the macho Latin culture has a similar event that confirms the time manhood takes place for the boys.

Jewish men know exactly when they become a man. It's called a *bar mitzvah*.

Last year my thirteen-year-old son, Chandler, attended his first bar mitzvah for one of his friends in the seventh grade. As I explained to Chandler what the bar mitzvah meant in the Jewish culture, it made me realize how few true celebrations we have in

Christian circles. Other than weddings and funerals, there are not many "events" that we celebrate to mark important milestones.

The Jewish culture emphasizes blessings by the father on the children. This is one of the reasons I believe the culture has survived so many centuries and why Jewish men I have known seem to have a sense of who they are and of their place in the world. They also have a sense that they are God's chosen people, as indeed they are.

I believe the health of any society depends on the health of the family. How much does the health of the family depend on the head of the family–the man–knowing his rightful role? How best to do this than to pass it down from father to son?

In this chapter I want to let you see what some fathers have done to help their sons make the transition into manhood with as little upheaval as possible.

The Father's Blessing

Patrick Means believes that sons need to receive a "father blessing" from their dads as part of a transition to manhood.[3] This was the Old Testament pattern with Abraham, Isaac and Jacob conferring their blessing–their approval of their sons–as a rite of passage into adulthood.

In the New Testament, this father blessing was modeled at Jesus' baptism in water in Matthew chapter 3. This is when Jesus inaugurated His public ministry. When Jesus rose out of the water, the Spirit of God in the shape of a dove descended upon Him, and a voice from heaven said, "This is my beloved Son, and I am fully pleased with him" (Matt. 3:16–17). "This benediction," writes Means, "sums up what all men need from their dads–a sense that they are *beloved,* and that the dads are well pleased with them."[4]

It has always struck me as poignant and wonderful that the Father was well pleased with Jesus before Jesus had done *any* of His earthly miracles or even begun His earthly ministry.

Preston Gillham writes about how he chased the mantle of

manhood from the time he was nine years old until after he had earned two college degrees. He pointed out several milestones when he realized he was getting closer to manhood. The first happened the Christmas he was nine years old and received a BB gun as a gift. On his twelfth birthday, he received a .22 caliber rifle–another milestone. Others included landing his first job and getting a driver's license. He had great expectations that at age eighteen the mantle of manhood would descend upon him.

"I was sure that upon arrival at age 18 manhood would come to rest upon my broadening shoulders," he wrote in *Things Only Men Know*. "After all, at 18 I could die for my country, vote, graduate, go to any movie I wanted, and drink beer if I chose to. I cut my long hair, grew a beard, paid my way through college, kissed a few girls, traveled some, and began thinking about a profession."[5]

But manhood seemed to be an elusive dream to him. Two college degrees later he was still searching for it. That's when he took matters into his own hands by taking full responsibility for his feelings of failure regarding his manhood, and he bestowed manhood on himself one day while he was out for a jog. "Although the honor was past due, I reasoned it was 'better late than never,'" he wrote. "And so I jogged home a man from a run that began as a boy."[6]

> **Frequent blessing should be a normal, routine part of a man's life. Coupled with a hug, pat, bump or kiss, these words communicate your unconditional acceptance.**

Gillham describes himself as an advocate of "creating a rite of passage that defines very clearly a fundamental change has occurred." He suggested that fathers prepare a blessing to give their sons to introduce them into manhood. More than the routine daily blessings that he believes men should pass on to their sons, the blessing of manhood is a formal declaration, given at one time and remaining with the sons as a point of reference. In other words, there can be many experiences of blessing, but only one blessing marking the passage into manhood. "You should regularly bless your ten-year-old son," Gillham advises, "but you should not transfer the mantle of masculinity to him."[7]

Gillham also believes that frequent blessing should be a normal routine part of a man's life. Coupled with a hug, pat, bump or kiss, these words communicate your unconditional acceptance and pride in your sons (and daughters). As Gillham suggested, some fathers have developed a method of blessing their sons that becomes a daily part of their family life.

David Welday, vice president of product development for Strang Communications, has worked for me for more than nineteen years. He began this practice several years ago with his three sons, David, Darren and Jason. Each morning before his sons leave for school, Welday imparts a spiritual blessing to each—something he considers a distinct act from praying for them, as many Christians fathers do. He points out that the Bible refers repeatedly to fathers who imparted a blessing to their children. Even Jesus "blessed" the little children who were brought to Him. He believes the act of blessing is more than imparting nice words or spiritual platitudes. The Bible speaks clearly of the authority of our words and of the power of those words to both bless and curse, to impact our natural world as well as the kingdom of heaven.

Welday says that parenting involves far more than raising our children to be "good," "successful" or even "Christian." We are to train our sons and daughters "in the way they should go." In other words, we are to ask God to show us the divine path, the destiny He has prepared before the foundation of the world, for each of our children. Each morning as he blesses his children, Welday uses that opportunity to speak into their young lives about the things God has shown him about the way they are to go.

Does Welday believe that this simple act of blessing his sons each day is having an impact? He believes it with all his heart. His boys may not express their desire for his daily blessing, but they let him know in other ways. A particularly poignant proof comes from his eldest son, David, who recently began high school. Welday takes the opportunity to drop David off at school on his way to work each morning.

"David is not particularly talkative in the morning (a huge understatement)," Welday says, "but I know my blessing is meaningful to him. If the radio is on as we approach the school, he will make a point of turning off the radio before we pull up so that I can bless him. Now, getting a teenaged boy to voluntarily turn off a radio—any radio—is truly an act of God!"

The New Covenant Bar Mitzvah

Gary Bergel, father of ten children and president of Intercessors for America, created his own Christian version of a bar mitzvah as a way to initiate his children into adulthood. First, he plans a trip to Israel with each of his boys on their twelfth or thirteenth birthday. While there, he schedules time for his son to be alone with God, often in the olive or citrus groves near the Sea of Galilee. Invariably, he says, the son is touched in some way by God.

When they get home, Bergel holds what he calls a "New Covenant Bar Mitzvah," inviting men who have been elders in the boy's life. They meet at a restaurant (Bergel picks up the whole tab to indicate that the son is important enough to spend a lot of money on). The son has been instructed in advance to prepare an outline of his testimony, plus Scripture verses that have meant something to him along the way. The evening is full of singing, remembering, looking forward and celebrating the completed childhood.

Without fail, Bergel says, the celebration changes their faith. They enter into a deeper relationship with Jesus. Bergel knows he cannot guarantee how his children eventually turn out, but I am convinced that his idea of a Christian bar mitzvah is powerful.

A Meaningful Moment in Time

James Ryle from Boulder, Colorado, is a close friend of mine. He is on the board of directors for Promise Keepers, and for many years was pastor to Coach Bill McCartney. Ryle is the one who persuaded me a couple of years ago to take up that expensive and frustrating habit called *golf*. Several years ago we did a big story on Ryle and his sons in *Charisma* magazine, dealing with the way that he has tried to help his own sons, Jonathan and David, attain manhood.

Ever since Ryle was a boy growing up in an orphanage, he promised to be a good father to his own sons. Now he wears many caps: father, disciplinarian, "dorm principal," "referee." "But all of the time, I'm a friend," he says. "That's the one hat I never take off."

"He's my best friend," David says.

Ryle has sought a genuine relationship with his sons. They talk honestly about their hopes, about sex, about wishing he could be home more often—something Ryle's preaching schedule does not always allow.

In a day when many grown men in America complain they never really got to know their dads, James Ryle has determined that his boys will never feel deprived of fatherly affection.[8]

In the June 1994 issue of *Charisma* magazine, James Ryle shared a secret that is helping his two teenage boys make the journey from childhood to manhood. Although that article was written several years ago, the principles that Ryle shares are things that can be used by fathers today. In fact, I think that many sons would be very grateful to have a father who cared enough to create this special experience.

A father's love
oldmannewman.com

David and Jonathan are the names Ryle gave his two sons. He says that the choice of their names was his way of blessing them at birth by expressing a father's hope that they, like their namesakes, would grow up to find their place in history. Ryle knows that their names alone cannot make his sons great. It takes prayer, vision, discipline and faithfulness on the part of their father who named them. And it takes trust, obedience, responsibility and desire on their part to grow up into the men God wants them to be. When these things work together, something wonderful happens. "I know, for I have seen it with my own eyes," Ryle writes. "It happened when my sons became men."[9]

Ryle believes that the passing from childhood into manhood should be a fixed point in time, a real place in history to which a man can look back with satisfaction. He points out that other societies have established a rite of passage to celebrate that event. But Western culture in general deprives boys of a definitive moment of transition into manhood. That is, of course, as long as we do not count what some men count as "entering manhood"—things like beer guzzling, immorality, wild parties or joining a gang. Not even the big events like getting a driver's license, graduating from high school or reaching age twenty-one are really worthy pivotal points in history that can count as "becoming a man."

> **Passing from childhood into manhood should be a fixed point in time to which a man can look back with satisfaction.**

Ryle says that he believes that for some men that time never comes. Many men today experience confusion and anxiety because they lack a definable moment when they "put away childish things." That is why we see grown men still living out the fears and fantasies of boyhood. Ryle did not want that to happen to his sons. He wanted to provide his sons with a meaningful ceremony that would forever stand out in their minds as the time and place they became men. As he prayed for wisdom on how to accomplish this, the Lord showed him what to do.

> I set aside their thirteenth birthday to give them each an unforgettable ceremony filled with symbolism and emotion—a Christian benchmark of maturity, somewhat akin to the Jewish bar mitzvah.[10]

Ryle tells us that this initiation into manhood included the following key elements:

Affirmation from the father

More important than *what* is said or done in this kind of ceremony is *who* is saying and doing it. Ryle believes that the greatest impact upon the son comes from knowing that it is his father who is saying the words and leading the service. A father's presence, along with his words and actions, carries great weight with his children.

Ryle and his own father never had a chance to be together while he was growing up. But God brought Ryle and his dad together in a wonderful way, and his father spent the final years of his life on earth praising and serving the Lord with all his heart and strength. Ryle tells what happened one night when his aging dad was staying with his family for an extended visit. As he went down to tuck his boys into bed, he passed the guest bedroom and heard his father's voice. He was praying. Ryle stood quietly, listening to a seventy-five-year-old man on the threshold of eternity talk quietly and sincerely to God. Of that moment, he says:

> Imagine my sense of wonder when I heard that my dad was praying for me!
>
> "Dear God," he said, "I pray for James. Where do I begin? How can I ever thank You for what You have done in his life? You have been a far better father to him than I could have ever been. As one dad to another, thank You for what You have done for my boy. I'm so proud of the man that You have made him."
>
> I stood speechless, completely overwhelmed with emotion. This transforming experience motivated me to do the same for my children.[11]

A desire for manhood

Ryle says that during his sons' ceremonial passages, he actually could see them "grow up" as they endeavored to act like men. They were not merely going along with his idea—they wanted this for themselves. And their desire and effort made it happen.

Support from friends

Ryle invited about eight close friends to join him for the ceremony. Each man came with symbolic gifts and specific blessings: a verse of Scripture, a prayer or some personal anecdote that he had prayerfully prepared beforehand. Each gift was presented to Ryle's son in light of its symbolic merit.

Ryle believes it is never too late to bless your son's life. Your son is never too old to hear you say, "I love you, and I am proud of the man you have become." God's Word tells us that the Spirit of God is moving on the hearts of men to turn "the hearts of the fathers to the children" (Mal. 4:6). Let Ryle's story inspire you to make the difference in the lives of your sons.

> Your son is never too old
> to hear you say, "I love you,
> **and I am proud of the man
> you have become.**

Mile Markers

For those of us who never had a formal transition into manhood, there is usually a point in our memories where we know the transition took place. For me, it was when I was eighteen years old. I had just graduated from high school, and my number one goal at that point was to attend the University of Florida where Steve Spurrier had won the Heisman Trophy a couple of years before, turning me into a lifelong Gator football fan.

Then my dad took a job more than two thousand miles away in California, messing up my neat plans for college.

After a great deal of anguish, a decision was made for me to stay in Florida and to attend the University of Florida. The day finally came when the moving van picked up the furniture and the family packed up the family car.

We had lunch together one last time, and after lunch I drove to my summer job bagging groceries while the family started their trip to California. I can remember following the family car for a few blocks before we had to go separate ways. As I watched the family drive off, I cried. I did not identify that moment until years later as the moment childhood ended and I became a man.

Suddenly I was on my own. At age eighteen, I did not leave home—my home left me. As young as I was, I was now responsible for my own schedule and actions. My parents still helped me with my college bills, but I was increasingly on my own financially—so much so that I was paying all my own bills by the time I was a senior.

It was painful to be alone so abruptly and at such a young age, but it made me grow up quickly. I was ready to settle down sooner than most young men my age. I was married three years later, almost to the day. And a couple of years after that I started a small Christian magazine for my local church. We called it *Charisma*. At age twenty-four I had found my life's work. I think it happened so young partly because I was forced to grow up and take care of myself at age eighteen.

Cameron's Transition to Manhood

The article on James Ryle and his sons in *Charisma* ran when Cameron was in high school, and I was eager to provide a similar rite of passage experience for Cameron. As I got to know Ryle and gradually heard about this rite of passage ceremony (long before the article ran), I told Cameron about it. But he did not share my enthusiasm. After a while, he greeted any mention of it in conversation with some remark about men going in the woods, beating their chests and baying at the moon. It was a reference, I am sure, to the stereotypical Robert Blythe "Iron Man" ceremonies that had become well known a few years earlier in the press.

I finally concluded that if Cameron did not want it, I could not force it on him.

Besides, I wanted something that fit his personality but would mark his transition to manhood. I just did not know what to do. Then Joy suggested that when he graduated from high school we have a little party in his honor. We reserved a room at a nearby hotel, had them cater a nice meal and arranged for fifty people to attend. Joy invited Cameron's grandparents and a few nearby aunts and uncles, totaling fifteen people—including her, Chandler and me.

Cameron was allowed to invite any thirty-five people he chose. I remember that for several evenings he pored over the invitation list with the intensity of Santa Claus checking his list to see what children were naughty or nice.

Finally the day arrived. The invited guests included a couple of favorite teachers and some high school friends. We showed some old video footage of Cameron growing up. Several people got to make little speeches about what a great guy he was or tell somewhat embarrassing stories about silly things he had done over the years. It was as much a *roast* as a *toast*. Then it was my turn.

I prepared a serious speech and told the story about James Ryle and how he helped initiate his sons into manhood. I said we never were able to do that for Cameron. I made some specific comments about how wonderful a son Cameron had been and how, as his father, I was very proud of him. I said that I considered that, having graduated from high school, he was now a man.

Then I prayed over Cameron. Being aware of the importance of the blessing, I made sure I prayed a blessing over his life. Then I shared a scripture I had learned from James Ryle.

In Jeremiah 12:5 it says, "If you have run with the footmen, and they have wearied you, then how can you contend with horses?" (NKJV).

Ryle uses it a little out of context, but in today's paradigms, it seems to tell us not to be wearied with mere footmen, but to charge into the future like horses. I had the scripture typeset so I could frame it for Cameron, and asked one of the art directors for the magazine to include a horse shaped like the logo for the Ford Mustang.

I presented it to Cameron, who was very moved by my speech— but unaware of the surprise waiting just outside the emergency exit for the small banquet room we were using. Then he recognized the Mustang logo and began to suspect something was going on. So I invited him and his guests to step outside to see a brand-new turquoise Mustang with a huge white bow around the car to make it look like a gift.

Joy and I had saved money and planned for some time to get him a new car when he graduated from high school. He had driven an inexpensive used compact car—a Dodge Spirit—during high school, and he needed a better car.

The Mustang was surprisingly reasonably priced, even though at the time it was considered a cool car. Besides, we rationalized, if we had been Jewish we would have spent far more on an elaborate bar mitzvah for Cameron than the cost of a new car!

The gift also gave us a lavish way to show Cameron our lavish love for him. We had encouraged him to avoid smoking or drinking. He had never been promiscuous or caused us heartache as many teenaged boys (including me) had done to their parents. This was our way of saying thanks! While I was not able to try out the "James Ryle style" rite of passage model on Cameron, our party accomplished the same thing in a way with which Cameron was comfortable. It marked the end of childhood and ushered him into being a man.

In college Cameron quickly took a leadership role at Oral Roberts University. He worked on the school paper and was its editor during his junior year because he was so mature—even though most editors are seniors. Now, only a couple years out of college, he has started his own media company. Can you tell I'm a proud papa?

The graduation party was a major "mile marker" in Cameron's life—and that is what I wanted. So maybe my example with Cameron shows that there are many variations of doing the rite of passage. You may not be able to do it as Ryle does—or as I did—but you can do something to let your son know he has become a man.

I have missed most major markers in life, or stumbled on them accidentally, so when there is an excuse to celebrate, I try to take it. I think it is important to reflect on God's goodness when there is reason to celebrate.

> " If we do not set up proper mile markers, our boys will set up their own. And if we do not experience healing of our own father-wounds, we will certainly pass them on. "

For this reason, we have celebrated *Charisma* magazine's anniversary every five years. We had a big dedication when we finished our new office building, and we celebrate all the birthdays ending in zero. None of those birthdays, however, are as meaningful as letting a boy know when he becomes a man. Without a meaningful mile marker, Christian boys are left—as are all the other boys in the culture—to pick one of their birthdays as their transition into manhood.

If we do not set up proper mile markers, our boys will set up their own. And if we do not experience healing of our own father-wounds, we will certainly pass them on, as I dealt with at the beginning of this book.

Of course, many of us had good dads. And even when our dads were less than perfect, we should still honor them, as the Bible says. In fact, I believe that forgiving our fathers is the starting point for becoming new men in other areas of our lives—it is definitely a key to a long life *and* a life that works (Eph. 6:2–3).

It is very difficult to heal from other types of wounds when the father-wound is still intact. We have a choice. We can let it fester, not address it and stunt our growth toward becoming a new man. Or we can delve into this issue with courage, choosing the right setting, whether it is with a friend, an accountability group or a Christian counselor.

I am so grateful to God that the issues that existed between my dad and I were cleared up before his sudden death in 1997. Yet now, several years later, I still have regrets. Did we gloss things over only on the surface? Did he really know how much I loved him? Did he really approve of me as a man? We did not talk a lot about these sorts of things. I think he felt uncomfortable about it, and so did I.

Yet just before he died, he and my mom spent an enjoyable weekend together, driving around the area looking for a place for them to live. My dad was having some health problems, and we suggested we help them find a house nearby so we could keep an eye on them. We also went shopping, and I talked my dad into buying some comfortable summer clothes for the hot Florida summers.

When my father-in-law passed away several years ago, the family was called to his bedside three times, being told he had only hours to live—and he continued to live several months. I subconsciously thought I would have the same warning when my dad died. Yet he dropped dead of an apparent heart attack the day after Mother's Day, so I never had an opportunity to say good-bye to him.

I cannot complain. Overall we had a good relationship. Yet there was still that empty place that was never really filled, and there was not the closure I wanted. But compared to many men, we had a good relationship, and there was no animosity. We had handled any major issues, and when he died so unexpectedly, I was at peace that it was his time to go. He had lived a long and happy life, faithfully served God, was married to the same women nearly forty-eight years and raised three children, all of whom have successful marriages and are serving God.

I mentioned all this at his memorial service, and it caught the attention of one of my friends who had driven from Jacksonville the two hundred or so miles to the small town of Brooksville, Florida, to attend the service to be supportive of me. My friend had been born out of wedlock. His mother had four children by four different fathers. One of her sons died of AIDS, another was a drug addict. Only my friend had escaped a similar fate. God saved him out of a life of drug addiction, and he trusted Christ while in college.

But my friend had never been reconciled to his father, who was two decades younger than his mother and who later had settled down, married and raised a family of his own.

My comments got my friend to thinking how important resolving these issues were. He came to me, and we talked about it. I encouraged him to take the initiative to call his father and ask if he could visit him. He did so, and his father invited him up for the weekend in another state. Over the course of a weekend, they talked through whatever outstanding issues they had. His father asked for his forgiveness for not being there as the boy was growing up. And he told my friend that he loved him.

A year later his dad also dropped dead of a heart attack. But my friend was able to accept his death because he had been reconciled to him. At the funeral, he was even accepted as a member of the family. Later, my friend thanked me for my remarks at my dad's funeral because it prompted him to seek a reconciliation he would not otherwise have had.

Empowering Your Sons

I let my son Cameron look over this chapter before we went to press, and he had some excellent suggestions that warmed my heart as a dad. I have already talked about how Cameron and I were not as close as I had wished when he was small. But we seem to be making up for lost time now that he is on his own and has started his own multimedia company.

Cameron wrote me in an e-mail about the book:

> I have an idea for your book. It is an aspect of fatherhood you are excellent at that you need to tell other fathers about. You are great at empowering your sons, something that not a lot of fathers grasp.
>
> Many fathers are controlling. They try to preplan their children's lives or belittle their career choices when they do not line up with their own preferences. You have never done that. You have spoken big dreams into my life. You have pushed me to follow God's call. You have led by example, which speaks louder than any words ever could.
>
> You really should add to the chapter about helping your sons transition into manhood. You need to add the aspect of empowering them to reach their fullest potential. This is something you have done my entire life. (Remember helping me to do the school paper in fourth and sixth grades? Not many dads would take the time). You need to challenge others to do the same. I am who I am today because you care enough about me to push me into my unique destiny. That is something I will forever be grateful for.

If you could see me now at this computer, you might see that my eyes are a little watery, but you could not see the lump in my throat as I write these words. Thanks, Cameron, for this advice.

Now it is time to deal with a very practical aspect of "getting your act together" as a new man in Christ—taking care of your body.

Talk about it   **Think** about it

Impacting Your Children: Speaking the Father's Blessing

Author's note: The father's blessing is a wonderful gift to give your son or daughter. In this chapter you have learned how several men have developed a way to speak blessing into their children's lives.

For more information on this topic (which we will add to as time passes) check out our www.oldmannewman.com website. Use the user id: **oldman** and the password **newman**. These are **case sensitive,** so use all lowercase letters and leave no spaces.

1. In what ways do you want to be like your father? In what ways do you not?

2. The clip from *New Man* that began this chapter reports that parents spend 14.5 minutes communicating with each child, and that the vast majority of this time is spent criticizing or correcting our children. How would you characterize the quantity and quality of your communication with your children?

3. What "father blessings" would you like your son to hear from you?

A clip from

New Man   January/February 1999

Pride + Men=Bad Health

Did you know that one-third of the male population has not been to the doctor in five years? In 1990, the American Medical Association concluded that men refuse seeing a doctor because it threatens male pride. It seems male aversion to doctors has been a running joke since the advent of medicine. But, as recent statistics bear out, the consequences can be far from funny. For instance:

- Man's life span is seven years shorter than a woman's.
- Men have a higher risk of cardiovascular disease than women.
- Men suffer from heart attacks 2.5 times more than women.
- Men have a higher risk of stress-related illness than women.
- Men are 30 percent more likely to have a stroke.
- 50,000 men die each year of emphysema, one of the most preventable diseases.

The bottom line: Avoiding doctors and ignoring changes in your health isn't macho; it's foolish (and possibly deadly).[1]

Health awareness

▶ oldmannewman.com

Chapter 14

Caring for Your Body: Getting Into Shape

OLD MAN   Exercises too little; eats too much; and
          has more fat than muscle.

NEW MAN   Establishes a fitness plan for building a
          healthy physical "temple."

Many Christians don't realize that taking care of your body is a spiritual discipline. This isn't taught much in the church, and most men don't have a physical fitness mentor. Too often men don't get into shape until they suffer their first heart attack and the doctor tells them they must get into shape or die young.

Physical fitness is important to God, and it should be important to us. Our bodies are indeed the temple of the Holy Spirit—but we don't want that temple to be a "mega-church."

David Stevens, M.D., a contributor to *New Man*, points out that 1 Corinthians 6:13, 15 and 20 tell us that our bodies were made for the Lord, and the Lord cares about our bodies. "Your bodies are actually parts of Christ. . . . So you must honor God with your body."

Proverbs 23:23 says, "Get . . . discipline." First Peter 5:8 says, "Be self-controlled and alert" (NIV).

God isn't talking about having a pro-wrestler-like body for the purpose of gaining power, success and admiration of women. Much more important than those things are the eternal issues at stake.

"God wants you to be healthy so you can serve Him better and longer," Stevens writes. God even promises that when you ask He will give you the power to be self-disciplined.

I come from a conservative Christian background that emphasized "holy living"—never going to the movies, no dancing and so forth. But there was a glaring blind spot when it came to taking care of the body. Of course, they emphasized no smoking—long before that was the vogue—and consumption of alcohol was totally taboo. Undoubtedly not drinking or smoking meant many of the Christians I grew up around were more healthy than people who drank or smoked.

But when it came to eating, some people I knew were anything but healthy. Mealtime was the major social event in our lives, both in the family and with friends. Evening services at church often ran late, and it was common to go out and get something to eat at Howard Johnson's—fried chicken, greasy gravy, ice cream and sugary pie.

God wants you to be healthy
so you can serve Him
better and longer.

I didn't see exercise modeled by many people in the church. Preachers used to justify this (usually tongue in cheek) by quoting 1 Timothy 4:8: "Physical exercise has some value, but spiritual exercise is much more important." Many of the preachers I knew were overweight and soft.

I was never encouraged to take up a sport, although I did play Little League baseball one year. People in our denomination were encouraged to attend church every time the doors were open. I don't remember anyone encouraring me to staying fit.

So by the time I graduated from college, I had no habit of

exercise and played no sports. The only reason I wasn't obese was my high metabolism. I had narrow shoulders and thin arms and what extra weight I carried, I carried around my middle. I didn't like going to the beach because I didn't like being seen without a shirt.

My first job out of college was to cover the police beat at the Orlando, Florida, *Sentinel Star* on a shift that started at 4 P.M. and ended at 1 A.M. When I got home, I was too pent-up to go to sleep, so I thought getting a little exercise would make me feel better.

I was so out of shape that I was winded by the time I'd run around the block. I also knew I didn't eat right. (I ate lots of sticky pastries out of the vending machine at the newspaper.)

About that time I read an article about elderly Senator William Proxmire from Wisconsin who jogged to the Capitol each day in Washington. The article told how he had been out of shape, but began to whip himself into shape slowly by jogging first to the next mail box and then walking to the next, then jogging to the next. Slowly he was able to jog the distance of two mailboxes, walk to the next and so forth. He was able to build up to running a block or two and then a mile or two without stopping.

I tried this simple formula, and it worked. I was able to build up slowly to where I was running several miles at a time, several days a week. I chose a path that led away from my apartment so that if I were too tired to keep running I would at least have to walk the distance back home.

I didn't realize I was getting aerobic exercise and it was speeding up my metabolism, making me healthier. But it encouraged me to do more—joining the YMCA where I would work out several days a week. It was there that I started playing racquetball, which is a regular habit of mine to this day. I even included a racquetball court and workout room in the construction of our warehouse building, at very little extra expense, so I and the other employees at the company can play racquetball or work out before or after work.

But an added dimension was needed: eating right. That didn't happen until Joy took a nutrition class at the University of

Central Florida with Pam Smith, a registered dietitian and founder of Nutritional Counseling Services in Orlando, Florida.

Smith, we learned later, is a Spirit-filled Christian, and we've since become good friends with her and her husband, Larry. Several years later we invited her to do a wellness program for our staff, testing our cholesterol levels and teaching us how to eat low-fat, balanced diets that would help improve our health. It was the first time I had my blood tested. I learned that with proper diet I could keep my cholesterol and triglyceride levels in line.

The relationship with Pam has led to our publishing seven books with her through Creation House, selling hundreds of thousands of copies and helping to launch Pam as a national expert on nutrition.[2] (Her seven books are listed in the Appendix, and you can get more information online.)

Meet Pam Smith
oldmannewman.com

The success of these books and my own interest in good health also caused us to launch an entire imprint of health books in 1999 called Siloam Press (so named for the pool of Siloam in the Bible where the angel of healing would visit and heal those who got into its healing waters.)

As with so many other things, some need in my life (such as my need to get into better shape physically) has been used by God, I believe, to help many other people also learn sound concepts of good health from a Christian perspective.

God Cares About Our Bodies

Your "bod" is important to God, and it should be important to you. I am always stunned to hear about a man in his fifties who has died, apparently out of the blue. This happened recently when I read an obituary for a man only three years older than me who died of a heart attack after playing a hard game of racquetball. I knew the man, although not well. Several years ago I'd played a spirited game of doubles in racquetball with him, a friend and Hue Grier, one of my key staff members who has placed first in the state of Florida for his age group in racquetball.

I hadn't kept up with my friend so I don't know what sort of shape he was in. So I am aware that men die for genetic reasons that cannot always be prevented by good physical fitness. Nevertheless, it seems that the stakes are higher the older we get, and it would be foolish to exclude exercise.

Your "bod" is important to God, and it should be important to you.

My friend Gary Beesley was more fortunate. At age forty-nine he went through quintuple bypass surgery. The doctor told him it was a miracle he hadn't had a major heart attack. Beesley pastors in Orlando after being Benny Hinn's associate for several years, so he believes in healing.

Beesley told me, however, that the scare he went through made a more long-lasting impression than if the Lord had just healed him. The reason: He became more aware of the genetic tendency he had for a heart condition—his dad died at age sixty-nine of a heart condition, and his grandfather died at age sixty-two of the same condition.

Even more important is that Beesley sees now that he was so busy with ministry responsibilities, which included travel and many hours at the computer, that he didn't take care of himself physically. When he traveled to crusades with Benny Hinn, he often ate huge meals late at night because it was the only time he could find time to eat. And he did very little exercise. Slowly his weight ballooned to eighty-five pounds over his ideal weight.

The tendency for most men is to not exercise or eat right as they get older. David Stevens, M.D., writing in *New Man* recently, said that men have a higher death rate for all of the fifteen leading causes of death. On average, men die seven to eight years younger than women do. And compared to women, men know a lot less about their health and simply don't take responsibility for their bodies.

If you think Christian men fare better, think again. A study from Purdue University showed that religious people are more overweight and out of shape than nonreligious people. "Instead of reflecting the image of God, His children often look like a bunch of pot-bellied Buddhas!" Stevens writes.

Most men also avoid going to the doctor. In our twenties, most of us men feel we'll live forever and never be sick. Yet most of us are not in good shape physically. So as you try to get your "act together" as a new man in Christ, there are some practical things you should know about taking care of your body. You'll look and feel better, and there are studies that show that (all other things being equal) that you'll live longer.

My interest in good health has also spilled over to *New Man* magazine. It regularly carries articles by my friend Joe Christiano, a motivational speaker and internationally recognized fitness trainer and the author of *My Body . . . God's Temple, The Seven Pillars of Health* and *The Answer Is in Your Bloodtype. New Man* also has a regular column on "Divine Health" by my own physician, Don Colbert, M.D., whose books are also published by Creation House and Siloam Press.

Recently in *New Man* magazine, managing editor Rob Andrescik suggested we run an article entitled "God and Your Bod," written by Dr. David Stevens. The entire article is available online, but here are some highlights:

Stevens tells us that the report cards are here—but the news isn't good. Men are failing when it comes to their health. He concentrates on giving men some important steps to help them bring up their grade. These steps include:

Exercise

A study of more than twenty-one thousand men showed that fitness—not leanness—is the secret to longevity. Stevens suggests that men should exercise their hearts through aerobic exercises like brisk walking, jogging, bicycling or swimming.

Then, build your muscles by lifting weights. Choose a program that works every muscle group. Repetitions build endurance, and increased resistance builds muscle mass. Repetition–aerobic exercise–leads to long thin muscles like runners have. Progressive overload–lifting heavier weights–enlarges and rounds muscles.

If you can do only one type of exercise, go the aerobic route. Aerobic exercise increases energy, causes fat loss, strengthens your heart and makes you "feel younger."  For more information on developing an exercise plan go to the website to check out the Couch Potato Busters.[3]

Diet

Studies have shown that most men want to lose weight, but aren't doing it. In fact, we're getting fatter and fatter. More than 50 percent of men are overweight or obese. And, like our belt sizes, that number expands every year.

How do you know if you're fat? Use the table on the last page of this chapter to determine your Body Mass Index. If it is over twenty-five, you're overweight. Over thirty, and you're obese.

Stevens tells us that fat causes many problems like high blood pressure, heart attacks, diabetes, snoring, sleep apnea, arthritis and clogged arteries from high cholesterol. Fat decreases your life expectancy and damages your libido.

"In plain English," Stevens writes, "you aren't going to live as long or have nearly as much fun."

Stevens advises us to forget crash diets, which damage muscles and slow metabolism, and to choose instead a balanced diet. He suggests that you include carbohydrates (fruits, vegetables and whole grains) to equal two-thirds of your food intake. Lean meats and other proteins should make up another 15 percent of your total calorie intake. Keep sugars to a minimum. And don't focus on the scales–focus on maintaining a good diet routine.

Physical exam

With a physical exam, a blood sample and an occasional test, you can avoid or detect problems before they get serious and damage the only body you have. Quit putting off routine maintenance! An ounce of prevention is worth a pound of pills.

In his *New Man* article, Stevens tells us that just as the right oil will make your motor last longer, there are some vitamins and supplements that can make your body run longer and better. Here are some of his recommendations.

After you turn forty, take a baby aspirin (81 mg. daily) to lower your chance for heart attack and stroke. A multivitamin with trace elements is a good idea as well. Vitamin E (400 I.U. daily) and Vitamin C (250–500 mg. daily) have antioxidant effects that may help to prevent cancer, heart disease and cataracts, and even slow the aging process.

Rest

Stevens advises, "Your peace of mind is also a part of living healthy." He gives two pieces of advice. First, you need seven to nine hours of sleep a night. If you are not getting enough sleep, go to bed two hours earlier and get up an hour sooner to exercise, have devotions and pray. It will revolutionize your life.

Examine your priorities

Your body is too important to ignore. Stevens recommends two books that can change your life. Both were written by Dr. Richard Swenson. They are *Margin* and *Overload Syndrome*. One very important priority for each of us is this: Take time today to talk to God about how you can make your bod a priority.[4]

Physical fitness has been Joe Christiano's world for several years. He is internationally known as a personal fitness trainer and speaker, and has worked with Hollywood celebrities, media personalities, international executives and people just like you. He has held the titles of Mr. Florida, first runner-up in the Mr. USA championships and fourth runner-up in the Mr. America bodybuilding championship. He believes that you can create a better quality of life only with a balance of physical and spiritual fitness.

> Our bodies are like massive pillars holding up the super-structure. Our physical well-being is dependent upon the strength and condition of each pillar. If a pillar is cracked or crumbling, the temple is subject to collapse. But when well maintained, these pillars of health will defend us from sickness, disease and a breakdown in the quality of life.[5]

In his book *Seven Pillars of Health*, Christiano lists seven pillars that play a vital role in protecting our health. They include:

■ Weight management

■ Diet

■ A clean "in"vironment (our "in"vironment is our environment inside our bodies)

■ A strong immune system

■ Exercise

■ Rest and relaxation

■ Anti-aging strategies

Christiano has pursued physical fitness many years. But he says a day came when something inside made him cry out, "What's it all for?" His answer may be the answer you've needed to get control of your physical fitness needs because it involved having priorities in order.

Christiano said he came to understand that he must give God first place in his life by giving Him his life and accepting Jesus as Savior. Then, remembering that God is the very giver of life itself, he began to understand that exercising and a healthy lifestyle are merely matters of being a "careful caretaker" of the healthy body that God had so graciously given him.[6]

My own personal physician, Dr. Donald Colbert, is extremely interested in a man's physical fitness. In his latest book, *What You Don't Know May Be Killing You*, he writes: "You were not placed on earth to be anemic, feeble and helpless. God wants you to live "more abundantly"—disease free and in maximum health."[7]

In his foreword to Colbert's book *Walking in Divine Health*, Benny Hinn tells about his own experience with health problems, teaching him to take care of his physical body—God's temple. During the 1980s Hinn began experiencing some occasional irregularities in his heartbeat, causing his heart to skip a beat every now and then.

As the condition continued, he became increasingly concerned about why God had not healed him. Although he was a part of a healing ministry, he was forced to take a pill every day. It didn't make any sense to him. He complained to God in prayer, totally frustrated: "Lord, I've prayed and I've prayed and I've prayed, and You have not healed me!" In the foreword he tells us what happened next:

> To my surprise the Lord rebuked me and said, "Don't blame Me for what is your own fault." I was shocked! I can still remember thinking, *My own fault? What have I done wrong?* I soon came to realize that I was neglecting to do what was right. I had not taken proper care of my body, and my ongoing neglect began to manifest itself through physical symptoms. Remember, faith begins where natural ability stops. I began an exercise program and started eating correctly. As I continued to modify my behavior, I noticed that my heart problem was less noticeable. Before long, it vanished completely.[8]

What would God say to you about your level of physical fitness? Have you been doing all that you can do to live healthy and be fit? Maybe it's time to begin.

Maintaining your physical fitness can become a consistent part of your life—even if you live a very busy, full life. I know that's true because my life is very busy—yet I've learned to make physical fitness a part of my daily life.

After I started jogging in the early 1970s, I joined the YMCA and later a health club where I could work out on a regular basis. I have found that when I exercise vigorously three times a week, it helps the way I feel. I handle stress better, and my energy level is higher. If I fail to work out for a week or so, I feel sluggish. That motivates me to get back into the gym—just so I feel better.

> ## God wants you to live "more abundantly"—disease free and in maximum health.

My lifestyle is so busy that often I must do two things at once. So when I exercise I am usually doing something else. Sometimes I will invite a friend or colleague to work out with me. That gives me a chance either to socialize with them, thus strengthening the relationship, or sometimes I am able to mentor a man whom I could not otherwise mentor, just due to time constraints.

Often, if I work out alone in the early morning or weekends in the fitness center our company provides for the staff. When I do, I will listen to a good teaching tape by someone like Jack Hayford or a motivational tape by Zig Ziglar. I have a tape series by both in the fitness center that I have listened to several times as I've worked out my body—working out my mind and spirit at the same time!

At other times I've listened to Bible tapes. I like to get God's Word hidden deep in my heart, and listening to the Bible on tape is a good way to do it.

The stronger our body, the better able we are to do everyday tasks, recreational activities and sports. The better shape our heart and lungs are in, the greater stamina we will have. Joe Christiano believes firmly in the benefits of exercise. He states that exercise does become a way of life—a wonderful way of life.

Once you start exercising on a regular basis, your body will enjoy the wonderful physical stimulation it receives from it.

Christiano asks, "Have you heard of 'the pump'? That's the physiological response of your muscles' being gorged with blood after you exercise. It's such a healthy feeling–having your muscles tight and firm. And just like stirring up and getting rid of sediment in your gas tank, your body gets to release many of the toxins that have been stored up. You experience a fresh sense of well-being."[9]

Christiano gives us seven principles that can help you with your fitness journey, which I try to do each time I work out. Start trying these today:

- Exercise a minimum of three times weekly.

- Exercise for a minimum of fifteen minutes.

- Warm up and cool down.

- Drink 12 to 16 ounces of water about twenty minutes before each workout session.

- Practice safety during exercise.

- Do a variety of exercises.

- Include family and friends.[10]

From the start of your fitness journey, remember that you are in a constant state of transition. You will have some hurdles to jump. There will be times when you won't see any progress, you won't get any compliments and you'll feel like quitting because you think you'll never reach your goals.

When any negative thoughts come in, just remember that you are in a state of transition. You're not there yet, but you're getting there. Keep the momentum going. I can testify that it is well worth the effort.

Here's an exercise from *New Man* magaine you may want to do. If you use it and like it, you will find it just a sample of other material we have added to our www.oldmannewman.com website. That is because there is just so much we can cram into a book. But there is no limitation like that on a website. In addition, we can keep adding material as we think it will add something to the reader. So use the website. In that way, this book becomes as interactive as a book can be. We've told you before how to find it, but it bears repeating: Use the user name: **oldman** and the password: **newman.** Since it is **case sensitive,** use all lowercase letters and no spaces between words on the user id and password. And, if you like the material you see, tell us when you log onto our website.

Take our quick test and find out for yourself.[11]   **Fit or Fat?**

To calculate your Body Mass Index (BMI), grab a pocket calculator and follow these steps:

1. Multiply your weight in pounds by 0.45.
2. Determine your height in inches: (12" x ft.) + in. = height in inches.
3. Multiply your height in inches by 0.025.
4. Multiply the answer by itself.
5. Divide the answer from step #1 by the answer of step #4.

If your BMI is:

- 19–24 you have minimal health risk
- 25–26 low risk
- 27–29 moderate risk
- 30–34 high risk
- 35–39 very high risk
- 40+ extremely high risk

Fit or Fat
oldmannewman.com

Talk about it   Think about it

Caring for Your Body: Getting Into Shape

Author's note:Yes, God does care how we take care of His temple—our bodies. Learn how to make lifestyle changes that will keep you in optimum health and fitness.

For more information on this topic (which we will add to as time passes) check out our www.oldmannewman.com website. Use the user id: **oldman** and the password **newman**. These are **case sensitive,** so use all lowercase letters and leave no spaces.

1. On page 247 this statement appears: "Your 'bod' is important to God, and it should be important to you." State why you agree or disagree with this.

2. The clip from *New Man* magazine that launches this chapter notes that on the whole men do not do a good job of monitoring their bodies and forming a vital health partnership with their doctors. Share with the group:

- When was the last time you went to the doctor?

- When was the last time you had a physical?

- What is your cholesterol level?

- What is your PSA level?

- What vitamins and supplements do you take? (The chapter recommends a multivitamin, a baby aspirin, Vitamin C and Vitamin E.)

Hold each other accountable to have a physical in the next few weeks *and to talk to your doctor about an exercise program.*

3. Page 255 gives you a formula to calculate your Body Mass Index. Share the results with the group, noting carefully what risk group each of you falls into. (The purpose of this is not to heap condemnation—it is to determine what is real so you can do something about it.)

4. On page 250 there appears this advice, "Your peace of mind is also a part of living healthy. First, you need seven to nine hours of sleep a night. If you are not getting enough sleep, go to bed two hours earlier and get up an hour sooner to exercise, have devotions and pray. It will revolutionize your life." Could you implement this in your life? Why or why not?

5. What do you think the benefits to you would be of having more sleep, regular exercise and a consistent devotional life?

A clip from

New Man May 1997

Generation Next, Please

Some call them Generation X. Now others are calling them Generation NEXT. "We don't have time for things that are fake," says Bill Haley of his generation. The 28-year-old Haley, director of outreach for The Falls Church (Episcopal), in Falls Church, Va., is organizing a conference for about 400 twenty-somethings in Washington, D.C. this year.

Says Haley: "Don't tell me Jesus loves me if you don't love me. We have been marketed to death, so that we can smell something fake a mile away. The church needs people like that."

But Haley's generation also seeks the wisdom of older leaders. "Sixty percent don't have a father," he says. "So mentor me, please!"[1]

Mentors wanted

oldmannewman.com

Chapter 15

Developing Male Relationships

OLD MAN — Feels isolated, alone with his problems and unable to trust anyone.

NEW MAN — Reaches out to others to be mentored and to mentor in turn.

I read once of a friendship that stands as a model through the centuries. According to the Roman statesman and author Cicero, Pythias was a young statesman in Rome who got into trouble with the government and was condemned to die. While he was awaiting execution, he indicated a desire to go home to his family and bid farewell to them.

His friend, Damon, took his place in prison as security for him while he was gone. The emperor, Dionysius, was so touched by this display of friendship that he granted them both a pardon, with the proviso that they include him in the secret of their friendship.

I believe most men want close friends in spite of the fact that as a group men tend to process things more individually than women might do. Even though much of a man's life is spent projecting a confident, strong, handle-what-comes image to himself and others, deep down he doesn't like being an island. Men long for "buds" that go beyond having someone to hang out with (although that's part of it).

For most men, myself included, it is difficult to swallow our pride or public image and work on the one area necessary for a real relationship: vulnerability.

Many of us don't know how to be vulnerable, and even if we did, we wouldn't want to be! Vulnerability involves real risk: risk of the soul, not just physical safety. Most men prefer risks that take place in the arena of business, sports or adventure, where failure may mean a bruised ego or body, but not outright rejection.

Vulnerability involves real risk: risk of the soul, not just physical safety.

I'm sure most men would rather hang glide, bungee jump, shoot whitewater rapids or skydive before they would open up with somebody about their real life struggles.

On the other hand, men can have terrific, sharpening, healthy and lasting relationships with other men. When we do, it meets one of our most profound needs. Healthy, long-lasting male relationships need to be established on a basis of trust.

That's true with any relationship, male or female. You can't have a relationship without trust. Therefore it is vitally important that we take the time to develop our trustworthiness and to exercise trust in another as that person learns to develop his trustworthiness.

With trust, it's easier to be vulnerable with one another. If I trust you, then I'm willing to show you who I really am—to a greater degree than I show my casual acquaintances. I will believe that I can trust you to keep my secrets, and I will be willing to keep yours. With a foundation of trust and vulnerability, closeness in relationship is possible.

Sam, a friend of mine, told me that many men want a meaningful men's ministry, but churches fail to provide it, so many men choose to remain an island—even in the church.

"We have our Sport Utility Vehicles and our power tools to protect us," Sam told me. "The hurt and problems run so deep in many men today (myself included) that it drives us away from the solutions that we need. I desire to one day have more real and honest relationships with men in my church."

Sam and other men like him need companionship and friendship with other men. Men need to be discipled by other men who will commit to spend time with them, hear their problems, pray with them, stick with them through thick and thin and encourage them to grow and become new men in Christ, fulfilling their destinies from God.

Encourage Spiritual Growth

As we develop relationships with other men, it will be important that we are growing spiritually ourselves, as well as encouraging our male friends to grow.

What are some practical things you can do to encourage yourself—and other men—to grow? First you can make it a point to develop a habit of daily communion with God. For me, that's first thing in the morning. Ideally I get up an hour early to study and pray.

I try to read through the Bible at least every other year. For me, I enjoy *The One Year Bible,* which includes a segment from the Old Testament and another from the New Testament each day so that you read through the Bible in one year. It also adds a passage from Psalms and Proverbs daily that will take you through those books twice a year.

This disciplined approach to reading the Bible helps you overcome the tendency to quit when you get to some long section of "begets" in the Old Testament.

There are many good books on prayer that will help you learn to talk to God in a personal way and to begin to hear the still, small voice as He speaks to you. On the accompanying website, I've recommended books that have blessed me, and we have included other materials to help you develop your prayer life. You should also learn to pray for the Lord to reveal truth to you as you read His Word each day.

I like to pray the Scriptures to get them into my heart and mind. My pastor, Sam Hinn, even teaches us to "sing" the psalms during our own prayer times. If singing aloud during your devotions isn't your "thing," Germaine Copeland's *Prayers That Avail Much* will bless you as they have blessed thousands.

If you look on my reading stand today, you'll find my friend John Mason's book, *Proverbs Prayers,* which turns the promises of Proverbs into prayers to pray each day for thirty-one days. As you use the Scriptures and books like this to pray, you will find that prayer becomes a vital part of every day for you.

You can also keep your mind on Jesus all day by listening to Christian radio or by putting on a Christian CD. I enjoy both praise and worship music and gospel music. Part of changing into the man of God that He wants us to be is learning to control our environment. We can do that by controlling what goes into our ears and minds.

Here's a practical idea: You can become one of the thousands of men who get our *New Man Booster* via e-mail every day. It's a short daily devotional that will give you a thought and a prayer each day as you open your e-mail. Go to www.newmanmagazine.com to sign up free of charge.

Frustration Factor

Kevin is a successful insurance agent who has an evangelistic outreach once a month at a country club in which they present the gospel to one hundred to one hundred fifty local business people. I spoke with Kevin about his own efforts at finding accountability partners.

He said that, after the height of Promise Keepers, he sincerely wanted to find someone to whom he could be accountable. He tried to form that type of relationship with a friend he had brought to a rally, but the friend's spiritual walk was not mature enough for Kevin to feel safe confiding in him. Since then, Kevin's efforts have been frustrated.

Even though he is the vice president of his church's evangelistic organization and a deacon at his church, Kevin still does not have the confidence or trust to be accountable to anyone in his social circle.

> " We were built for intimacy, this linkage of souls, but most of us men rarely experience it. And its scarcity breeds loneliness and fuels remoteness. "

From everything I know about Kevin, he's a strong Christian who is constantly growing in his faith. But his longing is one with which most of us can identify. It's to have good, meaningful friendships to provide accountability.

Frankly, it's the reason I started my men's group back in 1992. I've joked about the fact we were going to help each other through midlife crisis. But we had a higher calling. I remember asking the men what we could accomplish if we each challenged each other to become all we could become in Christ.

It would be easy to say these men who long for deep friendships aren't trying hard enough to form relationships and that they are blaming others for their own inability to open up. But we must remember that most men haven't been trained to be friends with others. And the very devil of hell tries to exploit men by keeping them in a type of solitary confinement. Author Preston Gillham says that the enemy of God and man perpetrates a uniquely masculine attack—isolation. We have tried to adapt, accept and accommodate masculine loneliness by glamorizing it in the movies and portraying men as independent and self-sufficient. But the fact is, men need men.

For all the competition and aggressiveness men exhibit toward each other, one of the deep needs in a man's life is masculine companionship.

Gordon MacDonald puts it this way: "We were built for intimacy, this linkage of souls, but most of us men rarely experience it. And its scarcity breeds loneliness *(I don't really know anyone)* and fuels remoteness *(No one really knows me)*."

I believe that much of this need for intimacy for those men who are married must be with our wives. For me, Joy is my best friend and has been since 1972. She is the one whose company I enjoy more than anyone else. Other friends come and go, but our commitment to each other is lifelong. Yet how many men can truly say that his wife is his best "pal"?

A mentoring relationship can be one of the most valuable, enriching relationships a man has.

But I also have men friends. Joy doesn't play racquetball, or golf or lifting weights—they are not "her thing." So Steve Beam, founder of Missionary Ventures, and I have become not only good friends, but "racquetball buddies." Bob Minotti, our vice president of advertising and a member of my men's group, is also my best "golfing buddy."

I just enjoy hanging around these guys. Along with the men in my men's group, I can be open with them and share my life with them. Because both are strong Christians, being with them inspires me spiritually.

What's the point? I'm giving examples from my own life of where these relationships have filled a real need. Cultivating these friendships is hard work and requires time. But to me, they are well worth the effort because they make life so much richer.

Why do so many men continue to feel isolated, alone with their problems and needs and unable to trust anyone to confide in? How can we solve this problem?

Gillham tackles the issue of isolation. He says that isolation is an awkward problem. Most of us agree we need other men in our lives, but knowing what to do when God brings them along is another matter. Friendship of this type is a modeled and learned behavior. If we haven't seen it enacted, creating it for ourselves is a formidable challenge, producing awkward emotions that can be avoided if isolation is maintained.

Gillham points out that if you think about the men discussed in the Bible, no matter how eccentric they were, whether in the Old Testament or the New, young or old, the men of God's Word were rarely alone. You can't really think of Moses without thinking of Aaron as well. And the same could be said for Elijah and Elisha, David and Jonathan, Paul and Barnabas, Paul and Silas and, of course, Jesus along with Peter, James and John. "If these men placed a premium on having other men in their lives," Gilham writes, "it seems apparent there is wisdom here we would be wise to consider."[2]

Mentors

A critical, and often missing, link in a man's life is mentoring, and I'd like to spend the balance of this chapter on this subject. I have described how mentoring has changed my life for the better. I know other men are in need of the same thing. I had a conversation one day with a man in his early thirties. When I mentioned the topic of mentoring, he was almost  beside himself wanting to know more. This young man had an enormous need for a mentor and said he hadn't a clue of how to find one.[3]

Pete, a man I met at church, confided his desire for a mentor. "I am jealous of others who have had a mentor in their life to help guide them," he told me. "This is something I have never known."

In the last several churches Pete attended he did not find it possible to become "one of the guys." So many people, he found, were in their own cliques and not willing to open the circle to newcomers. Sadly, after he and his wife both felt they had tried as hard as they could to form close friendships, they gave up trying and haven't attended church for a while.

Pete would be the first to admit that he needs a mentor who could help him sort through what has become a very difficult problem to solve. A good mentoring relationship would also fulfill some of the friendship need he has identified.

A good mentor gives you a living model to follow.

A mentoring relationship can be one of the most valuable, enriching relationships a man has. A mentor is someone who has achieved, learned and struggled through more than you have, perhaps in one specific area, and who is willing to pass that knowledge on to help you meet your goals in that area.

I have referred several times to the thirteen years when Jamie Buckingham was my mentor and friend. He let me attend "leader" meetings with him back when I was in my twenties. This let me learn what was happening, and it gave me credibility in the eyes of Jamie's friends who were much older than I.

Each month for a couple of years I drove to Melbourne, eighty miles away, to meet Jamie for lunch. I would pour out my frustrations and doubts, and Jamie would encourage me and challenge me to believe God and to think big. I'm the type of person who needs to "talk things through," and I was always able to talk to Jamie. I continued to talk over all major decisions with him up until only two weeks before he died.

I have been blessed to have had many good mentors over the years in various areas of my life. Now I am at a stage of my life where other men look to me as a mentor.

Actually, I have been mentoring people since my twenties when I began serving in a management role for *Charisma* and in a ministry role at my church. I felt at the time, however, that I was the one needing mentoring and didn't give much thought to the fact I had something to give to others.

Today I still look to Edwin Louis Cole or Jack Hayford as mentors. But I am aware that now there are more than a dozen men for whom I would have some sort of active mentoring role.

The main two, of course, are my sons Chandler and Cameron. I am first and foremost a father to them, especially Chandler who is a middle schooler. His older brother, Cameron, now seeks out my business advice since he has started his own company.

I mentor many of the men in my company. As president I have a responsibility for all my key staff members to grow and develop as professionals. However, some relationships develop that go way beyond what is required in a professional setting. One such relationship is Bob Minotti who heads up our advertising department.

When Bob was hired in 1988 he answered to another man. Then he was promoted when his boss resigned, and I began to relate to him directly. Often I would be frustrated with Bob because he was so aggressive—almost like a wild stallion with so much pent-up emotion and energy. But that's a good problem to have for someone in charge of sales!

Over the years I worked with Bob to hone his managerial skills. I helped him set goals and showed him how to get ahead financially. We spent hours together traveling on business or just enjoying recreational activities. I'd rather play golf with Bob than anyone else. We have also gone white-water rafting on the Arkansas

River in Colorado, horseback riding in North Georgia and fishing on the St. Johns River in Florida. We've been to Guatemala on a missions trip and attended five Promise Keepers events over the years. In the process we have become very good friends.

Another close friend is Scott Plakon who was one of the original members of my mens' group in 1992. Two years before that, our friendship bonded when he accompanied me on a trip to the former Soviet Union when it was still a communist dictatorship. Over the years we have been through many transitions together including three different jobs for Scott, three houses and the birth of three children (in addition to the two he had when we first met.) Scott is one of the men I would go to first to pray with me if I had a deep need.

Scott is seven years younger than I am, and I don't know whether I am his *mentor* or *peer.* Yet at crucial times, Scott has come to me for advice. When he was frustrated in a previous job, we met for breakfast at a family-style restaurant in Lake Mary near my office. I challenged him to look into a publishing opportunity I knew about.

One thing led to another, and Scott not only joined that company, but helped them go public. That was so lucrative for him it later provided capital for him to start his own publishing company specializing in directories for various industries. I'll let you guess where he first saw a model of how to be president of a publishing house! We don't have breakfast at that restaurant very often because Scott gets tired of my reminding him how much his life changed due to the advice I gave him that day!

Scott Nelson is another close friend in my men's group with whom I have attended Promise Keepers and gone on many "adventures." We enjoy each other's company. And while I am not the same sort of mentor to Scott that Jamie was to me, I challenge him to be a better husband and to pursue God more passionately. At the same time he challenges attitudes or motivations he sees in me that he thinks don't please God, earning him the well-deserved name in our group—"Brother Sandpaper."

The other two men in our men's group, Dr. Gene Koziara and Brian Walsh, are men I love and whom I consider peers. If there is mentoring at all, it's "mutual mentoring" in the group setting. I have learned much from both men.

When I lead a man to the Lord or pray with someone at the altar, I feel a responsibility toward that person for at least a few months. I want to see they are established in the Lord. I know it will not be a long-term mentoring relationship, but I want to pour into them some of what God has given to me.

I could give many other mentoring examples, but these will show that, in my own life, I not only seek out mentors, but I am also willing to mentor others as God brings them into my life. You need to be willing to do the same.

History is full of shining examples of mentoring relationships. Socrates mentored Plato, who mentored Aristotle, who mentored Alexander the Great—quite a line-up.

Leonardo da Vinci was mentored by a painter named Andrea del Verrocchio. Da Vinci then mentored another man, passing on all the knowledge he had gained. That man was Michelangelo.[4]

And, of course, Jesus was a mentor to His disciples for three years, though at a more intense level than most of us experience. Even then, there were some in Jesus' day who seemed to have long-distance mentoring relationships with Him. Take Joseph of Arimathea, for instance, or Nicodemus. These men are mentioned only a few times, but it is clear that Jesus' influence on them was profound. I am sure that was true of thousands who lived during those matchless days.

The Benefits of Having a Mentor

What, specifically, can a mentor offer you? Why would we spend the time investing in this kind of relationship?

1. Bridge to maturity

A mentor gives you a bridge to maturity, illuminating the path that is before you in life and inviting you to become a more settled, secure and effective person.

2. Career or personal advice

A mentor gives you advice on your career or personal goals. If you have chosen someone within your profession, he should be able to give you words of wisdom that will save you from pitfalls or help you through common struggles. Of course, advice must be acted upon.

3. Encouragement

A mentor gives encouragement. Having a mentor is not taking a shortcut around trials. You will still have to fight through certain tailor-made struggles in life that only you can fight through. But having someone on the sidelines cheering you on can make all the difference.

4. Skill improvement

A mentor passes on new or improved skills in your area of shared interest. On a practical level, you should be learning things that make you a more valuable commodity in the workplace or ministry.

5. Role modeling

A good mentor gives you a living model to follow. Not every situation can be predicted, and you will learn tremendously as you watch your mentor go through unexpected circumstances.

6. Access to opportunities and resources

A mentor gives access to opportunities and resources. If there is a job to be done, you might get the nod and a chance to prove yourself to your mentor and to others.

7. Visibility

A mentor gives you visibility in your profession or ministry. By taking you under his wing, he is putting a label on you that tells others you are trustworthy and available.[5]

Finding the Right Mentor

How do you find a mentor? It isn't that difficult. I told you earlier how I met Jamie Buckingham and over the course of a few lunches developed a mentoring relationship with him. You can probably think of people right now whom you would like to be mentored by, whether at work, church or elsewhere. I believe you need not one, but several mentors for different areas of life:

- Career
- Family
- Spiritual
- Health and fitness
- Educational
- Financial

In all of these areas, pick someone more successful than yourself. It is axiomatic in life that you become like the people you are around, and you will emulate your mentors. Pick someone who has a healthier family than you, who has greater spiritual depth and has been a follower of Christ for longer than you have, who has better health and fitness, and who makes more money than you do. As you get to know each of these men, you will begin to understand how he got to where he is.

Decide in what areas you want to grow. It would be nearly impossible to grow in all these areas at once, but maybe the Lord is leading you to one or two that you can focus on for a few months or a year. Identify in your mind what you want in a mentor and think of possible candidates. Then decide that establishing these friendships is important enough to spend time and money on. Put the names in order of priority.

Invite the potential mentor to breakfast or lunch (your treat). If the person can't or won't make time to meet with you for a free meal, it is likely that no relationship is meant to develop— but most men won't pass up a free meal. And, if you're willing to be patient long enough to fit into their schedule, I've found you can get an appointment with almost anyone.

Then ask the man about himself. Ask about his early history—

how he made it to where he is today. Ask him about his father (this reveals a lot about most men) and ask if he had a good mentor or if he is in a men's group. Ask a few leading questions about why he thinks it's difficult for men to form meaningful relationships with other men. Most men will open up and talk, but some won't. If a man won't open about these somewhat superficial topics, cross him off the list as a potential mentor.

> ## In a way, we are mentored by anyone who has spoken into our lives, even if they are now dead.

Then, if you feel comfortable doing it, open up about something that is somewhat revealing about yourself, but not so important that if it's repeated you'd feel embarrassed. For me, I might open up about my struggle to quit smoking when I turned over my life to the Lord in 1971.

I am not proud that I smoked (and today I can't stand to be in the same room with a smoker), but this "secret" isn't too humiliating if revealed. After you've done this, wait to see what he says. Most people will feel obligated to tell you something about themselves. If so, you're making progress.

Assess the meeting in your own mind. Did you feel comfortable together? Was there a free flow of conversation, or at least the possibility of a friendship? If so, ask if he would like to have breakfast or lunch again.

The second or third time, you might mention the topic of mentoring. But don't do it the first time! Most men will feel they are being led into a cage for experimentation and observation. Most men don't think of themselves as mentors, and most men are ashamed of some shortcoming in their lives that they are sure would disqualify them from mentoring anyone else.

In some cases, a mentoring relationship may develop simply because an older, more mature man takes an interest in you and begins to seek out times that he can spend with you.

Perhaps you remind him of his own son, or perhaps you remind him of the son he always wished he had. Maybe you are thrown together through a committee or group at work or some other social setting, and the two of you just "gel." In these cases, it's your mentor that chooses you—instead of you choosing him.

You can also be mentored by people you don't know very well. For example, I've always admired David Yonggi Cho and Pat Robertson from a distance. While I have the privilege of knowing both men, neither has been an active mentor to me as Jamie Buckingham was, or as Jack Hayford has been since Jamie died.

I've learned so much from Zig Ziglar that I consider him a mentor even though I have never talked to him. I've only heard him speak at the large Peter Lowe Success seminars.

Books can also mentor you. In a way, we are mentored by anyone who has spoken into our lives, even if they are now dead. I hope what I am writing is benefiting you in much the same way as if I could talk to you face to face after playing a hard game of racquetball or enjoying a cup of coffee at Starbucks.

Stages of Mentoring

According to Linda Phillips-Jones, the mentor relationship often goes through predictable stages.[6]

1. Admiration

First, there is the mutual admiration stage. This is assuming, of course, that a mentoring relationship develops. This is like a romance or a honeymoon. Both of you are anxious to please and retain a highly favorable view of the other. You are enjoying the chemistry of a relationship that seems to be working well. There may be a hint of uncertainty or fear of rejection, but these are not enough to derail the process.

2. Development

In the development stage the mentor plays the part of the wise teacher, and the student humbly and gratefully learns from him. At this stage, a mentor can become like a father, showing admiration for your accomplishments, taking pride in what you've learned. As a "student," you are happy when your teacher is happy.

Many mentoring relationships stay at this level for years. Or rather than moving on to the next two stages, your relationship with your mentor seems to change into one of strong friendship—with mutual admiration and respect that places you on equal footing.

This would be a natural progression as the one being mentored matures. At some point you no longer need the intensive mentoring you did to reach a level of maturity that corresponds to your mentor. But you have grown bonded in your relationship, and almost subconsciously you slip into a strong friendship.

Other mentoring relationships may find themselves going through these next stages.

3. Disillusionment

Disillusionment sets in as you begin to see a mentor's faults and shortcomings. You have learned enough to know what the mentor is doing wrong or right, and you begin to want to grow out from under that influence. At this point, a mentor might be frustrated because you are no longer so willing and passive a learner. This phase is as inevitable as the "let-down" phase in a marriage when romance fades.

Author Thomas Wolfe had a mentor in his editor, Maxwell Perkins, to whom he dedicated one of his books as a gesture of gratitude. But after a while, critics began claiming that Wolfe could not write his books without Perkins' help. This infuriated Wolfe, who became determined to break off the relationship with Perkins and show the world he could write books on his own.

A similar thing happened with Carl Jung, who was mentored by Sigmund Freud. After years of working under Freud as the "heir apparent," Jung began to feel trapped. He felt his own creativity being stifled under the mentor's demands and left, leaving Freud angry.

Disillusionment is the first step toward what must eventually happen.

4. Parting

A parting of the ways takes place after disillusionment. This is often awkward and uncomfortable for both parties as you have outgrown your role and no longer know how to relate to the mentor—as a peer or a teacher. Mentoring relationships usually only last a few months or years at most. But for maturity to continue, the mentoring relationship must end, and the next phase must begin.

5. Transformation

Transformation will occur as you assimilate all you have learned and allow it to propel you toward your goals. Some mentoring relationships will arrive at this stage after passing through the first two stages of admiration and development. Others will have to also pass through disillusionment and parting before they reach this final stage.

Hopefully, as you move into this final stage, your mentoring relationship will have the strength of the relationship that Paul and Timothy shared. Midstream in his mentoring with Timothy, Paul wrote these words to him: "But you, Timothy, belong to God; so run from all these evil things, and follow what is right and good. Pursue a godly life, along with faith, love, perseverance, and gentleness. Fight the good fight for what we believe. Hold tightly to the eternal life that God has given you, which you have confessed so well before many witnesses" (1 Tim. 6:11–12).

Those are the words of a mature, godly man who is anxiously trying to impart godly wisdom to a young immature Christian whom he is mentoring. But as their relationship developed, and as Timothy matured in the Lord, their relationship took on the nature of strong friendship.

As evidence of that, we read these words from Paul to Timothy: "Timothy, I thank God for you. Night and day I constantly remember you in my prayers. I long to see you again . . . and I will be filled with joy when we are together again. . . . Hold on to the pattern of right teaching you learned from me. And remember to live in the faith and love that you have in Christ Jesus. . . . Please come as soon as you can" (2 Tim. 1:3–4, 13; 4:9).

> # Paul developed a relationship with Timothy of mutual respect— and even dependence.

In these verses, Paul expresses a confidence in Timothy's maturity. He seems to have developed a relationship with Timothy of mutual respect—and even dependence. He is anxious to spend time with Timothy—probably as much for what Timothy can give to Paul as for what Paul gives to Timothy.

In my twenties I was a mentor-magnet. I needed and I gravitated toward men who filled this role in my life. One man was George Clouse, a godly man twenty-five years my senior who worked at the *Sentinel Star* (now known as *The Orlando Sentinel*) and who also attended Calvary Assembly, where Joy and I were members. I used to spend my coffee breaks with George, and over time we became close friends. He helped me understand the office politics at the newspaper, and he gave me advice on how to ask for a raise—advice I pass along elsewhere in this book.

One day I spoke with him about my need to earn a little extra money so my wife could quit her job and finish her last year of college. I told him I had an idea to start a small magazine at our church. George thought it sounded like a good idea, and so I pursued it. I will be eternally grateful for his encouragement because that magazine became *Charisma,* the cornerstone of our ministry.

At the same time Joy and I attended a home fellowship group led by George and his wife Mary Jo. We were powerfully ministered to during that time. But as time passed, circumstances evolved, and I began to see another man in the church as a potential mentor.

My first thought was that I didn't want to hurt George. I valued his friendship and advice, so I invited him to lunch and explained what was happening. He said the change sounded right, and he gave me his blessing. This mentoring relationship moved through transition to a good friendship. Today I'm still good friends with George, and his wife, Mary Jo, has worked in our organization for the past ten years.

Around the same time I related to one of the elders in the church, a wonderfully gifted man whose leadership style I still model today. He taught me how to dream big dreams, to work and build an organization, to recruit and successfully lead people. He was even the man who introduced me to the game of racquetball, and his example encouraged me to begin a lifestyle of physical fitness that I dealt with in an earlier chapter.

But our mentoring relationship never had the same sort of closure I had with George. Whether due to his personality or mine—or to some other reason—life took us our separate ways. Today I rarely see him. While I love and respect him, I still miss the closeness we once had.

Mentoring Pitfalls

There are some pitfalls to avoid in a mentoring relationship that may help you navigate it successfully.[7]

1. Don't demand too much of your mentor's time.

Determine how much you can reasonably ask for and how much you really need. Sometimes, less is more. Having lunch three or four times a year with a businessman you want to learn from is probably enough. On the other hand, you may want to meet twice a month with a spiritual mentor. In either case, be sensitive to taking up their time and don't overcommit, or you will both burn out quickly on the relationship.

2. Have realistic expectations of what a mentor can teach or give you.

Mentors are not super-humans; they have just gone down the road before you and have something to pass on—from their failures as well as their successes. Treat them like people, even if they are older and wiser.

3. Don't take advantage of your mentor's connections, especially if they are in your same profession.

No one wants to feel used, and the quickest way to get a mentor working against you is to make him feel like you are simply climbing the professional ladder and using his back as the next step.

4. Don't become overdependent on your mentor.

Keep a well-rounded life, listen to other advice, and allow other people to speak into your life. Then, when you transition out of a mentoring relationship with your mentor, you won't be left feeling high-and-dry, without other stable relationships.

Looking for and finding a mentor could make the difference in your life, no matter what your occupation or interests. Rather than going in circles or groping blindly, you will have the advantage of seeing through the eyes of a man who has been there. He will help you avoid the wrong paths and stay on the ones that lead to becoming a new man in Christ.

That leads us to the final chapter on becoming a man of God, and how to press in to the extravagant love of God.

Talk about it   Think about it

Developing Male Relationships

Author's note: Men need companionship and friendship from other men. Use the suggestions in this chapter to develop better friendships with the men you know and relate to.

For more information on this topic (which we will add to as time passes) check out our www.oldmannewman.com website. Use the user id: **oldman** and the password **newman**. These are **case sensitive,** so use all lowercase letters and leave no spaces.

1. The book identifies six areas where mentors can make a tremendous difference: career, family, spiritual, health and fitness, education, finance.

2. Who has helped mentor you in these areas in the past? Include books. (Note: The point here is not to be exhaustive—or *exhausting*—but rather to give helpful insight to others in the group.)

   In which of the six areas do you feel the most critical need for mentoring? Why?

3. Choose a potential mentor to invite to lunch. Share the name with the group so that they can joining you in praying for success. Be sure to share the results of the lunch with the group.

A clip from

New Man July/August 2000

Self-Realization Vs. Christ-Realization

Self-realization is a modern phrase. Nothing blinds the mind to the claim of Jesus Christ more effectually than a good, cleanly lived, upright life based on self-realization. If we are going to be His disciples, our ideal must be Christ-realization.

The one dominant note in the life of a disciple is:
> **Jesus only, Jesus ever,**
> **Jesus all in all I see.**

There is no devotion to principles or to a cause there, nothing but overwhelming, absorbing love to the person of Jesus Christ. "If anyone desires to come after Me, let him deny himself, and take up his cross, and follow Me."[1]

—Oswald Chambers

Christ realization
oldmannewman.com

Chapter 16

Becoming a
Man of God

OLD MAN   **Doesn't feel good enough to be completely,
overwhelmingly loved by God.**

NEW MAN   **Presses in to the extravagant love of God
and finds healing in His pleasure.**

Where does all this take us? If you've stayed with me this long, I can only assume you want to become a new man in Christ. I've opened my heart and shared my own odyssey, I've shared many stories and done a lot of research to help you see what it is to get over the old man and become the new man in Christ.

Yet you can get over the father-wound, you can have a good marriage by paying attention to your wife, you can get your finances in order, and you can get in shape physically. But one hundred years from today, none of that will matter. All that will matter then is your relationship with God.

I'm not even talking about whether you are saved. I assume you are. I am talking about whether you have a heart for God, whether you are pursuing God, as it says in Jeremiah 29:13: *"If you look for me in earnest,* you will find me when you seek me" (emphasis added).

People are tired of religion, but many have a heart for God. This is manifest even in our culture where "spirituality" is the vogue. Beyond all the excitement of doing high fives or bouncing beach balls, having a heart for God is what the appeal of Promise Keepers really is all about. It's why people flock to "revival" locations like the Toronto Airport Christian Fellowship or Brownsville Assembly of God where thousands have been impacted with almost daily services for the past several years.

It's why thousands have read Tommy Tenney's *God Chasers* or Henry Blackaby's *Experiencing God*.

So what do I have to add to what all these have written? To be honest, I have struggled more with writing this chapter than with any other in this book. I have procrastinated for weeks because I felt that anything I write will fall short.

> ## Our heavenly Father is a watching, running, weeping, laughing, embracing, kissing God.

Yet I also have a heart for God. I had a real experience with God at an early age, accepting Christ at age five and receiving the baptism in the Holy Spirit at age twelve. I didn't fully understand all that was happening to me. But I did have a genuine experience with God that sustained me through the time of rebellion in my late teenage years and brought me back to God as a twenty-year-old while I was a sophomore at the University of Florida.

My men's group has discussed spiritual issues many times. Over the eight years we've been meeting, there have been times we goofed off and just talked or joked or maybe even watched a sporting event. But many times we had meaningful discussions about what it means to pursue God, and we have spent time on our faces before God praying together and calling on Him for more of Him in our lives.

But that hasn't been easy either. Sometimes we feel awkward praying together or sharing our deepest thoughts about God. In some groups the men become so transparent about their struggles, they feel like hypocrites talking about pursuing God because the other men know their propensity to sin.

This type of thing comes out when I talk with other men. Many guys are really open about the things they struggle with. They want to love God, but they feel so unworthy. It's as if God won't accept them as a son because of their imperfections.

That's why a message by Mike Bickle, of Kansas City, Missouri, was so life-changing when we heard it at one of our Charisma conferences a couple of years ago.

Bickle is an amazing man. His book *Passion for Jesus* tells of his own odyssey to know God better. He reached a point in his life when although he was throwing all his efforts into his burning desire to please God and live for him, he knew he was failing miserably at it.

Used to achieving at whatever he attempted, filled with spiritual disciplines like praying at least an hour a day and memorizing large portions of Scripture and armed with a driving human zeal he had inherited from his father, Bickle says, "I felt like one big mess, one huge spiritual failure."

One day as he was reading the story of the prodigal son, the verbs regarding the prodigal's father suddenly came alive: "And he got up and came to his father. But while he was still a long way off, his father *saw* him, and *felt compassion* for him, and *ran* and *embraced* him, and *kissed* him" (Luke 15:20, NAS, emphasis added). Bickle tells us his reaction:

> In the midst of my spiritual coldness and failure I had wondered so many times how God felt about me. I'd even dreaded to imagine the expression on His face when He saw me coming back for forgiveness each time I let Him down. Suddenly I knew, for through the prodigal's father I glimpsed the face and heart of God. When God saw me trudging toward His throne with my head bowed in shame, like the prodigal's father, He was moved with

affection and tenderness for me. He was running toward me with joy and excitement. His arms were outstretched, reaching for me, longing to catch me up in His loving embrace and kiss away my guilt and failure.[2]

Bickle says that he recognized that his heavenly Father was a watching, running, weeping, laughing, embracing, kissing God! He was an encouraging, affirming, praising, affectionate kind of God. He was a God who loved him so much He couldn't keep from embracing him. "I was the apple of His eye," Bickle writes. "He was a God who loved my friendship and just wanted me to be with Him. A Father who bragged on me to anyone who would listen. A God who enjoyed me even in my failure and immaturity because He saw the sincere intentions of my heart. A God I didn't have to strive to make happy, because He'd been happy with me from the second I was born into His family. He was a Father who was always cheering me on from the sidelines. He enthusiastically called me His son."[3]

> ## Are you a sinner who struggles to love God, or are **you a lover of God who struggles with sin?**

I've known Mike Bickle more than ten years. He's a man's man who was a successful college football player. He is also a very loving man who gives everyone a hug and who is always surrounded by little kids who respond to his playful personality and genuine love.

Bickle is a powerful preacher and has ministered around the world. He has been a successful pastor, and recently he founded a ministry called International House of Prayer. Yet he is first and foremost a lover of God, and he has devoted his life to teaching people how to respond to the love of God the Father.

I invited him to speak at the conference because I knew he could lead people into God's presence. But I was blown away by the revelation he taught, which I've studied and is now the focus of this chapter.

Mike asks this question: *Are you a sinner who struggles to love God, or are you a lover of God who struggles with sin?*

The answer to that question will change your life and change your destiny. It determines how we look at ourselves and our relationship with God.

Because we know our own shortcomings—our tendency toward addictive behavior or whatever—we have trouble really understanding that God loves us and enjoys being with us. We think we must achieve some sort of spiritual perfection before we can be good enough for God to love us. It's a fear—a fear of rejection by God for whatever reason.

It paralyzes even Christian leaders who go through the motions but underneath have so much shame that they become bound and shackled by it.

Yet God loves us so much, and He wants to spend time with us. Not just with the women, who often seem more eager than men do to go off to a conference, read a Christian book or watch an anointed preacher on Christian television. God wants to spend time with men. He wants to show men the power of His love, to transform men into new men in Christ.

It is not that we men don't want to love God. We want and need His love—the love of the Father. But all too often we beat ourselves thinking we must be good enough for God to love us.

I've always liked Peter in the Bible—a character so great he preached the first great sermon on the Day of Pentecost and who went on to be the one on whom Christ built the church. Yet he was a man who struggled, denied Jesus and fled with all the others, except John.

We get a foreshadowing of what would happen later when Jesus talks to Peter in Matthew 16:13-19. This is a well-known scripture. In it, Jesus asks a question that is a key to understanding what I'm saying here. He asks the question: "Who am I?"

This is the most important question in your spiritual journey to becoming a victorious Christian. If you don't understand who Jesus is to you, you'll never become victorious or be effective in spiritual warfare. Your answer indicates how important God is in your life.

You remember the story. Jesus and His disciples must have been sitting around a campfire after a long day, and Jesus asked His disciples, "Who do men say that I, the Son of Man, am?"

They answered that some thought He was John the Baptist, some Elijah and others Jeremiah or one of the prophets.

Jesus asks the same question of us today: "Who do you say I am?" And if we're reared in the church, we may answer, like Simon Peter, "You are the Christ, the Son of the living God." Peter knew what to say! But look what Jesus said next: "Blessed are you, Simon Bar-Jonah, for flesh and blood has not revealed this to you, but My Father who is in heaven. And I also say to you that you are Peter, and on this rock I will build My church, and the gates of Hades shall not prevail against it. And I will give you the keys of the kingdom of heaven, and whatever you loose on earth will be loosed in heaven" (NKJV).

When I've studied this passage, I've often thought the most important parts of these verses were the parts about building the church and locking and opening, or as the King James Version says: "binding and loosing." Yet Jesus began by asking the disciples who men were saying that He is.

That day in our conference, as Bickle taught on this, I began to understand how important knowing who God is to us is in our process of becoming new men in Christ. Because it's not just *what we think about God*, but *what He thinks about us*. Until we understand how much God loves us, we will go in circles of spiritual fatigue.

When you comprehend what God thinks about you—you'll begin the journey into victory!

Answering the question of what God thinks about you is more than just learning to engage in spiritual warfare (being sure the gates of hell do not prevail against you). It's a matter of you beginning to understand what He is like. Knowing Him—really knowing His heart—is imperative to knowing how He thinks and feels when He looks at you.

Even though we may deny God by the way we live or with the sin we continue to commit, *He still loves us.*

In a later encounter with His disciples as they sat around a campfire late one night, Jesus was thinking about the fact that one of His disciples would soon betray Him. (See John 14 and 15.) He knew that they loved Him—but He also knew that at least one of them would betray Him. There's no greater tragedy in the life of a man who loves God than to sin grievously against the love in your heart toward God.

That's what betrayal is—it is that deep, desperate, sinking feeling we have when we sin against the one we love. It is the greatest crisis the true believer will ever face—and the way you respond to this crisis is very, very important. Many of God's men respond to it in exactly the wrong way.

Jesus is preparing His disciples for the crisis of failure that is going to happen in a few hours. In John 15:9, Jesus looks them right in the face and says: "I have loved you even as the Father has loved me."

Wait a second—*as the Father loves the Son?*

What a thought! What does the First Person of the Trinity feel about the Second Person of the Trinity?

Remember Jesus' baptism? It is as if the Father looked over the balcony of heaven and proudly proclaimed, "That's My Boy. I like Him. He's my Son, and I'm well pleased with Him."

When Jesus took His disciples with Him up on the mount of transfiguration, the disciples heard a voice that said, "This is my beloved Son, and I am fully pleased with him. Listen to him" (Matt. 17:6).

Once again, the Father was asserting His deep love for His Son. So when Jesus says, "As the Father loves Me," to the twelve disciples—He's telling them He loves them with the same indescribable, burning desire the Father feels for His Son, and that He takes infinite delight and enjoyment in them.

Can't you just see Jesus pausing at this point to let the power of His words touch them? He says, "Let Me tell you something—the same way the Father feels about Me—this is what I feel about you—even though tonight each one of you will deny Me!"

Let's let this truth sink in. Just hours before the disciples would turn their back on Him, Jesus was verbalizing this enormous love to them—the same love that God the Father has for Him. And now two millennia later, He says the same to us! Even though we may deny Him by the way we live or with the sin we continue to commit, *He still loves us.* And it is His love toward us that propels us to love Him in return.

Bickle believes that the greatest longing in the human heart is to have the assurance that we are enjoyed by God.

> **"I don't mean a stamped passport that we will go to heaven when we die,"** he told us at that conference. **"That's good to know we're going to heaven. But that's not what I'm talking about—it's the assurance—that when God looks at you— He enjoys you."**

As Bickle ministered this truth at our conference, you could almost see the "light bulbs" go on as people began to understand the importance of his words.

Men seemed to ask themselves, "God enjoys me now, and not in heaven only?" And almost immediately—as though this thought was too lofty to grab onto—they seemed to respond, "Well, maybe He will when I'm very mature spiritually, but not right now."

But, as though reading the minds, Bickle went on to say. "God enjoys the sincere believers when they are still immature."

If you can understand that one principle, the knowledge of God's love will empower you to grow into maturity.

> " God sees immaturity very differently than rebellion. God enjoys the **immature, and He judges the rebellious.** "

"God enjoys me even before I'm mature. He enjoys me while I'm struggling, and that pushes me to maturity." Bickle goes on to explain, "I enjoyed my son when he was two years old. I trained him, I disciplined him, I disagreed with things that he did. But I tell you I enjoyed him when he was two years old, not just when he grew up. If that's how we feel about our immature children, just imagine how strongly God must enjoy us."

Here's another point Bickle made that day about the difference between rebellion against God and the spiritual immaturity of many believers. It was so pivotal that one of my friends who was there that day specifically asked me to be sure this point was in this chapter. There is a great difference between immaturity and rebellion. Some preachers confuse them. They preach to immature believers—as though they were rebellious unbelievers. They hang them over hell on a rotten stick—just threatening to drop them into the pit. But many people sin out of immaturity, not rebellion against God.

On the outside, sinning by immaturity or rebellion may look the same, but depending on your spirit, they can be very different.

"God sees immaturity very differently than rebellion," Bickle says. "God enjoys the immature, and He judges the rebellious. There's a vast difference. In our zeal to get people motivated we can confuse those two and send new believers in a tailspin for many years."

God likes you.
God enjoys you.
You look good to God.

How true. I know men who have been Christians many years, yet who still are in a tailspin because they know they fall short. They fail to understand how much God the Father loves them—right now. They think God is mad at them

This is a very important reality. You see, if the greatest longing is the assurance that we are enjoyed by God even in our weakness, then the greatest fear is that God will reject us. If that fear is lodged in the core of our beings, it will have a colossal effect on how we look at ourselves—whether we live in fear or faith, and whether we run to God or from God.

This fear that we will fail in ministry—or in some other area—can be paralyzing even to leaders. There's a name for this: *shame*. And it's one of the most paralyzing realities in the lives of men who are trying to serve Jesus. As a result, we think, *Let my wife go to the conference. I'll stay home. It will never work for me. I'm not worthy for God to pour out His love and to give me greater anointing and blessing* (or whatever else we might be searching for).

Shame is the polar opposite of the assurance that God really likes us. This is how it works: Our vision of God determines what we think God thinks of us. For instance, if we believe God is disgusted with us, we're going to feel *disgusting*. And instead of running to

Him, we'll run from Him. But if we believe God really likes us, then we're going to feel *likeable*. And instead of running from God, we'll run to Him, appropriating the power and feeling the encouragement we need to live ever more victorious lives. That's why what we believe about God is so unbelievably important.

Many try to do that backwards. Many preachers will tell their people, "Change your behavior, change your behavior." We want to change our behavior because we think that if we do, then God just might start to like us. So we try harder for the kingdom, try to sin less, try give more. If we're sincere, we try our best to do it, but in the final analysis, we get beaten down emotionally, exhausted with feelings of self-hatred and self-disgust toward our ourselves.

What's the answer? It's not just persuading ourselves to feel better about ourselves like those syrupy self-help books encourage us to do. No, the answer is to understand how much God loves us.

God likes you. God enjoys you. You look good to God. Once this sinks in, you'll start to feel better and act differently!

But if you're struggling with some of the things we've discussed in this book, you might ask, "Can I *really* look good to God?" *It's not possible,* you might think, *because the God I worship isn't that happy. He's not that nice. He can't like what I look like—He can't enjoy me.*

But God does love you. He is a happy God who has a burning desire for *you*. And that's not all: You look good to Him; He *does* enjoys you.

On that day when Jesus was sitting with His disciples and telling them that they would soon deny Him, Peter began to argue with Him. "Oh no, Lord, not me! I'll never deny You. You must not understand—I'm different than the others!"

Let me expose a lie that was in Peter's heart, because many of us are operating in the same lie. I believe that Peter had more confidence in his own love for Jesus than he did in Jesus' love for him. The second part of the lie is this: Peter based his relationship on an inner vow he made that he would not sin or deny God. Of course he did not keep that vow. But he must have imagined that this vow not to deny Christ would make God like him more.

How many times have you promised God you wouldn't do some behavior? Have you been like me and gone to the altar, maybe even crying, making a vow to God, imagining this vow you are making will make God like you more? If so, then you and I aren't unlike Peter, who stands and declares, "I promise never, never, never will I fail."

Jesus knows Peter will fail. After all, He is God, and He is omniscient. He says in effect, "Peter, let Me describe how your heart works. There are two things in your heart, Peter, and you're all confused about them. First, you have a willing spirit, but you also have a weak human nature. There's a 'yes' in your spirit to Me, Peter, because I put it in you as a gift of the Spirit the moment you were born again. But your human nature is weak."

Of course Peter doesn't believe this, just as when we're sincerely calling out to God and vowing never to fail Him or fall back into the old, addictive behaviors. But Jesus knows that even though our hearts say "yes," our old man must still be dealt with.

How different it was just a few hours later when Peter stood alone at the fire of the Roman soldiers after Jesus had been arrested. Before he had the power to stop himself, Peter had denied Christ three times—just as Jesus said he would. His soul was wracked with the bitter reality of his cowardice as he lied about his Master to save his own neck. He was filled with self loathing and disgust—and with the terrible memory of his Master's eyes as they met his own at the very moment of his third denial.

That was the last encounter Peter and Jesus had before His death. And Peter wept bitterly. In his heart he must have been thinking, *Please don't go, Jesus; that's not what I meant to say. I love You—I really do.*

But Jesus was brutally crucified. And Peter feels like a pathetic hypocrite. He's broken in his heart.

Later when Jesus is resurrected, the angel appeared to Mary and told her to go tell the disciples—*and Peter*—that Jesus was alive. Even though Peter had failed miserably, it was as if Jesus wanted Peter specifically to know He loved him.

The next time we see Peter is when he is fishing on the Sea of Galilee. Now if you and I go fishing, it is probably for recreation. But Peter wasn't relaxing that day. He was a fisherman by trade, so he had gone back to what he knew to do to earn a living. He must have felt that he was finished in the ministry. This thing with following Jesus was over. It was back to business as usual.

We can imagine that Peter was hurting badly—aching inside with the kind of pain that is always in the background, always gnawing away. It brought with it a feeling of anxiety centered right in the stomach. The same thing happens to many of us when we sin. We believe we are hopeless hypocrites; we feel that God has written us off.

It's as if we are saying, "I just know that I'm going to mess it up. I can't reach for the highest thing in God because I know I'm going to fail. So rather than facing the high vision in failure, I'm going to bring the vision way down; I'm going to settle for second-class status with Jesus."

This second-class vision that we settle for isn't about what we do—whether we have a great international ministry or just maintain status quo in some little ministry in some nondescript setting. No, the second-class vision we settle for is the vision of who we are in God—are we the apple of God's eye, the one He runs to embrace, or are we just someone we hope He notices enough to let us slip into heaven? It's the second-class vision that hinders us from being an extravagant lover of God. This vision involves the passion of our heart. We settle for being a distant, dull, cold lover of God because the pain of reaching and failing is too great.

We resolve in our minds that we are second-class Christians, content to let others in the church be the ones who really have a passion for God. It's as if there is a fear that cries out, "Oh I would love to love God as I used to, but I have failed so many times, it's too painful to reach and fail.

I can identify with Peter. So I also identify with what Jesus said when He first saw Peter fishing that day. The very first question He asked him was, "Do you love Me?"

And that is what Jesus is saying to us today—"Do you love Me?" If we are to have any success in our Christian walk, it will be because we know, deep in our hearts, that we really are lovers of God. Do you know that deep within? Are you a lover of God?

> ## If we are to have any success in our Christian walk, it will be because we know, deep in our hearts, that we are really lovers of God.

Do you know what Peter was doing? He was defining his life by his struggle rather than defining his life by his pursuit for God. He looked through his struggles, his failings, "as through a glass darkly," to try to see the acceptance of Father God. His view was distorted by the dark shadows of his human failings. Just as Mary turned from the emptiness and grieving of the tomb where Jesus had lain to face Him with her back to the tomb, we must turn from the awareness of our struggle with sin to see Him face to face—straight ahead, and getting closer to us with every step of our pursuit.

Peter didn't realize—as many of us don't realize—that God wanted him just as he was. Though I am only a weak lover of God, *I am a lover of God nonetheless.* I want Him, and because He loves me and I love Him, I am successful in God's eyes, *no matter what happens.* That's what makes me successful in my heart.

Peter was also defining his value by his struggle. Do you struggle? Maybe it's a struggle with pornography, so you say, "I am not valuable to God, I am a pornography man." No! *You are a lover of God.*

I have a question for you: Are you a sinner who struggles to love God, or are you a lover of God who struggles with sin?

At the core or center of your being, if you see as yourself as a lover of God who still struggles with sin, then you have grasped the wonder of God's love for you. But if your struggle is to love God, then go back and read chapter five on how to know Jesus Christ as your Savior from sin. But if your struggle is with sin, then press into the extravagant love of God. Don't hide from God; find your healing in His pleasure.

Peter saw himself as a sinner who was struggling to love God. When Jesus said, "Peter, do you love Me?" Peter said, "You know I love You," and looked down, believing their conversation had ended. But Jesus knew that Peter had not really understood the question. So He asked Peter again, "Peter, do you love Me?"

Oh, Peter must have hated that question. He remembered that look in Jesus' eyes the night he denied Him. It's as if he wanted to say, "Jesus, I do love You. But I didn't know that I was going to deny You that night. Even though that terrible thing happened, please believe me, I do love You." He felt like a hopeless hypocrite—and was afraid that was how Jesus thought of him, too.

But Jesus was trying to tell Peter, "You are not a hopeless hypocrite. You are a lover of God. You don't have to give up on being a lover of God just because you failed." As Jesus paused for a moment, Peter looked down again, but not quite so far this time. And Jesus went on to ask the question a third time. Why do you think He asked it three times? Because Peter denied Jesus three times. By asking Peter to proclaim his love three times, Jesus was breaking the shame of failure off Peter.

For the third time, He asked, "Peter, do you love Me?"

In reply, Peter said, "You know everything (even about my denials), and You know I love You." That phrase—"You know everything"—is a key phrase. It tells me that an unspoken discussion was taking place between Peter and Jesus. It's as if Peter was saying to Jesus, "You know that I'm not a hopeless hypocrite; you know that I love You. I don't want to be a fisherman; I want to be a leader in Your kingdom. You know my heart; You know everything about me, things I don't even know. You say I am a lover of God; You know that I love You."

Jesus was reinstating Peter into the confidence that God

enjoyed him. If a man has the confidence that God enjoys him, he understands what being a new man in Christ is all about. Even in our weakness, no power in hell can take us down for long.

Jesus wants to reinstate you in the confidence that God enjoys you. Even though you may look at pornography again, or fall into some other sin, when you remember that God enjoys you and longs to embrace you, you won't stay in pornography very long. It's not about getting totally set free in a single instant; it's about the truth renewing you every time when you come back. In a matter of time, the besetting sin will be gone.

> **The devil wants you to define your success by your struggle, but God wants you to define your success by His love for you and your love for Him.**

The devil wants you to run from God, not to God. The devil wants you to define your success by your struggle, but God wants you to define your success by His love for you and by your love for Him—immature maybe, but genuine nonetheless.

Then you finally begin to believe: "I'm a lover of God; I'm not just a man who struggles with sin."

Consider the apostle John, who is the only writer of the Gospels who records the incredible statement from Jesus saying, "I have loved you even as the Father has loved me." He understood such love. Isn't it interesting that John is the only disciple who didn't run when Jesus was crucified?

When we understand this love, we'll also be able to stand strong, no matter what the devil throws at us, no matter what in our past would bring us down, no matter what addiction we are trying to overcome.

Perhaps you have given up on being an extravagant lover. You feel you've failed so many times that you almost want to give up on His high calling. You have given up on becoming a new man in Christ. You have accepted second-class status with God, not realizing how much God loves you.

Instead of doing that, pray a prayer with me, using whatever words you think of.

Tell Jesus how much you love Him. Tell Him that even though you have a weak flesh, you do have a willing spirit, and you do love Him!

Talk to Him quietly in your heart now. Take whatever sin there is in your life and don't lie about it. Put it right out there in front, and pray:

> **You know I am a lover of God. You know all things. You know I love You. I'm not a hopeless hypocrite. I am not just a guy hooked to pornography (or whatever you may struggle with), I'm not just an angry guy, I'm a lover of God. Do I struggle? Yes! But I am a lover of God, and I am the one God likes.**
>
> **Now, I am going to throw away this argument that makes me live second class.**
>
> **Lord Jesus, here I am. I want to do away with the old man; I want to become a new man in Christ.**

If you prayed this prayer, or if you understand what I'm writing here about God loving you, then you are a new man in Christ. You understand why I have written this book. And I hope you see that you don't have to stay in the muck and mire of sin, but that you can begin to soar with God and that you can go on to great exploits for Him—just as Peter did.

There is a place in God where we don't have to go three steps forward and two steps back. But getting there takes more than reading a book. It takes making a decision to change and moving ahead, being accountable to others who love you and renewing your mind—all the things we have talked about.

With the condition of our society, and even the condition of many in the church, we may begin to feel as if everyone is struggling and no one is making it spiritually. That's not true! Many men are living victorious lives in God.

If this book has ministered to you, I want to hear from you. You can write me directly at www.oldmannewman.com or post your comments about your spiritual odyssey for others to read. In that way, this book becomes a two-way communication as we continue our journey together to become in Christ the new men we were meant to be.

Talk about it Think about it

Becoming a Man of God

Author's note: God loves you more than you know. He wants you to know how passionately He longs for an intimate relationship with you. Read how you can grow closer to Him than you have ever seen before.

For more information on this topic (which we will add to as time passes) check out our www.oldmannewman.com website. Use the user id: **oldman** and the password **newman**. These are **case sensitive**, so use all lowercase letters and leave no spaces.

1. Mike Bickle used the story of the prodigal son to help us understand the Father's great love for us. How have each of the following been expressed to you from God?

   - God saw you.

   - God felt compassion for you.

   - God ran to you.

   - God embraced you.

   - God kissed you.

2. Bickle advised us not just to think about God, but to think about what He thinks about us. What do you think God thinks about you?

3. In order to mature spiritually, we must begin to define our lives by our pursuit of God—not by our struggles. In what ways can you pursue God more passionately than you have in the past?

Appendix

Important Reading for New Men

Here is a list of the fifty-two books cited in this book. Almost without exception I have read each book, some of them several times. I believe reading good books will enrich your life. That is why I am calling attention to the book besides listing each in the Notes section. We have repeated this list at www.oldmannewman.com. You can log on using the user id: **oldman** and the password **newman.** There you will find more information on each book listed—only one of many things we have done on the website to make it interactive with this book.

Anderson, Neil T. *A Way of Escape.* Eugene, Oregon: Harvest House, 1998.

Annacondia, Carlos. *Listen to Me, Satan!* Lake Mary, Florida: Creation House, 1998.

Arterburn, Stephen; Stoeker, Fred; Yorkey, Mike. *Every Man's Battle.* Colorado Springs, Colorado: Waterbrook Press, 2000.

Bettger, Frank. *How I Raised Myself From Failure to Success in Selling.* Prentice Hall, 1992.

Bickle, Mike. *Passion for Jesus.* Lake Mary, Florida: Creation House, 1993.

Blanton, Brad, Ph.D. *Radical Honesty.* DTP, 1996.

Bottari, Pablo. *Free in Christ.* Lake Mary, Florida: Creation House, 2000.

Buckingham, Jamie. *The Promise of Power.* Ann Arbor, Michigan: Servant Publications, 1998.

Buford, Bob. *Halftime.* Grand Rapids, Michigan: Zondervan, 1994.

Christiano, Joseph. *My Body–God's Temple.* Trinity Publishing and Marketing Group, 1998.

———*Seven Pillars of Health.* Lake Mary, Florida: Siloam Press, 2000.

Christiano, Joseph; Weissberg, Steven M., M.D. *The Answer Is in Your Bloodtype.* Personal Nutrition USA, 1999.

Colbert, Don, M.D. *Walking in Divine Health.* Lake Mary, Florida: Creation House, 1999.

———*What You Don't Know May Be Killing You.* Lake Mary, Florida: Siloam Press, 2000.

Copeland, Germaine. *Prayers That Avail Much.* Tulsa, Oklahoma: Harrison House, 1997.

Crossland, Don. *A Journey Toward Wholeness.* Little Rock, Arkansas: Journey Press, 1998.

Dalbey, Gordon. *Father and Son: The Wound, the Healing, the Call to Manhood.* Nashville, Tennessee: Thomas Nelson, 1997.

Freidzon, Claudio. *Holy Spirit, I Hunger for You.* Lake Mary, Florida: Creation House, 1997.

———*Treasure in Jars of Clay.* Lake Mary, Florida: Creation House, 1999.

Gillham, Preston H. *Things Only Men Know.* Eugene, Oregon: Harvest House, 1999.

Hart, Archibald D., M.D. *The Hart Report: The Sexual Man.* Dallas, Texas: Word Publishing, 1994.

Hayford, Jack. *The Beauty of Spiritual Language.* Dallas, Texas: Word, 1996.

Hybels, Bill. *Honest to God?* Grand Rapids, Michigan: Zondervan, 1992.

Lahaye, Tim and Beverly. *The Act of Marriage* (revised). Grand Rapids, Michigan: Zondervan, 1998.

Mason, John. *Proverb's Prayers.* Tulsa, Oklahoma: Insight Publishing Group, 1999.

Maxwell, John. *The 21 Irrefutable Laws of Leadership.* Dallas, Texas: Nelson, 1998.

Means, Patrick. *Men's Secret Wars.* Grand Rapids, Michigan: Fleming H. Revell, 1999.

Morley, Patrick. *The Man in the Mirror.* Grand Rapids, Michigan: Zondervan, 2000.

———*Second Wind for the Second Half.* Grand Rapids, Michigan: Zondervan, 1999.

———*The Seven Seasons of a Man's Life.* Grand Rapids, Michigan: Zondervan, 1998.

Mossholder, Ray. *Marriage Plus.* Lake Mary, Florida: Creation House, 1990.

Munroe, Myles. *Understanding Your Potential.* Tulsa, Oklahoma: Destiny Image, 1992.

Phillips-Jones, Linda. *Mentors and Proteges.* Arbor House, 1982.

Pickett, Fuchsia. *Stones of Remembrance,* Lake Mary, Florida: Creation House, 1998.

Powell, John. *The Secret of Staying in Love.* Argus Communications, 1974.

Rainey, Dennis, *The Tribute and the Promise.* Dallas, Texas: Nelson, 1997.

Rea, John, Th.D. *Charisma's Bible Handbook on the Holy Spirit.* Lake Mary, Florida: Creation House, 1998.

Roberson, Dave. *The Walk of the Spirit—the Walk of Power.* Tulsa, Oklahoma: Dave Roberson Ministries, 1999.

Roberts, Ted. *Pure Desire: Helping People Break Free From Sexual Struggles.* Ventura, California: Regal Books, 1999.

Rosenau, Dr. Douglas E., *A Celebration of Sex.* Nashville, Tennessee: Thomas Nelson, 1996.

Schuller, Robert. *Move Ahead Through Possibility Thinking.* New York: Doubleday, 1967.

Smith, Pam. *Eat Well—Live Well.* Lake Mary, Florida: Creation House, 1992.

——*The Food Trap.* Lake Mary, Florida: Creation House, 1990.

——*Food for Life.* Lake Mary, Florida: Creation House, 1994.

——*Food for Life Study Guide.* Lake Mary, Florida: Creation House, 1997.

——*The Good Life.* Lake Mary, Florida: Creation House, 1996.

——*Healthy Expectations.* Lake Mary, Florida: Creation House, 1998.

———*Healthy Expectations Journal.* Lake Mary, Florida: Creation House, 1998.

Swenson, Richard, M.D. *Margin.* Colorado Springs, Colorado: NavPress, 1992.

———*Overload Syndrome.* Colorado Springs, Colorado: NavPress, 1999.

Weiss, Douglas, Ph.D. *The Final Freedom.* Fort Worth, Texas: Discovery Press, 1998.

Wilkerson, David. *The Cross and the Switchblade.* Grand Rapids, Michigan: Zondervan, 1986.

Notes

Author's note: Let's face it, endnotes are usually boring, but necessary. Here are our endnotes, to satisfy all the librarians of the world. But these endnotes are more! Think of them as hyperlinks to our www.oldmannewman.com website. There, you can find more information on each one listed. Often you will read the entire article or at least find out where you can buy the book or link to the website of the author.

Sound cool? Read more about it on page xiii. And log on using the user ID: **oldman** and the password: **newman**. Remember that the Internet is **case sensitive**, so use only lowercase letters.

CHAPTER 1
MEN: MUST WE STRUGGLE TO SERVE CHRIST?

1. Mike Bickle, *Passion for Jesus* (Lake Mary, FL: Creation House, 1993), 182–183.
2. Douglas Weiss, Ph.D., *The Final Freedom* (Fort Worth, TX: Discovery Press, 1998), n.p.

CHAPTER 2

FATHERLESSNESS: THE ROOT OF THE PROBLEM

1. "What Will Your Kids Engrave on Your Tombstone," *New Man* (July/August 1994), 13, from *Dad the Family Mentor* by Dave Simmons, Victor Books. **Website resource: Sons about fathers.**
2. Gordon Dalbey, *Father and Son: The Wound, the Healing, the Call to Manhood* (Nashville, TN: Thomas Nelson, 1997).
3. Ibid.
4. Ibid.
5. Ibid.
6. Edwin Louis Cole, "The Fatherless Syndrome," *New Man* (January/February 2000), 70. **Website resource: Healing fatherlessness.**
7. "Seeking Guidance," *New Man* (September/October 1995), 18.
8. *Update*, November 1999.
9. *Update*, September 1999.
10. *Update*, June 1997.
11. *Update*, August 1999.
12. "Lessons from Dad," *New Man* (May/June 1995), 33. **Website resource: He was always there.**
13. Mike Yorkey, "Champs for Children," *New Man*, (July/August 1998), 31.
14. Preston H. Gillham, *Things Only Men Know* (Eugene, OR: Harvest House, 1999), 114. **Website resource: When fathers fail.**
15. Ken R. Canfield, "One Size Fits All," New Man (May/June 2000), 57. **Website resource: A father's legacy.**
16. "Lessons from Dad," *New Man* (May/June 1995), 36–38.
17. Patrick Means, *Men's Secret Wars* (Grand Rapids, MI: Fleming H. Revell, 1999), 62.

CHAPTER 3

SEXUAL PROBLEMS: ARE THEY ALWAYS AN ISSUE?

1. "The Masturbation Puzzle," *New Man* (July/August 1998), 21. **Website resource: Analyze the need.**

2. Dr. Archibald D. Hart, *The Hart Report: The Sexual Man* (Dallas, TX: Word Publishing, 1994), 1.
3. Ibid., 5.
4. Ibid., 59.
5. "Tiger tears off woman's arm," AP, May 25, 2000.
6. Ted Roberts, *Pure Desire: Helping People Break Free From Sexual Struggles* (Ventura, CA: Regal Books, 1999), 27.
7. Ibid., 46.
8. Don Crossland, "Escape From the Trap of Addiction," *New Man* (January/February 1995), 52. **Website resource: Released by God.**
9. Stephen Arterburn, Fred Stoeker, Mike Yorkey, *Every Man's Battle* (Colorado Springs, CO: Waterbrook Press, 2000), 29–30.
10. Roberts, *Pure Desire*, 32.
11. For more information–**Website resource: Admit secret sins.**
12. "Letters," *New Man* (March/April 1995), 12.
13. Ibid.
14. For more information–**Website resource: See poll results.**
15. "The Masturbation Puzzle," *New Man* (July/August 1998), 21. **Website resource: A self-centered exercise**

CHAPTER 4
THREE STEPS FORWARD: TWO STEPS BACK

1. "The XXXtent of the Problem," *New Man* (May 1997), 33, from Ken R. Canfield, president, National Center for Fathering. **Website resource: Revealing results.**
2. "Lightning fells huge Ohio oak tree," Associated Press, May 25, 2000.

CHAPTER 5
SALVATION: BRINGS NEW LIFE

1. "Object of His Love," *New Man* (May 1997), 19, from *The Journey Home* by Bob Benson & Karen Dean Fry (Beacon Hill Press, 1997). **Website resource: He found me!**
2. Ed Donnally, "The Love Bug," *New Man* (March/April 2000), 25–29. **Website resource: Deep-down fulfillment.**

3. Patrick Morley, *Second Wind for the Second Half* (Grand Rapids, MI: Zondervan, 1999), 13–16.
4. Bob Buford, "What's in the Box?" *New Man* (July/August 1996), 75. **Website resource: Don't be miserable.**
5. Morley, *Second Wind for the Second Half.*
6. Bill Hybels, *Honest to God?* (Grand Rapids, MI: Zondervan, 1992), 12–15.
7. Michael Zigarelli, "Business by the Book Pays Off," *New Man* (March/April 2000), 55–56. **Website resource: A rededicated business.**

CHAPTER 6

DELIVERANCE: BREAKS SIN'S HOLD

1. Adapted from Pablo Bottari, *Free in Christ* (Lake Mary, FL: Creation House, 2000), 39–40.
2. Sherry Andrews, "The Deliverance of James Robison," *Charisma* (December 1983), 34–41. **Website resource: Joy, peace and freedom.**
3. Neil T. Anderson, *A Way of Escape* (Eugene, OR: Harvest House, 1998), from the foreword by Charles Mylander.
4. Bottari, *Free in Christ,* 109.
5. Carlos Annacondia, *Listen to Me, Satan!* (Lake Mary, FL: Creation House, 1998), 136.
6. Bottari, *Free in Christ,* 70.
7. Adapted from Claudio Freidzon, *Holy Spirit, I Hunger for You* (Lake Mary, FL: Creation House, 1997), 53–57.
8. Ibid., 183.

CHAPTER 7

RECEIVING THE HOLY SPIRIT: EMPOWERS YOUR LIFE

1. Adapted from John Rea, Th.D., *Charisma's Bible Handbook on the Holy Spirit* (Lake Mary, FL: Creation House, 1998), 160-162.
2. David Wilderson, *The Cross and the Switchblade* (Grand Rapids, MI: Chosen Books, 1986), 151–155.
3. Fuchsia Pickett, *Stones of Remembrance* (Lake Mary, FL: Creation House, 1998), 26–33.

4. Jack Hayford, *The Beauty of Spiritual Language* (Dallas, TX: Nelson, 1996).
5. Ibid.
6. Ibid.
7. Ibid.

Chapter 8
Accountability: Keeps You in Touch

1. "For New Surfers: The Top 10 for Men," *New Man* (September/October 1999), 18. **Website resource: Great websites.**
2. Stephen Strang, "My Group of Loyal Friends," *New Man* (September/October 1998), 37. **Website resource: Develop friendships.**
3. Brad Blanton, Ph.D., *Radical Honesty* (n.p.: DTP, 1996).
4. Ibid.
5. Gary Rosberg, "We're in This Together," *New Man* (November/December 1995), 63. **Website resource: Joining the team.**
6. Ibid., 65.**Website resource: Take off the mask.**
7. Gillham, *Things Only Men Know,* 190.
8. Terry Etter, "Seven Tips for a Great Men's Group," *New Man* (September/October 1994), 51–54. **Website resource: Small group ideas.**
9. Gillham, *Things Only Men Know,* 190.

Chapter 9
Getting a Life Vision: Finding Your Purpose

1. "The Makings of a GREAT MAN," *New Man* (January/February 2000), 20, copyright 1999 by Patrick M. Morley. **Website resource: Making a great man.**
2. Jamie Buckingham, *The Promise of Power* (Ann Arbor, MI: Servant Publications, 1998).
3. Myles Munroe, *Understanding Your Potential* (Tulsa, OK: Destiny Image, 1992), from the foreword by Jerry Horner.
4. Ibid., 5.
5. Ibid., 64–65.
6. Morley, *Second Wind,* n.p.
7. Ibid., 174–176.

Chapter 10
Renewing Your Mind: Changing the Way You Think

1. Dan Ewald, "Hollywood, Hip-Hop & Heaven," *New Man* (January/February 1999), 12. **Website resource: The void is filled.**
2. Jodi Wilgoren, "Words of Advice for Graduates on the Threshold of the Millennium," *New York Times* (September 29, 2000).
3. Karen Spears Zacharias, "Straight From the Heart," *New Man* (March/April 1999), 40. **Website resource: No magic formula.**
4. Roberts, *Pure Desire*, 37.
5. Dave Roberson, *The Walk of the Spirit—The Walk of Power* (Tulsa, OK: Dave Roberson Ministries, 1999).

Chapter 11
Ordering Your Finances: Gaining Freedom to Soar

1. "Keys to Becoming Debt-Free," *New Man* (January/February 2000), 13, from Larry Burkett, *A Guide to Family Budgeting*, Christian Financial Concepts, (770) 534-1000. **Website resource: Become debt-free.**
2. Morley, *Second Wind*, 14–15.
3. *Tycoon* magazine, Spring 2000.
4. For more information—**Website resource: Twenty-five years.**
5. Charles Ross, "Financial Life Cycles," *New Man* (July/August 1999), 19. **Website resource: Five life cycles.**
6. Morley, *Second Wind*, 88.
7. Maureen Eha, "Letting Go to Hold On," *Power Up!* for the week of June 5, 2000. **Website resource: Sowing to reap.**
8. John Maxwell, *The 21 Irrefutable Laws of Leadership* (Dallas, TX: Nelson, 1998).

Chapter 12
Working on Your Marriage: Making It Great

1. "10 Ways to Sabatage Your Marriage," *New Man* (July/August 2000), 21, from *God Is in the Small Stuff for Your*

Marriage (Promise Press), by Bruce Bickel and Stan Jantz. **Website resource: Avoid sabotage.**

2. Source obtained from the Internet: "Chuck Shepherd's News of the Weird," www.newsoftheweird.com.
3. Tessie Guell, "When Love Broke Through," *Charisma* (February 1996), 29–30. **Website resource: Don't give up.**
4. National Center for Health Statistics.
5. Gary Whetstone with Lee Grady, "And the Two Became One Again," *Charisma* (February 1991), 51–57. **Website resource: Marriage restored.**
6. John Powell, *The Secret of Staying in Love* (n.p.: Argus Communications, 1974).
7. Ray Mossholder, *Marriage Plus* (Lake Mary, FL: Creation House, 1990).
8. Patrick Morley, *The Seven Seasons of a Man's Life* (Grand Rapids, MI: Zondervan, 1998).
9. Ibid., 195.
10. "Americans Say Yes to Monogamous Sex," *New Man* (January/ February 1995), 12.
11. Roberts, *Pure Desire*, 98.

CHAPTER 13

IMPACTING YOUR CHILDREN: SPEAKING THE FATHER'S BLESSING

1. "Bullish on Fathers," *New Man* (July/August 1998), 15, from *ESPN Magazine*, April 6, 1998.
2. "Quality time," *New Man* (July/August 1998), 16, from *Building Strong Families* by William Mitchell and Michael Mitchell (Broadman & Holman, 1997). **Website resource: Fathers at home.**
3. Means, *Men's Secret Wars*, 53.
4. Ibid.
5. Gillham, *Things Only Men Know*, 101–103.
6. Ibid.
7. Ibid., 226–227.
8. Joe Maxwell, "A Typical Suburban Dad–'NOT!'" *Charisma* (June 1994), 20–21. **Website resource: A father's love.**
9. James Ryle, "When My Sons Became Men," *Charisma* (June 1994), 19.
10. Ibid., 21.
11. Ibid., 21–22.

CHAPTER 14
CARING FOR YOUR BODY:
GETTING INTO SHAPE

1. "Pride + Men = Bad Health," *New Man* (January/February 1999), 13, from Phenix & Phenix. **Website resource: Health awareness.**
2. For more information—**Website resource: Meet Pam Smith.**
3. David Stevens, M.D., "God and Your Bod," *New Man* (May/June 2000), 36–40. **Website resource: Aerobic exercise.**
4. Ibid.
5. Joseph Christiano, *Seven Pillars of Health* (Lake Mary, FL: Siloam Press, 2000).
6. Ibid.
7. Don Colbert, M.D., *What You Don't Know May Be Killing You* (Lake Mary, FL: Siloam Press, 2000), 4.
8. Don Colbert, M.D., *Walking in Divine Health* (Lake Mary, FL: Creation House, 1999), 10–11.
9. Christiano, *Seven Pillars of Health*, 126.
10. Ibid.
11. For more information—**Website resource: Fit or Fat.**

CHAPTER 15
DEVELOPING MALE RELATIONSHIPS

1. "Generation Next, Please," *New Man* (May 1997), 18. **Website resource: Mentors wanted.**
2. Gillham, *Things Only Men Know*, 29.
3. For more information—**Website resource: The missing link.**
4. Linda Phillips-Jones, *Mentors and Protégés* (n.p.: Arbor House, 1982).
5. Ibid.
6. Ibid.
7. Ibid.

CHAPTER 16
BECOMING A MAN OF GOD

1. "Self-Realization vs. Christ-Realization," *New Man* (July/

August 2000), 17, taken from *Approved Unto God* by Oswald Chambers, copyright 1936. **Website resource: Christ-realization.**

2. Bickle, *Passion for Jesus,* 40.
3. Ibid.